Normative Motherhood

Regulations, Representations, and Reclamations

Edited by Andrea O'Reilly

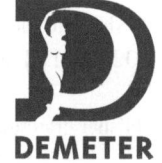

DEMETER

Normative Motherhood
Regulations, Representations, and Reclamations

Edited by Andrea O'Reilly

Copyright © 2023 Demeter Press

Individual copyright to their work is retained by the authors. All rights reserved. No part of this book may be reproduced or transmitted in any form by any means without permission in writing from the publisher.

Demeter Press
PO Box 197
Coe Hill, Ontario
Canada
K0L 1P0
Tel: 289-383-0134
Email: info@demeterpress.org
Website: www.demeterpress.org

Demeter Press logo based on the sculpture "Demeter" by Maria-Luise Bodirsky www.keramik-atelier.bodirsky.de

Printed and Bound in Canada

Cover artwork: Vanessa Marr
Cover design and typesetting: Michelle Pirovich
Proof reading: Jena Woodhouse

Library and Archives Canada Cataloguing in Publication
Title: Normative motherhood: regulations, representations, and reclamations / edited by Andrea O'Reilly.
Names: O'Reilly, Andrea, 1961- editor.
Description: Includes bibliographical references.
Identifiers: Canadiana 20230157114 | ISBN 9781772584479 (softcover)
Subjects: LCSH: Motherhood. | LCSH: Motherhood–Social aspects.
Classification: LCC HQ759.N67 2023 | DDC 306.874/3—dc23

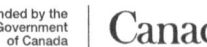 The publisher gratefully acknowledges the support of the Government of Canada

Contents

Introduction
Normative Motherhood: Regulations, Representations, and Reclamations: An Introduction
Andrea O'Reilly
7

Part 1.
Regulations
35

1.
Contemporary Motherhood Is Mothering for Success
May Isaac
37

2.
Does My Mothering Look Normal to You? A Poetic Exploration of Formal Guidelines and Internet Spaces
Elizabeth A. Bennett and Lori E. Koelsch
55

3.
Social Media and the Management of Normative Motherhood
Megan Marshall
67

4.

Social Conditions, Cultural Inheritances, and
Normative Motherhoods in Times of COVID-19 in Brazil:
Gender Relations and Historical Inequalities
Ana Carolina Eiras Coelho Soares and Sônia Maria de Magalhães
85

5.

The Misogyny of Lactivism: Why Breastfeeding Is
Central to the Discourse of Normative Motherhood
Karla Knutson
111

Part 2.

Representations

129

6.

Artwork: Upholding the Mother
Vanessa Marr
131

7.

Childrearing by the Book: Motherhood Manuals
from Birth to Nineteenth-Century America
Denise Hill
135

8.

The Perils of Embracing Respectability Politics: Maternal
Conformity and Normativity in Alice Walker's *The Abortion*
and Nafissa Thompson-Spires's *Belles Lettres*
Zsuzsanna Lénárt-Muszka
153

9.

"What Finally Dragged Her under the Water and Who Carried the Spark": The Intergenerational Trauma of Normative Motherhood in Celeste Ng's *Everything I Never Told You* and *Little Fires Everywhere*

Andrea O'Reilly

169

10.

Buzz Kill and Eye Candy: Normative Motherhood Disrupted and Matricritics in Courtney Kessel and Chloé Clevenger's *In Balance With*

Natalie Bruvels

189

Part 3.

Reclamations

209

11.

The Death of the God Mother: Deconstructing Normative Motherhood and Its Resistance

Isabelle Portelinha

211

12.

Supermom's Support Group: Exploring and Resisting Normative Motherhood

Rachel E. Stough and Elizabeth A. Bennett

231

13.

The Art of Mothering with a Disability: Challenging Normative Motherhood

Amy Wagner, Susan Smith, and Amy Crocker

245

14.
Older First-Time Moms in Twenty-First-Century Canada:
Challenging (and Changing) the Norms of Normative
Early Motherhood
Rosann Edwards
261

15.
Throw Down Your Bundles: An Anishinaabeg Mother's
Perspective on Anishinaabeg Normative Motherhood
Renée E. Mazinegiizhigoo-kwe Bédard
279

Notes on Contributors
301

Normative Motherhood: Regulations, Representations, and Reclamations, An Introduction

Andrea O'Reilly

Each year, I open my second year "Mothering-Motherhood" course at York University asking students to define good motherhood in contemporary culture: What does a good mother look like? What does she do or not do? Students usually comment that good mothers, as portrayed in the media or popular culture more generally, are white, middle class, heterosexual, cisgender, able bodied, married, and in a nuclear family with usually one to two children. Such words as "altruistic," "patient," "loving," "selfless," "devoted," "nurturing," and "cheerful" are frequently mentioned. For the students, good mothers put the needs of their children before their own, are available to their children whenever needed, and should the mother work outside the home, her children rather than her career should be at the centre of her life. Good mothers are the primary caregivers of their children: care other than that provided by the mother (e.g., daycare) is viewed as inferior and deficient. Children and culture at large do not see mothers as having a life before or beyond motherhood. As well, although students typically agree that our culture regards mothering as natural to mothers, that same culture paradoxically requires mothers to be well-versed in theories of childrearing. Several students remarked that good mothers today are concerned with their children's educational or more general psychological development; good mothers, thus, ensure that their children have many and varied opportunities for enrichment, learning, and self-growth. And, of course, mothers are not sexual.

I then ask how many students in the room are good mothers as defined by these normative images of motherhood. (Or if they are not mothers themselves, I ask if they were they raised by this so-called ideal mother.) Seldom has a hand been raised. Of course, we all know that mothers come from all races and ethnicities, that mothers are both young and old, that mothers are both urban and rural, straight and queer, that many women mother with disabilities, that many mothers are poor or working class, that most mothers work outside the home in paid employment, that social and political activism is a part of many mothers' lives, that women mother older children as well as young children, that some mothers live apart from their children, that many women raise children with whom they have no biological relation as with adoption and in blended families, and finally that all these mothers are good mothers who raise their children with love and care equal to that of the normative and idealized good mother. However, we also know that normative motherhood, though representative of very few women's lived identities and experiences of mothering, is considered the normal and natural maternal experience: To mother otherwise is to be abnormal or unnatural. Mothers who, by choice or circumstance, do not fulfill the profile of the good mother—they are too young or too old, or they do not follow the script of good mothering, or they work outside the home or live apart from their children—are deemed bad mothers in need of societal regulation and correction.

A central aim of motherhood studies is to examine and theorize normative motherhood. Where does it come from? What are its defining features and demands? How does it work as a regulatory discourse and practice across differences of age, class, race, ability, sexuality, and region? What is the impact of normative motherhood on women's lives? What does an intersectional analysis of normative motherhood reveal? How is normative motherhood reflected and enacted in public policy, workplace practices, family arrangements and so on? How is normative motherhood represented and resisted in literature, art, photography, and film? How do or may women resist normative motherhood? This collection explores these questions of normative motherhood under three interrelated topics: regulations, representations, and reclamations. This introduction will first consider my use of the term "normative motherhood" and then move to a brief history of the emergence of normative motherhood from the mid-twentieth century to contemporary times, examine the discourse and practice of intensive mothering as the current enactment of normative motherhood, and then consider explanations for the emergence of intensive mothering as the current mode of normative motherhood. The final section will introduce the chapters under each section.

Why the Term "Normative Motherhood"?

The term "normative motherhood" is used in motherhood studies to signify the concept of good motherhood as discussed above. However, at times, building upon the work of Adrienne Rich, the term "patriarchal motherhood" is used to denote this concept of good motherhood, which has led researchers to ask what is the difference between the terms "normative" and "patriarchal"? In *Of Woman Born*, Rich distinguishes "between two meanings of motherhood, one superimposed on the other: the potential relationship of any woman to her powers of reproduction and to children; and the institution—which aims at ensuring that that potential—and all women —shall remain under male control" (7). For Rich, the term "motherhood" refers to the patriarchal institution of motherhood, which is male defined and controlled and is deeply oppressive to women, whereas the word "mothering" refers to women's experiences of mothering and is female defined and centred and potentially empowering to women. The reality of patriarchal motherhood, thus, must be distinguished from the possibility or potentiality of empowered mothering. In other words, whereas motherhood operates as a patriarchal institution to constrain, regulate, and dominate women and their mothering, mothers' own experiences of mothering can, nonetheless, be a site of empowerment. Patriarchal motherhood, thus, centres on how mothers and their mothering are defined and restrained by patriarchal culture, whereas normative motherhood expands upon this to consider how the concept of good motherhood is not only derived from patriarchal culture but also formed in and through racism and classism. As noted above, not only is the good mother required to be the selfless wife in a patriarchal nuclear family, but she is also coded as white and middle class.

The term "normative motherhood" is thus employed to denote and emphasize how the concept of good motherhood operates as a regulatory institution, both discursively and materially, to construct mothers who are not white or middle class as de facto bad mothers. In their introduction to *Bad Mothers: Regulations, Representations, and Resistance*, Michelle Hughes Miller, Tamar Hagar, and Rebecca Jaremko Bromwich argue that "the Bad Mother trope arises from the cultural inculcation of the Good Mother and its successful institutionalization" (6). Moreover, they go on to explain that "the Good Mother shapes the Bad Mother through its mechanism of accountability to the expectations that it holds" (6). The tropes of the good and bad mother are thus divergent yet symbiotic: The meaning of one depends on that of the other. Under normative motherhood, the good and idealized mother is white and middle class, and her dichotomous other is the bad and demonized racialized and working-class or poor mother. Thus, racialized and working-class/poor mothers are uniquely and specifically oppressed by the institution of motherhood in its normative constructions along with its patriarchal ones.

Judgment, surveillance, and regulation are also central to normative motherhood and are explicitly enforced and enacted in the construction of racialized and poor mothers as de facto bad mothers. In her recent book *Small Animals: Parenthood in the Age of Fear*, Kim Brooks argues that "[All mothers] feel watched and judged. [All] wonder who is doing it the right way; all feel guarded and anxious; [we all] evaluate someone's mothering ... forming categories, erecting columns" (55, 60). However, and as noted by Asian American author Jessamine Chan and explored in her recent novel *The School for Good Mothers* (2022), much of the control, judgment, and surveillance mothers experience is based on race and class (Miller). In Chan's dystopian novel, Frida, the central character and an Asian American mother, loses custody of her eighteen-month-old daughter after leaving her alone for a couple of hours and is punished with a yearlong sentence at a state-run, Big Brother-like institution, which will train Frida to be a good mother and determine if her daughter will be returned to her. Unsurprisingly, most of the mothers at the School for Good Mothers are poor and/or racialized. Only a handful of the mothers are white; Frida is the only Asian American mother. This representation, as Chan explains, "gestures to the fact that the way we are surveilled is different depending on race and class. And that we don't all face the same monitoring from the government or the police" (qtd. in Cook). Upon arrival at the school, the instructor tells the mothers: "Bad parents must be transformed from the inside out. [They must learn] the right instincts, the ability to make split-second, safe, nurturing, loving decisions" (83). The mothers must continually repeat the school's refrain: "I'm a bad mother, but I am learning to be good" (83). At the school, the mothers are under constant surveillance, continually monitored and assessed, and must perform normative motherhood to regain custody of their children. I mention Chan's novel here because it lucidly elucidates how the institution of motherhood oppresses and regulates mothers differently, and that for racialized and poor mothers, it is the normative configurations of good motherhood rather than its patriarchal ones that cause these mothers to be under heightened surveillance and deemed as de facto bad mothers in need of correction and punishment. In my writings, I use the term "normative motherhood" over "patriarchal motherhood" to signify and emphasize these racialized and classed configurations of the institution of motherhood and how they are enforced through surveillance and regulation.

A History of Normative Motherhood

In my book *Matricentric Feminism: Theory, Activism, Practice*, I survey the emergence of normative motherhood and then consider how and why normative motherhood becomes the only legitimate discourse and practice of motherhood and how it is used to oppress and regulate mothers and their mothering. I introduce here what I have termed the ten dictates of normative motherhood: essentialization, privatization, individualization, naturalization, normalization, idealization, biologicalization, expertization, intensification, and depoliticalization. Essentialization positions maternity as the basis of female identity, whereas privatization locates motherwork solely in the reproductive realm of the home. Similarly, individualization causes such mothering to be the work and responsibility of one person, and naturalization assumes that maternity is natural to women—that is, all women naturally know how to mother—and that the work of mothering is driven by instinct rather than intelligence and developed by habit rather than skill. In turn, normalization limits and restricts maternal identity and practice to one specific mode—the nuclear family, wherein the mother is a wife to a husband and she assumes the role of the nurturer and the husband assumes that of the provider. The expertization and intensification of motherhood—particularly as they are conveyed in what Sharon Hays terms "intensive mothering" and what Susan Douglas and Meredith Michaels call "the new momism"—cause childrearing to be all consuming and expert driven. Idealization sets unattainable expectations of and for mothers, and depoliticalization characterizes childrearing solely as a private and nonpolitical undertaking, with no social or political import. Finally, biologicalization, in its emphasis on blood ties, positions the cisgender birth mother as the real and authentic mother. Normative motherhood is only available to mothers who can enact and fulfill these ten dictates. Mothers who cannot, or will not, do so because they are young, queer, single, racialized, trans, or nonbinary, are defined and positioned as de facto bad mothers.

Building on Rich's insight that motherhood is a cultural construction, I argue that normative motherhood discourses are rewritten in response to, and as a result of, significant cultural and economic changes. Numerous works detail how the modern image of the full-time stay-at-home mother—isolated in the private sphere and financially dependent on her husband—came about as result of industrialization. Industrialization took work out of the home and repositioned the domestic space, at least among the middle class, as an exclusively nonproductive and private realm, which is separate from the public sphere of work. At the end of World War II, the discourse of the "happy homemaker" made "the stay-at-home-mom-and-apple pie" mode of mothering the normal and natural motherhood experience. The view that stay-at-home motherhood is what constitutes good motherhood emerged only in the postwar period to effect social reorganization and, more particularly, to redesign feminine gender behaviour and roles. During World War II in North America, there was an unprecedented increase in women's employment to include white, middle-class mothers who had previously not been engaged in full-time employment. Thus, in the war period, mothers were encouraged to work and were celebrated for doing so, particularly in the propaganda films and literature. With the end of the war and the return of the soldiers, women were forced to give up their wartime employment. This was orchestrated and facilitated by an ideological redesign of what constitutes good motherhood. Buttressed by the new psychological teachings, notably John Bowlby's attachment theory, two beliefs emerged in the 1950s: Children require full-time stay-at-home mothering, and children, without full-time mothering, would suffer from what was termed "maternal deprivation." According to Bowlby, as noted by Shari Thurer in *The Myths of Motherhood: How Culture Reinvents the Good Mother*, "maternal deprivation was as damaging in the first three years of life as German measles in the first three months of pregnancy: mother love in infancy is as important for mental health as proteins and vitamins for physical health" (276).

Sacrificial motherhood, as described above by my students, thus emerged as the dominant view of good mothering in the postwar period, or approximately seventy years ago. Sacrificial motherhood is characterized by three central themes. The first defines mothering as natural to women and essential to their being, conveyed in the belief, as Pamela Courtenay Hall notes, that "women are naturally mothers, they are born with a built-in set of capacities, dispositions, and desires to nurture children ... [and that this] engagement of love and instinct is utterly distant from the world of paid work" (60). Second, the mother is to be the central caregiver of her biological children. And third, children require full-time mothering, or in the instance where the mother must work outside the home, the children must always come before the job. Hays argues that intensive mothering emerged in the postwar period. I contend, in contrast, that even though the origins of intensive mothering may be traced back to this time, intensive mothering, in its fully developed form, developed in the late 1980s and early 1990s. Hays argues that intensive mothering is characterized by three themes: first, "the mother is the central caregiver"; second, "mothering is regarded as more important than paid employment"; and third, "mothering requires lavishing copious amounts of time, energy, and material resources on the child" (8). I argue that whereas the first two characterize mothering from the postwar period to present day, only mothering of the last thirty years can be characterized by the third theme—namely, children require copious amounts of time, energy, and material resources. The postwar discourse of good motherhood demanded that mothers be at home full-time with their children;

however, such a demand did not require the intensive mothering expected of mothers today. I see the postwar discourse of motherhood—what I term "custodial motherhood" or the "flower-pot" approach—covering the period between 1946 to the late 1980s and understand it as different from intensive mothering. Intensive mothering, in contrast, emerged in the early 1990s and is practiced by the daughters born after the baby-boom era and who became mothers in the early 1990s and onwards. Although intensive mothering emerges from custodial mothering, I emphasize that it is a distinct motherhood discourse specific to its historical period.

To illustrate the difference between custodial motherhood and intensive mothering and to locate this transition in the early 1990s, I share one of my own mothering experiences. In 1988, when my eldest daughter was two, she attended a dance class held on York University campus, where our family lived. The mothers would arrive with large mugs of coffee every Saturday morning, and we would leave our children with the dance instructor. As our toddlers exercised their rambunctious energy, the mothers enjoyed a much-needed hour of peace and companionship. Three years later in 1991, I enrolled my youngest daughter in the same program and arrived again with my huge mug of coffee looking forward to that much-needed hour with the other mothers. However, as I was about to exit the gymnasium after dropping my daughter off, the same instructor explained that I was to stay, as this was a "moms and tots" dance class. I do not know who was more surprised and dare I say disappointed that day: my daughter, who was looking forward to an hour with her friends, or I, who would have rather been drinking a cup of coffee hanging out with the other mothers. This is in no way to suggest that I do not enjoy spending time with my daughters or that mothers and their children should not dance together (in fact, I still do, although my children are now adults). I am only suggesting that there is a time and place for everything. Indeed, after experiencing both types of programs, I argue that the one where the children danced with other children without their mothers' interference was more beneficial to both my daughters and me.

Most research on motherhood, however, does not distinguish between custodial motherhood and intensive mothering or consider how and why the latter emerged in the 1990s; rather, both are characterized as postwar mothering or more generally twentieth-century mothering. To fully understand how patriarchal ideologies of good motherhood function as culturally constructed practices—ones that are continuously redesigned in response to changing economic and societal factors—there must be a distinction made between custodial motherhood and intensive mothering because these two discourses emerged in response to two very different cultural transformations.

Normative motherhood in the postwar era required full-time mothering, but the emphasis was on the physical proximity of mother and child (i.e., the mother was to be at home with the children) and not on the mother needing to be continuously attuned to the psychological, emotional, or cognitive needs of her children. My mother, for example, remembering the early 1960s, recalls "airing" my sister and me on the front porch each morning while she tended to the housework. Domesticity—keeping a clean house and serving well-prepared dinners—was, more so than children, what occupied the postwar mother's time and attention. In the 1950s and 1960s, as well, there was a clearer division between the adult world and the world of children. Children would spend their time out in the neighbourhood playing with other children; children would seldom look to their parents for entertainment or amusement. And children were rarely enrolled in programs, except for the occasional Brownies or club meeting in the school-aged years. Fast forward to the mid-1990s and the type of mothering I received and enjoyed as a child would be regarded as deficient under the new discourse of intensive mothering.

Contemporary Enactments of Normative Motherhood: Intensive Mothering

Hays argues, as noted above, that intensive mothering is characterized by three themes: first, "the mother is the central caregiver"; second, "mothering is regarded as more important than paid employment"; and third, "mothering requires lavishing copious amounts of time, energy, and material resources on the child" (8). Moreover, intensive mothering "tells us that children are innocent and priceless, that their rearing should be carried out primarily by individual mothers and that it should be centered on children's needs, with methods that are informed by experts, labor intensive, and costly" (21). She emphasizes that intensive mothering is "a historically constructed cultural model for appropriate childcare" (21). She continues:

> Conceptions of appropriate child rearing are not simply a random conglomeration of disconnected ideas; they form a fully elaborated, logically cohesive framework for thinking about and acting toward children.... [W]e are told that [intensive mothering] is the best model, largely because it is what children need and deserve. This model was not developed overnight, however, nor is intensive mothering the only model available to mothers. (21)

Intensive mothering, in contrast to custodial mothering, dictates the following: 1) children can only be properly cared for by the biological mother; 2) this mothering must be provided 24/7; 3) mothers must always put children's needs before their own; 4) mothers must turn to the experts for instruction; 5) mothers must be fully satisfied, fulfilled, completed, and composed in motherhood; and finally; 6) mothers must lavish excessive amounts of time, energy, and money in the rearing of their children. In the introduction to her book *Intensive Mothering*, Linda Ennis perceptively provides concrete examples of how these mandates are enacted in the day-to-day work of childrearing:

> They include but are not limited to mothers doing homework for their children; mothers being friends with their children's friends; mothers' social lives revolving around their children; mothers encouraging children to continually phone or text them; mothers spending all their free time with their children; mothers always putting the children's needs before their own; mothers doing everything for their children such as laundry, driving, and lunches; mothers speaking for their children; all conversations with friends and family revolving around their children; mothers feeling empty after their children leave home for school or move out; mothers who won't allow their children to sleep over at friends' homes or go to overnight camp and/or children who won't leave home for any length of time. (6)

Today, intensive mothering demands more than mere physical proximity of the mother and child: Contemporary mothers are expected to spend, to use the discourse of the experts, "quality time" with their children. Mothers are told to play with their children, read to them, and take classes with them. As the children in the 1950s and

1960s would jump rope or play hide and seek with the neighbourhood children or their siblings, today's children dance and swim with their mothers in one of the many "moms and tots" programs. And today, children as young as three months old are enrolled in a multitude of classes—water play for infants, French immersion for toddlers, karate for preschoolers, and competitive skiing, skating, or sailing for elementary school children, to name just a few. (An article I read recently also recommends reading and singing to your child in utero.) It was not until the rise of intensive mothering that the patriarchal mandates of expertization and intensification became fully enacted and enforced. "We all know the ideal of the good mother," Susan E. Chase and Mary Rogers assert in their book *Mothers and Children: Feminist Analysis and Personal Narratives*, and they proceed to give a list of her characteristics:

> Above all, she is selfless. Her children come before herself and any other need or person or commitment no matter what. She loves her children unconditionally, yet she is careful not to smother them with love or her own needs. She follows the advice of doctors and other experts, and she educates herself about child development. She is very present in her children's lives when they are young, and when they get older, she is home every day to greet them as they return from school. If she works outside the home, she arranges her job around her children so she can be there for them as much as possible, certainly whenever they are sick or unhappy. The good mother's success is reflected in her children's behavior—they are well mannered, and respectful to others; at the same time, they have a strong sense of independence and self-esteem. They grow up to be productive citizens. (30)

Indeed, as Bonnie Fox has remarked:

> Expectations about the work needed to raise a child successfully have escalated at a dizzy rate; the bar is now sky high. Aside from the weighty prescriptions about the nutrition essential to babies' and children's physical health, and the sensitivity required for their emotional health, warnings about the need for intellectual stimulation necessary for developmental progress are directed at mothers. (237)

Even though today mothers have fewer children and more labour-saving devices—from microwaves to takeout food—mothers spend more time, energy, and money on their children than their mothers did in the 1960s. And the majority of mothers today, unlike sixty years ago, practice intensive mothering while engaged in full-time employment. Mothering today is more expert driven than postwar mothering. Moreover, under the ideology of intensive mothering, mothering is more child centred than the "children-should-be-seen-but-not-heard" style of mothering that characterized the postwar period. Contemporary mothering, thus, demands far more from mothers than was asked of them from the 1950s to 1980s.

The ideology of intensive mothering, as Hays notes, "advise[s] mothers to expend a tremendous amount of time, energy and money in raising children" (8). However, as Hays continues, "In a society where over half of all mothers with young children are now working outside the home, one might wonder why our culture pressures women to dedicate so much of themselves to child rearing" (x). Indeed, again to quote Hays, "Today ... when well over half of all mothers are in the paid labor force, when the image of a career women is that of a competitive go-getter, and when the image of the family is one of disintegrating values and relationships, one would expect a de-emphasis on the ideology of child rearing as labor-intensive, emotionally absorbing work" (3). One would expect to locate the ideology of intensive mothering in the postwar period when middle-class mothers, engaged in full-time motherhood, had more time and energy to devote to childrearing. Instead, the emergence of intensive mothering parallels the increase in mothers' paid labour force participation.

Explaining the Emergence of Intensive Mothering as the Contemporary Discourse and Practice of Normative Motherhood

Theorists of motherhood and mothers alike offer various explanations to account for the emergence of intensive mothering as the normative practice of motherhood over the last twenty-five years. Hays, for example, argues the following:

> The ideology of intensive child rearing practices persists, in part, because it serves the interests of men but also capitalism, the

state, the middle class and Whites. Further, and on a deeper level ... the ideology of intensive mothering is protected and promoted because it holds a fragile but nonetheless, powerful cultural position as the last best defense against what many people see as the impoverishment of social ties, communal obligations, and unremunerated commitments. (xiii)

I argue that intensive mothering emerged in the late 1980s in response to changing demographics of motherhood. Today, for the majority of middle-class women, motherhood is embarked upon only after a career is established and when the woman is in her thirties. For these mothers, the hurriedness of intensive mothering is a continuation of their busy lives as professional women. Whereas once mothers' daybooks were filled with business lunches, office meetings, and the like, now as intensive mothers who are home with their children, their daybooks are full of Gymboree classes, moms and tots programs, and library visits. Often these professional, highly educated women—who are unfamiliar and perhaps uncomfortable with the everyday, devalued, invisible work of mothering and domesticity—fill up their days with public activities that can be documented as productive and visible work. With fewer children, and more labour-saving devices and household help, childrearing—or more accurately the enrichment and amusement of one beloved child—becomes the focus of the mother's time and attention, as opposed to cooking and cleaning as it was in my mother's generation. And when these professional women return to their careers, intensive mothering, as practiced in the evenings and weekends, is the way a working mother, consciously or otherwise, compensates for her time away from her children; it bespeaks the ambivalence and guilt contemporary working mothers may feel about working and enjoying the work that they do. Intensive mothering's emphasis on enrichment—toys, books, games, activities, programs, camps, holidays, theatre, and so forth for children—has also emerged in response to mothers earning an income of their own and having a say on how household money is spent. Mothers, more so than fathers, are the consumers of items children need and want; as a mother's earnings and economic independence increase, more money is spent on children. Mothers today are having fewer children, which makes intensive mothering possible. They can devote all their time and attention to one or two beloved children. Now children must also turn to their mothers, rather than siblings or neighbours, for companionship. Finally, some argue that just as custodial mothering emerged in the postwar period in response to new psychological theories that stressed the need for mother-child attachment, intensive mothering in our time has arisen in response to new scientific research that emphasizes the importance of the first five years of life in the intellectual, behavioural, emotional, and social development of the child. Whatever the economic or social explanation may be, the ideology of intensive mothering measures good mothering in accordance with the amount of time, money, and energy a mother spends on childrearing. Raising one child today, as my mother frequently remarked, demands more time, energy, and money than rasing four in the postwar period. Indeed, the demands made on mothers today are unparalleled in history.

In her article, "Motherhood as a Class Act: The Many Ways in Which 'Intensive Mothering' is Entangled with Social Class," Fox argues that intensive mothering requires, signifies, and reproduces middle-class status. From her interviews with forty couples (nine working-class and thirty-one middle-class ones), Fox finds that middle-class women "are more likely to have the material and personal resources necessary to give themselves over completely to mothering; [thus middle-class women] are more likely to develop intensive mothering practices" (251). These resources include not only the obvious one of money—being free from economic pressures and financial worries—but also those of efficacy and time. Middle-class women, Fox argues, come to motherhood with a sense of accomplishment and competence and thus have "a strong sense of self-efficacy ... to take on and persist in the considerable challenges of intensive mothering" (250). The middle-class women interviewed by Fox also "displayed a sense of ownership of time," and, in particular, successful women in the labour force "felt entitled to spend their time on the baby and able to overcome feelings that they needed to accomplish more than baby care" (255). Given the nature of intensive mothering, middle-class circumstances and resources—in particular financial security, time, and efficacy—seem to be, Fox concludes, "the pre-requisites for its accomplishment" (243).

One mother interviewed by Fox remarks: "Having a woman at home full-time is the new marker of being middle class" (256). However, although intensive mothering may signify class privilege, it is, as Fox emphasizes, acutely gendered: "As being home with a baby and doing intensive mothering may detract from women's class status given how much more recognition paid work is regularly shown, it may bolster men's class status" (257). I argue further that different from the postwar era, when having a stay-at-home wife marked the achievement of middle-class status, today middle-class status is signified not only by a stay-at-home mother but one who engages in intensive mothering. In this way, intensive mothering is specifically a marker of middle-class status. Fox also considers how mothering practices reproduce social class: "It is possible that intensive mothering reproduces social class, in that babies cared for in this manner are somehow better prepared for success later in life" (256). However, Fox concludes that "the theoretical and empirical grounds on which to build such a case are not at all obvious" (256). Although I agree with Fox that it is impossible to prove that intensive mothering reproduces social class, I argue that what is at issue here is that middle-class parents believe that intensive mothering does reproduce class status and privilege. Parents are committed to intensive mothering precisely because they believe, to quote again from Hays, that "by lavishing copious amounts of time, energy, and material resources on the child" (8) their children will succeed in life and achieve, or perhaps more accurately inherit, middle class status.

In her book *Parenting Out of Control: Anxious Parents in Uncertain Times*, Margaret K. Nelson argues that the parenting styles of what she refers to as the "professional middle class" compared with those from the middle to "working" classes are quite distinct. Parenting among the professional middle class includes the following:

> A lengthy perspective on a child's dependency, a commitment to creating "passionate" people, personalized and negotiated guidance in the activities of daily life, respectful responsiveness to children's individualized needs and desires, a belief in the boundless potential, ambitious goals for achievement and an intensive engagement with children. (7)

By way of contrast, Nelson notes that "the working class and middle-class parents are more concerned with skills that will ensure self-sufficiency, and there are clear rules of authority within the family" (8). Why do professional middle-class parents engage in this style of parenting? This mode of childrearing—alternatively called "intensive mothering" or "helicopter parenting" or in Nelson's words, "parenting out of control"—is due to, according to the author, "anxieties about the children's future, from the nostalgia for the way they imagine families used to live, and from assessment of dangers to children in the world today" (174). Speaking specifically on parents' anxiety about their children's future, Nelson comments:

> Anxious to secure their children's competitive advantage in a world marked by increasing anxiety about college acceptance and increasing inequality (and perhaps shrinking options for elite status), professional middle class parents seize opportunities for educational success and enroll even their very young children in a dazzling array of "extracurricular" activities. They assume that their children are, if not perfectible, blessed with boundless potential. In response they nurture children to become the best they can possibly be; they also provide them with the "best" social, cultural and economic capital. (8)

Of interest here, particularly in relation to Fox's argument on the relationship between social reproduction and social class, is Nelson's argument that professional middle-class parents engage in intensive mothering to preserve class privilege to ensure, in Nelson's words, "secure status reproduction" (76). Indeed, when mothers engage in intensive mothering, they are, as Hays explains, "grooming their children for their future class position by providing them with the appropriate cultural capital and demonstrating their own class status relative to mothers who cannot afford such luxuries or do not recognize them as an essential element of good childrearing" (159). They are engaging in what Melissa A. Milkie and Catherine H. Warner term "status safeguarding" (66). Thus, the issue is not that the intensive mothering reproduces social status and class but that anxious professional middle-class parents in uncertain times practice intensive mothering in the belief that it will. Nelson attributes parental anxiety about children's futures among the professional middle class to several social and economic factors and all of them centre on giving children a competitive advantage and providing them with social and economic capital. Though not named as such by Nelson, professional middle-class anxiety about their children's future and their concern with capital and advantage, I argue, is the result of the specific political and economic context of our times—namely, the ideology of neoliberalism. The ideology of neoliberalism rests on the following assumptions and practices: the rule of the market, as seen in laissez-faire economics and free-trade policies; the cutting of public expenditure for social services, such as education and healthcare; minimal governmental intervention and deregulation; privatization, which results in the public paying even more for its needs; and the elimination of the concept of the "public good" or community to be replaced with individual responsibility (Martinez and Garcia). Susan Braedley and Meg Luxton, in their article "Competing Philosophies: Neoliberalism and Challenges of Everyday Life," argue that neoliberalism has negatively affected women in several ways. Melinda Vandenbeld Giles in her introduction to *Mothering in the Age of Neoliberalism* discusses these themes as follows:

1) Women's work is so poorly remunerated that women are the majority of poor people in the world, and this is only made worse by neoliberal policies. 2) While neoliberalism identifies women only as economic actors, the work of mothering must still be performed and is in fact integral to the reproduction of future neoliberal workers. However, due to the neoliberal commitment of reducing state expenditures such as paid maternity leave and childcare, mothers are left with no support systems. 3) Despite the emancipatory potential within the "feminization of society," neoliberalism remains an inherently male paradigm in terms of who controls the capital assets. (6)

Neoliberalism, as Braedley and Luxton write, "allows space for women who are willing or able to be like men, who present themselves as men do and who are able to compete as men do" (15).

Focusing on intensive mothering, rather than mothers and motherhood more generally as do the authors above, I argue that the rise of intensive mothering in the 1990s grows out of the emergence of neoliberalism in the same decade. Once again, the meaning and practice of normative motherhood are rewritten as a result of and in response to significant cultural and economic changes. With privatization and deregulation, many of the services once provided by government—schooling, education, culture, arts, recreation, health, fitness, and carework—have been downloaded to mothers. Moreover, with neoliberalism's emphasis on individual responsibility, mothers today are responsible not only for this downloaded work but also for how their children fare under neoliberalism. If children do not succeed, the blame rests solely with the mother, as it was her responsibility to ensure that they could and should. The forces of neoliberalism and intensive mothering have created the perfect storm for twenty-first century motherhood, as mothers today must do far more work with far less resources. Indeed, neoliberalism has created the "anxious parents in uncertain times" as theorized by Nelson, which is the subtitle of her book, and has produced the practice of intensive mothering, which seeks to alleviate this anxiety and uncertainty through the social reproduction of class privilege and status, as discussed by Fox. And again, these changes in the ideological and material conditions of mothering are due to the larger economic and social transformations brought about by the rise of neoliberalism in the 1990s.

Today's intensive mothering is also, as was custodial mothering in the postwar era, a normative ideological construction that functions as a backlash discourse, and like all backlash discourses, it functions to regulate women, or more specifically in this instance, mothers. Drawing on Naomi Wolf's theory of the "beauty myth," I argue that the current discourse of intensive mothering has emerged in response to women's increased social and economic independence, which includes the following: their increased labour participation, their entry into traditionally male areas of work, the rise in female-initiated divorces, the growth in female-headed households, and improved educational opportunities for women that took place in the 1970s and early 1980s. It seems that just as women were making inroads and feeling confident, a new discourse of motherhood emerged that made two things inevitable—that women would forever feel inadequate as mothers and that work and motherhood would be forever seen as in conflict and incompatible. I believe that the guilt and shame women experience in failing to live up to this impossible ideal are neither accidental nor inconsequential; rather, it is deliberately manufactured and monitored. Just as the self-hate produced by the beauty myth undercuts and undermines women's sense of achievement in education or a career, the current discourse of intensive mothering gives rise to self-doubt or, more specifically, to a guilt that immobilizes women and robs them of their confidence as both workers and mothers. Given that no one can achieve intensive mothering, all mothers see themselves as failures. This is how the discourse works psychologically to regulate mothers through guilt and shame. And, some mothers, believing that perfect motherhood could be achieved if they "just quit work," leave paid employment. This is how the discourse regulates on the level of the social and the economic.

A few years ago, a colleague shared with me a story that I believe illustrates well the argument I am making here. My colleague attended a conference where a presenter was speaking on the merits of intensive mothering. At the conclusion of the talk, she suggested to the presenter that intensive mothering was incompatible with paid work, to which the presenter agreed. My colleague then asked: "If a woman cannot practice intensive mothering while employed, what is she to do?" The presenter responded: "She should marry a rich man." Her response forcefully exemplifies how intensive mothering functions as a backlash discourse to undo the achievements of feminism through the redomestication of women. Intensive mothering thus, I argue, emerges as the normative ideology and practice of motherhood in the 1990s in response to changing demographics (discussed earlier), the rise of neoliberalism, and as a backlash to the advancements of women in earlier decades.

The discourse of intensive mothering as enacted in normative motherhood is oppressive not because children have needs but because we, as a culture, dictate that only the biological mother is capable of fulfilling them, that children's needs must always come before those of the mother, and that children's needs must be responded to around the clock and with extensive time, money, and energy. Petra Bueskens acknowledges that infancy and early childhood "are periods of high emotional and physical dependency ... and not a pure invention of patriarchal science" (81). However, as Bueskens continues, "The problem is not the fact of this requirement but rather that meeting this need has come to rest exclusively, and in isolation, on the shoulders of biological mothers" (81). Indeed, as author Toni Morrison has commented: "If you listen to your children and look at them, they make demands that you can live up to. They don't need all that over-whelming love either. I mean, that's just you being vain about it" (270-71). Although sacrificial motherhood, and in particular intensive mothering, requires the denial of the mother's own selfhood in positioning the children's needs as always before her own, these enactments of normative motherhood may be resisted, and women can and do find other ways to mother—ones that allow them both their selfhood and power in motherhood.

Regulations, Representations, and Reclamations: Introducing the Three Sections of the Book

The opening section on regulations explores the defining features and demands of normative motherhood, considers how it works as a regulatory discourse, examines the impact of normative motherhood on mothers and their mothering, and surveys how normative motherhood is reflected and enacted in social discourses, workplace practices, digital spaces, breastfeeding promotion, and social media.

In the opening chapter, "Contemporary Motherhood Is Mothering for Success," May Isaac argues that current conceptualizations of contemporary motherhood as intensive and neoliberal fail to capture fully how motherhood is socially constructed today and introduces "mothering for success" as a new concept that better defines the normative frame-work of contemporary motherhood as a social institution. Mothering for success is articulated as an ideology comprising of five doctrines that underpin its practice—namely, determinism, future orientation, professionalism, caring consumerism, and pervasive responsibility. It conveys how the defining characteristic of contemporary motherhood is the joint pursuit of neoliberal specific notions of success both for the child and for the mother. This fresh perspective on contemporary motherhood, which illuminates how maternal subjectivities align with and are actively shaped by neoliberalism's values, is critical because COVID-19 has increased the work of mothers and further entrenched neoliberalism's hold.

In the following chapter, "Does My Mothering Look Normal to You? A Poetic Exploration of Formal Guidelines and Internet Spaces," Elizabeth A. Bennett and Lori Koelsch explore how mothering norms are enacted and, at times, policed in mothering spaces. The authors employ autoethnographic and dialogic poetry as a means of evocatively playing with mothering discourses, as experienced both within digital community spaces and from regulatory bodies. In particular, the authors present an argument that is particularly timely three years into the COVID-19 pandemic, which has forced many mothers into exclusively online spaces to learn normative mothering. In her chapter, "Social Media and the Management of Normative Motherhood," Megan Marshall explores how social networks serve to reify ideological narratives of normative motherhood even while appearing to encourage mothers to express and perform resistance to these same ideals. She cites how the structural design of popular social media platforms maintains the visibility of normative narratives of motherhood while filtering and/or redirecting points of view that seek to resist these same ideological and patriarchal representations. However, rather than place blame squarely with social networks, she problematizes her argument by looking at how she (and others) may be complicit in keeping normative motherhood on the centre stage of social media. In the next chapter, "Social Conditions, Cultural Inheritances, and Normative Motherhoods in Times of COVID-19 in Brazil: Gender Relations and Historical Inequalities," Ana Carolina Eiras Coelho Soares and Sônia Maria de Magalhães explore the partial results of a broad investigation on the impacts of COVID-19, in the first half of 2020, on the life of mothers at a Brazilian university. The research, initially developed to think about the cultural heritages of Brazilian society in pandemic times, evidenced through the respondents' data entrenched legacies of normative motherhood.

In the final chapter of the section, "The Misogyny of Lactivism: Why Breastfeeding Is Central to the Discourse of Normative Motherhood," Karla Knutson explores how lactivism functions as a form of misogyny. She argues that lactivism imposes a normative version of motherhood by using shaming, misogynist rhetoric to monitor and discipline mothers who do not abide by the normative discourse of "breast is best." Drawing upon philosopher Kate Manne's theory of misogyny, Knutson illustrates how an example of lactivism, the article "Increasing Milk Supply," from the website *Ask Dr. Sears*, harnesses misogyny through two patriarchal mechanisms: positioning the reading mother as someone who must identify with the normative social role of maternal giver and policing women's future behaviours by admonishing and shaming.

The next section on representations examines how normative motherhood is interrogated in art, motherhood manuals, contemporary women's fiction, and feminist performance art. The section opens with Venessa Marr's three hand-embroidered artworks that visualize the ideals of normative motherhood—such as being saintly, desirable, and fertile—and how they are inspired by art, religion, and iconography. Her use of embroidery hints at the legacy of a stitch that has both empowered and disempowered women, which is embellished upon a vintage cloth that anchors the mother in the feminine expectations that surround her. In her historical tracing of motherhood manuals, Denise Hill, in her chapter "Childrearing by the Book: Motherhood Manuals from Birth to Nineteenth-Century America," demonstrates that from the Middle Ages to the present, maternal advice books have played a powerful role in prescribing normative mothering practices. Shifts in the genre over centuries reflect not only fluctuating norms but also changes in who is allowed agency to shape those norms. Hill demonstrates that the genre has vacillated between empowering women and stripping them of authority, a tug of war that continues today under "the watch of a digital panopticon." In "The Perils of Embracing Respectability Politics: Maternal Conformity and Normativity in Alice Walker's *The Abortion* and Nafissa Thompson-Spires's *Belles Lettres*," Zsuzsanna Lénárt-Muszka examines the representations of normative motherhood and respectability politics vis-à-vis Black American motherhood in two contemporary short stories by African American women writers: Alice Walker's *The Abortion* (1981) and Nafissa Thompson-Spires's *Belles Lettres* (2018). It discusses the narrative ramifications of prioritizing the figure of the ideal mother and reflects on the personal and social implications of adopting or resisting the imperatives of respectability politics.

In the following chapter "'What Finally Dragged Her Under the Water and Who Carried the Spark': The Intergenerational Trauma of Normative Motherhood in Celeste Ng's *Everything I Never Told You* and *Little Fires Everywhere*," I explore how Celeste Ng's two novels—*Everything I Never Told You* (2014) and *Little Fires Everywhere* (2018)—incisively contribute to a critique of normative motherhood in their portrayal of the frustrated ambitions, forsaken dreams, and lost selves of the novels' two mothers, Marilyn and Elena. More specifically the chapter argues that the novels do more than just detail and document what sociologists term the "motherhood penalty," they also perceptively and uniquely show the cost of this penalty for the daughters of these mothers. The final chapter of this section, "Buzz Kill and Eye Candy: Disruptions to Normative Motherhood in Courtney Kessel and Chloé Clevenger's *In Balance With*" by Natalie Bruvels, examines how this iterative performance disrupts the dictates of normative motherhood and the consequences on the act of viewing. More specifically, the chapter argues how operating outside the bounds of normative motherhood, though necessary and radical, likely results in a subconscious disappointment (buzz kill) for the viewer by not facilitating Kristeva's mechanism of primary narcissism of the Madonna form. Using Heal's concept of matricritics, which emphasizes description over interpretation, among other strategies, the chapter offers an alternative method of engagement with *In Balance With*.

The final section on reclamations explores how normative motherhood may be disrupted and destabilized through alternative representations of motherhood and the creation of empowered mothering support groups and from multiple maternal perspectives and practices, including Indigenous, older, and disabled mothering, and how, in so doing, these mothers claim empowered mothering. The opening chapter, "The Death of the God Mother: Deconstructing Normative Motherhood and its Resistance," by Isabelle Portelinha, investigates the imperviousness of (hegemonic) normative motherhood to alternative representations of motherhood. The silencing of the mothers' voice and, with it, the maintenance of the representational status quo are examined in light of sociopsychological processes of influence relating to normative beliefs. While offering a conceptual clarification of normative motherhood, Portelinha promotes the normative figure of the good mother to that of the god mother to foreground its power of influence and role in the muzzling of forms of everyday resistance. Beliefs in the god mother are ultimately related to the value-laden realm of neoliberal subjectivity, and the death of the god mother is considered to move beyond the pervasive and desolidarizing silencing of the mothers' voice—of the voices within. In the following chapter, "Supermom's Support Group: Exploring and Resisting Normative Motherhood," Rachel E. Stough and Elizabeth A. Bennett critique the aspects of normative motherhood that result in social isolation as well as consider the support structures that at first attempt to alleviate that isolation but instead serve to reinforce oppressive norms. Through the well-worn metaphor of the supermom, these mother-scholars vulnerably offer their own experiences of trying and failing to "do it all" in mothering, highlighting the psychological harms of the maternal ideal. Finally, in an effort to spark resistance against the oppression of normative motherhood, the authors call for a reconceptualization of mothering support groups.

In the next chapter, "The Art of Mothering with a Disability:

Challenging Normative Motherhood," Amy Wagner, Susan Smith, and Amy Crocker discuss how mothers with disabilities challenge the concept of normative motherhood. They describe the lived experience of mothering with a disability, which may serve as a cultural critique, as well as define medical and social models of disability and their impact on full inclusion and participation for disabled mothers. The authors point to the work of artist and disabled mother Alison Lapper, who through her artwork and as a subject of art challenges the normative motherhood ideal of able bodiedness and illuminates the full continuum of motherhood. The following chapter, "Older First-time Moms in Twenty-First-Century Canada: Challenging (and Changing) the Norms of Normative Early Motherhood" by Rosann Edwards, situates the phenomena of delayed childbearing in the Canadian context and explores the links between older first-time mothers and intensive mothering. Using her doctoral work on older first-time mothers and breastfeeding, Edwards argues that through the small acts of resistance, older mothers are finding the space that allows them to practice empowered motherhood while being true to themselves as mature human beings. In the final chapter, "Throw Down Your Bundles: An Anishinaabeg Mother's Perspective on Anishinaabeg Normative Motherhood," Renée E. Mazinegiizhigoo-kwe Bédard looks at normative motherhood through the lens of Anishinaabeg maternal cultural teachings. Through story, ancient prophecy teachings, and personal experiences, Bédard shares unique perspectives on the complexities of normative motherhood from an Indigenous worldview.

Conclusion

The Oxford dictionary defines the word normative as "establishing, prescribing, relating to, or deriving from a standard or norm, especially of behavior and relates to negative sanctions to enforce normative behavior." This collection explores the workings of normativity in relation to motherhood and examines how this normativity prescribes, sanctions, and enforces maternal discourses and practices to regulate mothers and their mothering. But the collection also shows how normative motherhood may be interrogated and resisted in both representation and action across various maternal subjectivities, including African American, Asian American, Indigenous, Brazilian, older, single, and disabled. In *Of Woman Born*, Rich writes: "We do not think of the power stolen from us and withheld from us in the institution of motherhood" (275). It is the aim and hope of this collection that in understanding the workings of normative motherhood, and by showing how they may be contested and changed through resistant counter- narratives and dissident maternal subjectivities, mothers may achieve the empowered mothering denied to them in the institution of normative motherhood.

Works Cited

Braedly, Susan, and Meg Luxton. "Competing Philosophies: Neoliberalism and Challenges of Everyday Life." *Neoliberalism and Everyday Life*, edited by Susan Braedly and Meg Luxton, McGill-Queens University Press, 2010, pp. 3-21.

Brooks, Kim. *Small Animals: Parenthood in the Age of Fear.* Flatiron Books, 2018.

Bueskens, Petra. "The Impossibility of 'Natural Parenting' for Modern Mothers: On Social Structure and the Formation of Habit." *Journal of the Association for Research on Mothering*, vol. 3, no. 1, 2001, pp. 75-86.

Chan, Jessamine. *The School for Good Mothers.* Simon & Shuster, 2022.

Chase, Susan E., and Mary F. Rogers. *Mothers & Children: Feminist Analysis and Personal Narratives.* Rutgers University Press, 2001.

Cook, Diane. "Who Decides What Makes a Good Mother." *Electric Literature*, 12 Jan. 2022, electricliterature.com/jessamine-chan-novel-the-school-for-good-mothers/. Accessed 8 Feb. 2023.

Douglas, Susan J., and Meredith Michaels. *The Mommy Myth: The Idealization of Motherhood and How It Has Undermined Women.* Free Press, 2004.

Ennis, Linda Rose. "Intensive Mothering: Revisiting the Issue Today." *Intensive Mothering: The Cultural Contradictions of Modern Motherhood*, edited by Linda Rose Ennis, Demeter Press, 2014, pp. 1-23.

Fox, Bonnie. "Motherhood as a Class Act: The Many Ways in Which 'Intensive Mothering' Is Entangled with Social Class." *Social Reproduction: Feminist Political Economy Challenges Neo-Liberalism*, edited by Kate Bezanson and Meg Luxton, McGill-Queens University

Press, 2006, pp. 231-62.

Hall, Pamela Courtenay. "Mothering Mythology in the Late Twentieth Century: Science, Gender Lore, and Celebratory Narrative." *Canadian Woman Studies*, vol. 18, no. 1-2, 1998, pp. 59-63.

Hays, Sharon. *The Cultural Contradictions of Motherhood*. Yale University Press, 1996.

Martinez, Elizabeth, and Arnoldo Garcia. "What Is Neoliberalism?" *Corpwatch: Holding Corporations Accountable*, www.corpwatch.org/article.php?id=376. Accessed 8 Feb. 2023.

Milkie, Melissa A., and Catherine H. Warner. "Status Safeguarding: Mothers' Work to Secure Children's Place in the Social Hierarchy." *Intensive Mothering: The Cultural Contradictions of Modern Motherhood*, edited by Linda Rose Ennis, Demeter Press, 2014, pp. 66-85.

Miller, Michelle Hughes, Tamar Hagar, and Rebecca Jaremko Bromwich. *Bad Mothers: Regulations, Representations, and Resistance*. Demeter Press, 2017.

Miller, Stuart. "How Novelist Jessamine Chan Created the Dystopian 'School for Good Mothers.'" *The Orange County Register*, 8 Jan. 2022, www.ocregister.com/2022/01/08/hownovelist-jessamine-chan-created-the-dystopian-school-for-good-mothers/. Accessed 8 Feb. 2023.

Morrison, Toni. "A Conversation with Bill Moyers." *Conversations with Toni Morrison*, edited by Danielle Taylor-Guthrie, University of Mississippi Press, 1994, pp. 262-274.

Nelson, Margaret K. *Parenting out of Control: Anxious Parents in Uncertain Times*. New York University Press, 2010.

Oxford Languages. languages.oup.com/google-dictionary-en/. Accessed 8 Feb. 2023.

O'Reilly, Andrea. *Matricentric Feminism: Theory, Activism, Practice*. 2nd edition. Demeter Press, 2021.

Rich, Adrienne. *Of Woman Born: Motherhood as Experience and Institution*. 2nd edition. W.W. Norton, 1986.

Thurer, Shari. *The Myths of Motherhood: How Culture Reinvents the Good Mother*. Penguin, 1994.

Vandenbeld Giles, Melinda. "Introduction: An Alternative Mother-

Centered Economic Paradigm." *Mothering in the Age of Neo-Liberalism,* edited by Melinda Vandenbeld Giles, Demeter Press, 2014, pp. 1-30.

Wolf, Naomi. *The Beauty Myth.* Anchor Books, 1991.

Part 1.
Regulations

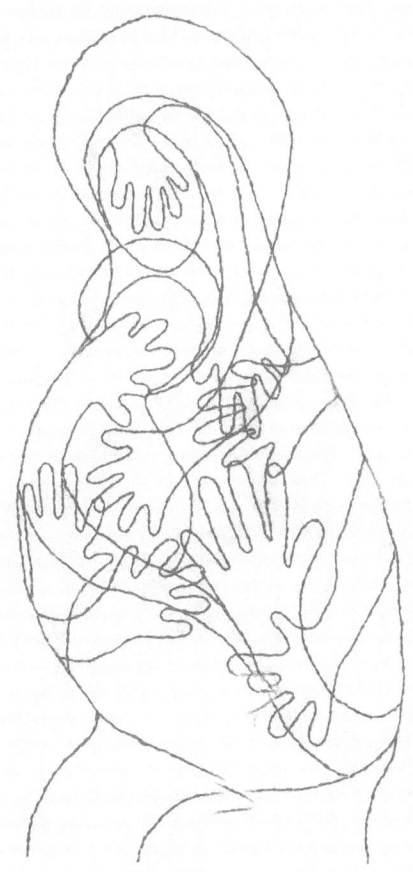

THE SAINTLY MOTHER

Chapter 1.

Contemporary Motherhood Is Mothering for Success

May Isaac

Introduction

The profound, intense, and life-altering motherhood experience is eulogized, lamented, and parodied in popular culture, wherein "mother" has become both a swearword and an instance of the sacred divine. Similarly, motherhood's resonance as pervasive and essential to human existence is reflected in the palimpsest of academic writing on its theorization, experience, and practice. Uniting both realms, however, is an acknowledgement that the concept of motherhood is not static. Instead, motherhood both affects and is affected by society, including medicine, law, culture, economics, technology, and politics. Therefore, notions of what constitutes motherhood are dynamic and adaptive responses to the broader political, economic, and cultural environment. In other words, motherhood is socially constructed. It is created and recreated constantly by members of society through everyday interactions, discourses, and social practices via dynamic activities and ever-evolving relationships (Glenn).

Although motherhood research is inherently cross-disciplinary—including such disciplines as anthropology, cultural studies, economics, history, law, literature, politics, psychology, and sociology—maternal studies have recent antecedents as a separate field of study. For example, Adrienne Rich's canonical text *Of Woman Born* was the first theoretical work to distinguish between the institution of motherhood and the experience of mothering. Drawing from the disciplines of anthropology, feminist theory, psychology, as well as from her personal reflections on mothering, Rich explores the two meanings of motherhood: the patriarchal institution that is male defined and controlled and deeply oppressive to women; and mothering, which includes women's experiences of mothering that are female defined and centred and potentially empowering to women.

Building on these insights, this chapter deconstructs and theorizes contemporary motherhood to articulate the normative doctrines that compose it, the practices that sustain it, and ideologies that uphold it. Its point of departure is the new parenting culture (Lee et al.)—that is, the broad and progressively global consensus about the informal rules and codes of conduct that define how parents should raise their children. Extant literature on the new parenting culture, though vast and encompassing several disciplines, is disparate, piecemeal, and spread across four areas: maternal studies, childhood studies, socio-political economy analyses, and parenting culture studies. Maternal studies draw attention to how the new parenting culture remains heavily gendered, with mothers bearing the bulk of responsibility for childrearing. This body of scholarship relies heavily on the concept of "intensive motherhood" to characterize contemporary maternal practice as child centred, expert guided, emotionally absorbing, labour intensive, and financially expensive (Hays). Intensive motherhood claims hegemonic status and casts heavy conceptual shadows over parenting culture and childhood studies, which simply reuse the well-worn label "intensive" to describe motherhood today. Studies from political economy and feminist political economy also employ intensive motherhood to guide their thinking. However, they make explicit the links between contemporary motherhood and neoliberalism—the present-day hegemonic expression of the continuum of capitalism. These studies probe "neoliberal motherhood" (Boyer) to identify how neoliberalism actively shapes maternal subjectivity and practice in contemporary society.

This chapter challenges the conceptual capacity of intensive motherhood and neoliberal motherhood to capture entirely contemporary motherhood. Despite the global ascendency of the logic of the market via neoliberalism and the enormous sociocultural, economic, and technological shifts this has wrought, intensive motherhood has persisted in locating its logic as separate from that of the market. This neglect of neoliberalism's influence on contemporary motherhood results in a failure to interrogate whether intensive motherhood as a concept still grasps the social construction of motherhood adequately in neoliberal times. Compounding this vacuum is the sparsity of rigorous theorizing on motherhood and its practice in critical and feminist political economy scholarship. Despite being driven by the desire to expose and explore how neoliberal femininities are constructed and lived today, the persistence of intensive motherhood as a guiding concept has resulted in a lack of attention to how neoliberal motherhood itself should be defined and its maternal practices described as an alternative to intensive motherhood.

This chapter fills this knowledge void and advances theorizing on contemporary motherhood by synthesizing scholarship from motherhood, parenting culture, and childhood studies and deepening this integration with critical and feminist political economy insights. This chapter introduces "mothering for success" as a new concept to build a theoretical bridge between intensive and neoliberal motherhoods through such a fusion. Its central argument is that mothering for success updates intensive motherhood for neoliberal times via a normative framework that defines, describes, and contextualizes contemporary motherhood as a social institution and dictates its practice. Mothering for success is articulated via five doctrines under-pinning its practice: determinism, future orientation, professionalism, caring consumerism, and pervasive responsibility. These doctrines provide fresh perspectives on intensive motherhood's child-centred, expert-guided, emotionally absorbing, labour-intensive and financially expensive characteristics. Crucially, they convey how under neoliberalism, the logic of intensive motherhood no longer stands apart from the logic of the market but is instead subsumed by it.

Specifically, the five doctrines help to illuminate how neoliberalism shapes contemporary maternal subjectivities practice by entwining moral and economic imperatives in motherhood to infuse the core of contemporary motherhood with a neoliberal-specific purpose of success for both mother and child, which is best expressed as "mothering for success." Mothering for success as a bridging concept between intensive motherhood and neoliberal motherhood provides a normative framework that helps us see neoliberalism's hues, tones, and influences on contemporary motherhood. Without mothering for success, we would continue our journey towards understanding contemporary motherhood on two separate paths—one that remains resistant to how the logic of the market has merged with the logic of motherhood and one that suggests several avenues for exploring this fusion without providing a detailed road map on how to do so. A reconceptualization of contemporary motherhood as mothering for success will broaden and deepen our engagement with motherhood for our times. Critically, mothering for success can enrich our understanding of how the individual actions of mothers and their experience of motherhood are embedded within, and dictated by, the institution of contemporary motherhood, which as the dominant ideology dictates the rules, norms, and conventions of the new parenting culture that contemporary mothers must engage with as a social institution regardless of whether they conform to it.

This chapter proceeds in three broad sections. The first amalgamates extant motherhood literature with critical political economy to justify the need for the new concept of mothering for success. The second section builds on this literature by incorporating insights from parenting culture and childhood studies to outline the framework of mothering for success via the five doctrines. Each doctrine illustrates how neoliberalism shapes the maternal subjectivities latent in intensive motherhood. The final section concludes the chapter with a summary of the implications of mothering for success.

Current Limitations and the Need for a New Concept

Despite the lack of theoretical consensus on motherhood, a central vein from which motherhood scholarship draws is the recognition that motherhood is socially constructed. The seminal articulation of this approach is Sharon Hays's concept of "intensive motherhood," which describes an ideology of childrearing that is child centred, expert guided, emotionally absorbing, labour intensive, and financially expensive. Even though it contradicts the broader cultural emphasis on market values, this ideology sets the normative gold standard for contemporary motherhood and dictates that even if the logic of the workplace operates in a mother's life, the logic of intensive mothering has a stronger *claim* (Hays). Since its coinage, intensive motherhood has provided the conceptual currency underpinning a plethora of academic work seeking to unpack the meanings of contemporary motherhood. As a result, empirical scholarship inspired by the notion of intensive motherhood has, over time, nuanced, broadened, and operationalized the concept in a variety of ways.

However, absent within intensive motherhood analysis is a robust investigation of the adequacy and potency of the concept itself to scrutinize whether the notion still reflects how motherhood is socially crafted in contemporary times. Instead, the literature has tended to dwell on the cultural contradictions inherent in the original concept, despite motherhood being continually reconstituted in messy, locally constructed, and globally influenced ways (Sherfinski). This neglect is salient, particularly given the enormous and significant changes in the social, political, economic, cultural, and technological environment since intensive motherhood's coinage in 1996. The gender reversal in education as well as the advent of social media, identity politics, globalization and, more recently, COVID-19 have significantly affected contemporary motherhood. To enhance our understanding of contemporary motherhood and advance our theoretical grasp of its social construction, we must take stock of intensive motherhood to ensure that our conceptual equipment still does what we think it does and want it to do (Bell and Green).

The penetrative insights of critical and feminist political economy scholars are relevant in this endeavour. These scholarship streams focus on neoliberalism, which operates as the "common sense" of our times (Humpage). Indeed, despite the term's slipperiness, conceptual sprawl, and ambiguity, it is hard to deny neoliberalism's hegemonic status globally in three forms—as an ideology, a mode of governance, and a policy package. Neoliberalism is a particular form of capitalism that ascended in the 1980s. Premised on the notion of a rational and self-interested individual, neoliberalism prioritizes and promotes freedom of choice, responsibility, and risk averseness via a reduced role for the state through deregulation, liberalization, and privatization policies. Essentially, neoliberalism extends market logic as a guiding principle for all human action (Harvey). However, so hotly contested is neoliberalism as a scholarly term that it is far better to deconstruct the term into doctrines and ideas that compose it and then relate them to particular practices (Gamble).

This chapter deconstructs neoliberal doctrines and ideas and traces their relation to the new parenting culture. Parenthood is a cultural, historical, and socially situated practice embedded in societal structures. Parents and children are defined through their mutual dependence; parents' actions actively shape children's lives in ways that make parenthood impossible to understand without relating it to childhood (James and Prout). The nature and meaning of intimate relations have been dramatically reshaped over the decades. Indeed, neoliberalism's fundamental role in this reshaping of care relationships is not only accentuated but elevated to a crisis (Fraser).

Parenthood epitomizes one of the most intimate social relationships. Therefore, the extension of neoliberal market logic into parenting fuses the economic and moral actor (Khoja-Moolji) in the mother, who both drives and fulfils the neoliberal need for specific types of compliant, individualized worker-citizens. The conflation of moral and economic imperatives is what constitutes the neoliberal self (McGuigan), the good neoliberal citizen (Randles and Woodward), and neoliberal motherhood (Boyer). These notions expose how maternal subjectivities align with, and are actively shaped by, the values of neoliberalism. The logic of intensive motherhood no longer stands apart from the logic of the market but is instead subsumed by it. A critical political economy framework can show us how the good mother of intensive motherhood is now the good neoliberal mother within contemporary motherhood.

The Normative Framework of Mothering for Success

Current theorization on contemporary motherhood is at an impasse. Specifically, intensive motherhood scholarship has neglected to keep pace with and scrutinize how neoliberalism shapes the social institution of contemporary motherhood. Critical and feminist political economy proponents, in contrast, delve deeply into how neoliberalism shapes the self and the maternal but have yet to provide a framework that defines, describes, and contextualizes neoliberal maternal practices as a coherent and updated replacement for intensive motherhood.

Concept formation lies at the heart of all social science endeavours. It is only through interpretative battles over terms and definitions that progress occurs in the cultural sciences (Gerring). New concepts are necessary when we seek to draw distinctions, grasp commonalities, describe new empirical phenomena, or adopt new perspectives on old ones (Schedler). Hence, in this spirit, this chapter introduces mothering for success as a new concept to build a theoretical bridge between intensive and neoliberal motherhoods. Mothering for success allows us to grasp the commonalities between contemporary mothering and present-day neoliberalism by updating and aligning intensive motherhood to better reflect the influence of neoliberalism on parenting culture. Mothering for success captures how the ideology of contemporary motherhood has been subsumed by the logic of the market rather than existing in contradiction to it. As such, it provides a framework for neoliberal motherhood practice by elucidating how the child-centred, expert-guided, emotionally absorbing, labour-intensive, and financially expensive characteristics of intensive motherhood have morphed into a new parenting culture in which motherhood is not just intensive but intensive with purpose—a neoliberal specific definition of success, both for the child and for the parent. This purposeful joint pursuit of success is the linchpin of contemporary motherhood as a social institution.

In the rest of this section, this chapter will discuss the metamorphosis of intensive motherhood into mothering for success by unpacking the five doctrines of contemporary motherhood practice: determinism, future orientation, professionalism, caring consumerism, and pervasive responsibility. Each has a neoliberal pursuit of success at its core. Together, these doctrines provide the normative framework for contemporary motherhood as a social institution.

Determinism

The deluge of media attention on the impact of parenting on children, a myriad of government family policy initiatives, and the globalization of child welfare concerns could well make the twenty-first century the "century of the parent" (Hartas). More than any other time, parenting actions in everyday life are now deemed to have a causal and robust link to children's future wellbeing and success (Dermott and Pomati), resulting in a kind of parental determinism (Füredi). Fuelling this determinism is the neoliberal doctrine of individualism, which reshapes the relationship between individuals and society (Beck) and makes individuals responsible and continuously self-reflective and self-producing to mitigate against an increasingly risky and insecure social, political, and economic environment. Determinism absolves community involvement in raising children and makes them the sole responsibility of parents. This responsibility places extraordinary focus on everyday parental behaviour through explicitly linking the minutiae of daily private parenting practices with the public good of society. In this way, the success of the parent is tied to the future success of not only the child but also the society. Furthermore, determinism makes private parent behaviour a matter of public moral debate and creates an environment where there is pressure to display good parenting.

Within neoliberal determinism, childhood is endowed with a pervasive sense of vulnerability, which is mitigated by appropriate parental behaviour. However, mothers overwhelmingly bear the burden of determinism as primary producers, consumers, and reproducers of the neoliberal world (Giles). Determinism demands unremitting embodied emotional work by mothers, who are expected to protect their children from risk by moderating and regulating their behaviour to ensure future success for their children. Determinism captures how neoliberalism's merging of moral and economic imperatives has shifted the child-centred focus of intensive motherhood into more of an emphasis on the behaviour of the mother. One example of determinism is how maternal behaviour is regulated through breastfeeding (Hamilton). The expectation for a mother to breastfeed is no longer a personal decision. Instead, within neoliberalism, breastfeeding is reshaped as a moral decision that a mother makes to ensure good outcomes for her child, thus contributing towards shaping future societies. Framed alternatively, a good breastfeeding mother is mothering for success—her own, her child's, and her society's. She is demonstrating her status as a good neoliberal citizen and contributing towards the future outcome of her child as one.

Future Orientation

Running parallel with determinism is the future orientation focus of contemporary motherhood. Rather than a relationship focussed on the present, a future orientation reconstitutes the mother-child relationship as a constantly pedagogical and future-success-focused one laden with educational opportunities, for both child and mother, in everyday life. Parents are expected to assume responsibility for ensuring their child's future social and economic success in an increasingly competitive, uncertain, and global marketplace. One example of future orientation includes how parents are urged to enrol preschool-aged children in organized enrichment activities based on the premise that future educational success of children is dependent on parental investment in the preschool years. Mothers are encouraged to do all they can to give their child a head start on learning (Smyth). Another example of future orientation is how parents expose their children to cosmopolitanism to teach them flexibility and open-mindedness to mitigate against and benefit from globalization as adults rather being motivated to share a sense of global connectedness among their children (Weenink).

Future orientation also underpins the concerted cultivation of children (Lareau), which requires enrolling children, at private cost, in a range of extracurricular academic, sporting, musical, and other activities designed to draw out children's talents and skills and increase their future competitiveness in the economy. Mothers are expected to raise self-sufficient and self-regulating children who excel in a range of academic and nonacademic areas and eventually become ideal neoliberal citizens. At the heart of future orientation is the merging of the logic of the market with the logic of intensive motherhood. A successful mother is one who can ensure the future success of her children by making the strategic optimizing of life opportunities an integral part of her child-rearing practice. In this way, future orientation coalesces the labour-intensive and financially expensive aspects of intensive motherhood and infuses it with the neoliberal purpose of success. Future orientation also helps us to expose how neoliberalism promotes and glamorizes middle-class values as exemplars of ideal neoliberal citizens. In particular, it can crystallize the ideal mother as the ubiquitous, middle-class, and professional wife and mother (McRobbie) as the ideal vision of neoliberal motherhood success who is most likely to raise successful children.

Future orientation within mothering for success refines and updates the emotionally absorbing element of intensive motherhood. Conflating the logic of the ideology of intensive motherhood with the logic of the market makes motherhood a proactive and vigilant status safeguarding not only the child's future but also the mother's success. The successful neoliberal mother is a pedagogical one, who is capable of actively cultivating cognitive and emotional skills in her children (Edwards and Gillies) through her own emotional literacy in being constantly alert and able to interpret shifts and fluctuations in her child's feelings (Füredi). The emotionally absorbing element of intensive motherhood, which is child focused, becomes an emotionally pedagogical practice for both mother and child under mothering for success. Future orientation resonates with how neoliberalism produces and modifies emotions for competitive self-advancement through personal strategies and opportunities. Therefore, mothering for success through future orientation can help us understand and explain how neoliberalism constructs motherhood as an exercise in self-learning (Jezierski and Wall) to facilitate the transfer of neoliberal virtues—such as resilience (Henderson and Denny; Hoffman), continual self-improvement through the "cult of passion" (Aarseth), and the self-regulation of emotional wellbeing (Hartung, Wright and Halse)—to children.

Professionalism

In conceptualizing intensive motherhood, Hays identifies an increased reliance on expert advice to guide mothering. Within mothering for success, parents and mothers are now expected to be the experts of their children in a neoliberal inspired trend of self-responsibility, professionalism, and managerialism in parenting. The construction of childrearing as a complex and challenging job requiring particular knowledge and skills (Füredi) has intensified even more since the coinage of the term "intensive motherhood." Added now is the expectation that mothers learn the skills necessary for parenting and then execute them to demonstrate their success as mothers and ensure their children's success (Shpakovskaya and Chernova). This entrepreneurial approach to parenting guides neoliberal policymaking, which aims to increase the competence of the family, which is evidenced through state-sponsored parent education programs. Parents, particularly mothers, are taught how to become independent problem solvers, as motherhood is increasingly defined as what a mother does (Ramaekers and Vandezande) in her role as a parent. A crucial component of professionalism is the mother's success in managing her children's emotions to develop resilience (Hoffman) to ensure their current wellbeing and future success.

Professionalism places an enormous burden on mothers. Not only are mothers the experts and risk managers of their children, but they must also model emotional wellbeing and constantly keep their own behaviour in check by practising appropriate self-care, for example, "me-time" (Reece), to carefully balance the intensity of motherhood.

Professionalism lends a managerial culture to parenting (Ramaekers and Suissa), which, for mothers, translates into entrepreneurial, do-it-yourself management of the self (Hartung). Hence, mothering for success via professionalism captures the conflating of neoliberalism and feminism, which constructs motherhood as a path to individual empowerment (Thornton). Professionalism corporatizes motherhood framing the mother as the family CEO (Medved and Kirby). The mother, as Family CEO deftly multitasks and balances family and work responsibilities. She demonstrates a form of confidence mothering (Holloway and Pimlott Wilson), for example, as a yummy mummy or mompreneur who can do it all and make it look easy. Professionalism within mothering for success also aligns with the postmodern concern of searching for identity, meaning, and self-actualization in a complex world (Giddens). In this context, motherhood offers a new sense of cohesion, direction, and sense of self-identity. Professionalism imbues motherhood with a sense of neoliberal purpose and makes mothering an identity, which mothers can constantly work at. Motherhood thus becomes a meaningful profession, which if carried out successfully leads to successful outcomes for the children. Mothering for success via professionalism can help integrate and explain the notion of maternal gatekeeping, which occurs when mothers protect their motherhood status and identity by restricting, inhibiting, or controlling the amount and nature of involvement of others in childrearing.

Caring Consumerism

Caring consumerism illuminates how neoliberalism has nuanced the financially expensive characteristic of intensive motherhood. In intensive mothering, mothers regard spending financial resources on childrearing as essential to good motherhood. Mothering for success updates this with the notion of caring consumerism to refine our understanding of the specific ways neoliberal ideology and the logic of the market guide financial spending in contemporary motherhood. Consumerism has traditionally been explored within economic parameters and only recently has a critical gaze turned towards understanding the cultural roots of consumerism as well as why and how neoliberalism fuels and drives forms and expressions of financial spending. Of specific relevance to mothering for success is how the cultural roots of neoliberal consumerism warp the desire to become and be with the desire to have (Wolff). In other words, to become and be a good mother, the neoliberal mother must buy and possess the correct consumer goods. Through such a reading, we can unpack and reveal the broader projects, desires, and ongoing narratives self-actualizing parenthood embedded within neoliberal consumerism.

Critiques of neoliberal consumerism culture help us identify how intimate and intrinsic qualities—such as care, love, and commitment to children—become intertwined with the logic of the market, which results in financial spending fundamentally underpinned by neoliberal ideas (e.g., self-responsibility, individualism, choice, competition, and risk aversion). This fusing is particularly relevant for motherhood, such as when moral and ethical choices can influence consumer choices. The frame of mothering for success can illuminate and further this analysis by interpreting neoliberal spending by mothers as caring consumerism. Specifically, we can use it to interrogate how the figure of a bad parent, central to the common sense of neoliberalism, merges with the notion of the neoliberal ideal—that is, a citizen consumer. Here, again, motherhood combines both moral and economic interests. Caring consumerism can advance intensive motherhood by showing how determinism, future orientation and professionalism, separately and together, contribute to making contemporary neoliberal mothering financially expensive. In other words, we can examine how success at making the right consumer choices not only validates the success of mothers but underpins their belief that it leads to successful outcomes for their children. Mothers often make ethical and moral choices as neoliberal consumers for their children. Some examples include purchasing environmentally friendly diapers (Takeshita) and feeding their children organic food (Cairns, Johnston, and Mackendrick). Mothering for success via caring consumerism can update intensive motherhood by showing how mothers' love, commitment to their children, and desire to be a good mother are incorporated within and exploited by the logic of the market. Perhaps, Tracey Jensen (38) expresses this best in noting that motherhood has progressed from "by the book" to "buy the book" (38).

Pervasive Responsibility

The concept of intensive motherhood is based on data from mothers of young children collected in the 1990s, which probed their ideas about motherhood rather than their everyday practice. This approach led, understandably, to the presumption that motherhood intensity tapers off as children mature. Consequently, intensive motherhood literature focuses primarily on younger mothers or mothers with young children. In comparison, the maternal experiences of mothers with older children and older mothers with young children have been mainly ignored, even though increasing evidence shows that intensive motherhood practices continue with older children—for example, when adult children go to university (Schiffrin et al.). Care for older children can even continue beyond menopause (Dillaway). Significantly, the transition to adulthood—hitherto traditionally defined by leaving the parental home, entering the labour force, getting married, and becoming a parent—is now increasingly extended, disorderly, deconcentrated, and unpredictable. Although the global nature of delayed adulthood has been noted and its structural causes have been examined (Newman), its impact on motherhood has largely been neglected. Employing the idea of pervasive responsibility within the frame of mothering for success can update intensive motherhood to include examining the effect of delayed adulthood on mothers.

Pervasive responsibility can also help incorporate how the proliferation of technology makes parenting of older children even more demanding, complex, and exhausting. Everyday mothering practices now routinely include monitoring children's social media use (Clarke) and interacting with technology to ascertain children's safety and whereabouts (Bernstein and Triger). The longer time frame of motherhood, caused by delayed adulthood, and the omnipresence required by contemporary mothering well justifies the identification of pervasive responsibility as a core feature of contemporary neoliberal mothering. Adapting the frame of mothering for success to pervasive responsibility allows us to investigate how the invisible mental labour of mothering (Lupton), as risk managers of their children, becomes unrelenting across a woman's life course, demanding her total responsibility for her children. Finally, pervasive responsibility can also reveal how notions of good motherhood now include responsibility for the quality of fatherhood and explore how they remain primarily responsible for the organization, if not the conduct, of caring work within the family. Studying this in the context of the longer life course of contemporary motherhood and delayed adulthood could yield rich results.

The Implications of Mothering for Success

This chapter focussed on mothering for success as an updated conceptualization and normative framework for contemporary motherhood as a social institution. Future research can explore how this institution influences the experience of mothers today. Future orientation, for example, can broaden and deepen inquiries into how a focus on the future rather than meaningful interactions in the present shapes family relations. In addition, pervasive responsibility can explore the impact of delayed adulthood on contemporary mothers. More generally, we can ask what are the consequences of mothering for success? Who mothers for success and why? How does intersectionality affect mothering for success? What role do fathers play in mothering for success? How can we think critically about the neoliberal ideology inherent in mothering for success and defy, resist, and subvert its agenda? The last question is significant because COVID 19 continues to harshly affect mothers and to deepen neoliberalism's nexus with motherhood (Güney-Frahm).

The normative framework of mothering for success, which defines the social institution of contemporary motherhood, deepens maternal studies' theoretical and practical engagement with contemporary motherhood. Of course, all new concepts need further testing and developing. However, we now have a conceptual road map for the journey towards a better understanding of the normative framework of contemporary motherhood as a social institution.

Works Cited

Aarseth, Helene. "Fear of Falling—Fear of Fading: The Emotional Dynamics of Positional and Personalised Individualism." *Sociology*, vol. 52, no. 5, 2018, pp. 1087-1102.

Beck, Ulrich. *Risk Society: Towards a New Modernity*. Sage Publications, 1992.

Bell, Kirsten, and Judith Green. "On the Perils of Invoking Neoliberalism in Public Health Critique." *Critical Public Health*, vol. 26, no. 3, 2016, pp. 239-43.

Bernstein, Gaia, and Zvi Triger. "Over-Parenting." *UC Davis L. Rev.*, vol. 44, 2010, p. 1221.

Boyer, Kate. "'Neoliberal Motherhood': Workplace Lactation and Changing Conceptions of Working Motherhood in the Contemporary US." *Feminist Theory*, vol. 15, no. 3, 2014, pp. 269-88.

Cairns, K., J. Johnston, and N. Mackendrick. "Feeding the 'Organic Child': Mothering through Ethical Consumption." *Journal of Consumer Culture*, vol. 13, no. 2, 2013, pp. 97-118.

Clarke, Juanne N. "A Study of the Portrayal of Bullying in Magazines for Parents: It Is Everywhere and It Is Growing." *Children & Society*, vol. 31, no. 6, 2017, pp. 441-51.

Dermott, E., and M. Pomati. "'Good' Parenting Practices: How Important Are Poverty, Education and Time Pressure?" *Sociology*, vol. 50, no. 1, 2016, pp. 125-42.

Dillaway, Heather. "Good Mothers Never Wane: Mothering at Menopause." *Journal of Women & Aging*, vol. 18, no. 2, 2006, pp. 41-53.

Edwards, Rosalind, and Val Gillies. "'Where Are the Parents?': Changing Parenting Responsibilities between the 1960s and the 2010s." *Parenting in Global Perspectiv: Negotiating Ideologies of Kinship, Self and Politics*, edited by Charlotte Faircloth, Diane M. Hoffman, and Linda L. Layne, Routledge, 2013.

Fraser, Nancy. "Can Society Be Commodities All the Way Down? Post-Polanyian Reflections on Capitalist Crisis." *Economy and Society*, vol. 43, no. 4, 2014, pp. 541-58.

Füredi, Frank. *Paranoid Parenting: Why Ignoring the Experts May Be Best for Your Child*. Chicago Review Press, 2002.

Gamble, Andrew. "Neo-Liberalism." *Capital & Class*, vol. 25, no. 3, 2001, pp. 127-34.

Gerring, John. "What Makes a Concept Good? A Critical Framework for Understanding Concept Formation in the Social Sciences." *Polity*, vol. 31, no. 3, 1999, pp. 357-93.

Giddens, Anthony. *Modernity and Self-Identity: Self and Society in the Late Modern Age*. Polity, 1991.

Giles, Melinda. "Introduction: An Alternative Mother-Centred Economic Paradigm." *Mothering in the Age of Neoliberalism*, edited by Melinda Vandenbeld Giles, Demeter Press, 2014, pp. 1-31.

Glenn, Evelyn. "Social Constructions of Mothering: A Thematic

Overview." *Mothering Ideology, Experience and Agency*, edited by Evelyn Glenn, Grace Chang, and Linda Forcey, Routledge, 1994, pp. 1-29.

Güney-Frahm, I. "Neoliberal Motherhood During the Pandemic: Some Reflections." *Gender, Work and Organization*, vol. 27, no. 5, 2020, pp. 847-56.

Hamilton, P. "The 'Good' Attached Mother: An Analysis of Postmaternal and Postracial Thinking in Birth and Breastfeeding Policy in Neoliberal Britain." *Australian Feminist Studies*, vol. 31, no. 90, 2016, pp. 410-31.

Hartas, Dimitra. *Parenting, Family Policy and Children's Wellbeing in an Unequal Society: A New Culture War for Parents*. Palgrave Macmillan, 2014.

Hartung, Catherine. *Conditional Citizens Rethinking Children and Young People's Participation*. Springer Singapore, 2017.

Hartung, Catherine, Jan Wright, and Christine Halse. "The Possibilities of Happiness: Australian Mothers' Aspirations for Their Children in Neoliberal Times." *Families, Relationships and Societies*, vol. 3, no. 1, 2014, pp. 67-78.

Harvey, David. *A Brief History of Neoliberalism*. Oxford University Press, 2005.

Hays, Sharon. *The Cultural Contradictions of Motherhood*. Yale University Press, 1996.

Henderson, J., and K. Denny. "The Resilient Child, Human Development and the "Postdemocracy." *Biosocieties*, vol. 10, no. 3, 2015, pp. 352-78.

Hoffman, Diane. "Risky Investments: Parenting and the Production of the 'Resilient Child'." *Health, Risk & Society*, vol. 12, no. 4, 2010, pp. 385-94.

Holloway, S., and H. Pimlott Wilson. "New Economy, Neoliberal State and Professionalised Parenting: Mothers' Labour Market Engagement and State Support for Social Reproduction in Class Differentiated Britain." *Transactions of the Institute of British Geographers*, vol. 41, no. 4, 2016, pp. 376-88.

Humpage, Louise. "'A Common Sense of the Times'? Neo Liberalism and Changing Public Opinion in New Zealand and the Uk." *Social

Policy & Administration, vol. 50, no. 1, 2016, pp. 79-98.

James, Allison, and Alan Prout. *Constructing and Reconstructing Childhood: Contemporary Issues in the Sociological Study of Childhood.* Routledge, 2015.

Jensen, Tracey. *Parenting the Crisis: The Cultural Politics of Parent-Blame.* Policy Press, 2018.

Jezierski, S., and J. Wall. "Changing Understandings and Expectations of Parental Involvement in Education." *Gender and Education,* vol. 31, no. 7, 2017, pp. 1-16.

Khoja-Moolji, Shenila. "Producing Neoliberal Citizens: Critical Reflections on Human Rights Education in Pakistan." *Gender and Education,* vol. 26, no. 2, 2014, pp. 103-18.

Lareau, Annette. *Unequal Childhoods: Class, Race, and Family Life.* University of California Press, 2011.

Lee, Ellie, et al. *Parenting Culture Studies.* Palgrave Macmillan, 2014.

Lupton, Deborah. "'I'm Always on the Lookout for What Could Be Going Wrong': Mothers' Concepts and Experiences of Health and Illness in Their Young Children." (2012).

McGuigan, Jim. "The Neoliberal Self." *Culture Unbound: Journal of Current Cultural Research,* vol. 6, no. 1, 2014, pp. 223-40.

McRobbie, Angela. "Feminism, the Family and the New 'Mediated' Maternalism." *New Formations,* vol. 80, no. 80, 2013, pp. 119-37.

Medved, Caryn, and Erika Kirby. "Family Ceos: A Feminist Analysis of Corporate Mothering Discourses." *Management Communication Quarterly : McQ,* vol. 18, no. 4, 2005, pp. 435-78.

Newman, Katherine. "Ties That Bind: Cultural Interpretations of Delayed Adulthood in Western Europe and Japan." *Sociological Forum,* vol. 23, no. 4, 2008, pp. 645-69.

O'Reilly, Andrea. *From Motherhood to Mothering: The Legacy of Adrienne Rich's of Woman Born.* State University of New York Press, 2004.

Ramaekers, Stefan, and Annabel Vandezande. "'Parents Need to Become Independent Problem Solvers': A Critical Reading of the Current Parenting Culture through the Case of Triple P." *Ethics and Education,* vol. 8, no. 1, 2013, pp. 77-88.

Randles, Jennifer, and Kerry Woodward. "Learning to Labor, Love, and Live: Shaping the Good Neoliberal Citizen in State Work and Marriage Programs." *Sociological Perspectives*, vol. 61, no. 1, 2018, pp. 39-56.

Reece, Helen. "The Pitfalls of Positive Parenting." *Ethics and Education*, vol. 8, no. 1, 2013, pp. 42-54.

Rich, Adrienne. *Of Woman Born: Motherhood as Experience and Institution*. Norton, 1986.

Schedler, A. "International Encyclopedia of Political Science." *International Encyclopedia of Political Science*, edited by B. Badie, D. Berg-Schlosser, and L. Morlino, Sage Publications, 2011, pp. 371-82.

Schiffrin, Holly, et al. "Helping or Hovering? The Effects of Helicopter Parenting on College Students' Well-Being." *Journal of Child and Family Studies*, vol. 23, no. 3, 2014, pp. 548-57.

Sherfinski, Melissa. "Book Review: Mothering in the Age of Neoliberalism." *Contemporary Issues in Early Childhood*, vol. 17, no. 4, 2016, pp. 456-60.

Shpakovskaya, L., and Z. Chernova. "The Professionalization of Parenthood: Between Common Sense and Expert Knowledge." *Zhurnal Issledovanii Sotsial'noi Politiki*, vol. 14, no. 4, 2016, pp. 521-34.

Smyth, C. "Boost Your Preschooler's Brain Power! An Analysis of Advice to Parents from an Australian Government-Funded Website." *Women's Studies International Forum*, vol. 45, 2014, pp. 10-18.

Takeshita, C. "Eco-Diapers: the American Discourse of Sustainable Motherhood." *Mothering in the Age of Neoliberalism*, edited by Melinda Giles, Demeter Press, 2014, pp. 117 - 131.

Thornton, Davi. "Transformations of the Ideal Mother: The Story of Mommy Economicus and Her Amazing Brain." *Women's Studies in Communication*, vol. 37, no. 3, 2014, pp. 271-291.

Weenink, Don. "Cosmopolitanism as a Form of Capital: Parents Preparing Their Children for a Globalizing World." *Sociology*, vol. 42, no. 6, 2008, pp. 1089-106.

Wolff, Kenya. "When More Is Not More: Consumption and Consumerism within the Neoliberal Early Childhood Assemblage(s)." *Global Studies of Childhood*, vol. 3, no. 3, 2013, pp. 328-38.

Chapter 2.

Does My Mothering Look Normal to You? A Poetic Exploration of Formal Guidelines and Internet Spaces

Elizabeth A. Bennett and Lori E. Koelsch

Introduction

In a text dedicated to the concept of normative motherhood, we consider it imperative to examine the ways in which such norms are carried out. Other writers in this volume seek to explore the notion of normative motherhood itself; here, we focus on how normative motherhood is enacted—and, often, enforced. In other words, we seek to partially answer Andrea O'Reilly's question: "How does [normative motherhood] work as a regulatory discourse and practice?" (478). We explore normative motherhood primarily through the use of autoethnographic and dialogic poetic inquiry, and we follow in the footsteps of Sandra Faulkner and others who explore and resist aspects of motherhood through poetry. Christopher Poulos defines autoethnography as "an autobiographical genre of academic writing that draws on and analyzes or interprets the lived experience of the author and connects researcher insights to self-identity, cultural rules and resources, communication practices, traditions, premises, symbols, rules, shared meanings, emotions, values, and larger social, cultural, and political issues" (4). He adds that "autoethnographers who are poetically inclined use poetry and poetic language to accomplish things straight prose cannot" (70) and notes that although most autoethnographic work is solo authored, there is a promising future for collaborative autoethnographies.

Through this process of poetic writing, we are especially interested in communal spaces in which norms of mothering are shared, enacted, and understood. We specifically explore mother spaces on the internet, such as digital groups for which mother identity is the primary criterion for membership. We are particularly interested in self-disclosure and transparency within these platforms and how norms of "good" or "ideal" mothering may be upheld through fear of public shaming.

Many mothers, us included, were forced into isolation throughout the COVID-19 pandemic and relied on internet support and advice to help navigate the challenges associated with raising children. Even before the pandemic, mothers sought support from social media (Basden Arnold and Martin). We seek to explore and problematize how norms are enacted in these spaces—ones in which mothers have the opportunity not only to interact with parents from different backgrounds and traditions but also to enter and exit these spaces freely, such that we can seek likeminded individuals who reinforce the same perceived norms. An integral part of this exploration is our understanding that the norms associated with motherhood are tied to culture and are perhaps more fluid than they initially appear. In addition to communal spaces, we will focus on the normative function of formal guidelines as set forth by regulatory bodies, such as the American Academy of Pediatrics. We consider how these guidelines are resisted and reified in parenting circles. In doing so, we question the notion of normative motherhood—in that what seems normative is regulated by the spaces one frequents and is learned generationally, locally, and through expert opinion.

Given the autoethnographic components to this chapter, it is important to situate ourselves within this exploration. We are both white, heterosexual, and married mothers of two young children, and we are both interested in the ways in which normative motherhood is enacted across a variety of milieus. Elizabeth has few friends "in real life" who are mothers and, as such, has relied heavily on digital spaces for mothering community and advice seeking. Lori, in contrast, prefers to seek parenting advice and support from friends who are also mothers, her children's pediatrician, and parenting books. Lori has been wary of joining both in-person and online parenting groups but has some experience lurking around in digital spaces. Elizabeth is a somewhat active member of her digital groups and spaces, although she has not joined an in-person parenting or mothering group. The bulk of this chapter is rooted in Elizabeth's experiences, although we situate them in dialogue with Lori's, via both prose and poetic response.

Gaining Entry to Digital Mothering Spaces

We begin this exploration with the norms for digital mothering spaces. Many of these spaces require interested mothers to respond to a series of questions and attest to having read the community guidelines before gaining access. Such questions include the following:

1) How many children do you have?
2) What are your children's birthdays?
3) Why do you want to join this group?
4) Do you commit to maintaining a supportive environment?

Remember! No MLM, no spam, be kind!!! You can only post from your side hustle on Tuesdays—look out for the business post!

The above are a sample of questions/disclaimers that we pulled directly from digital groups on Facebook and Instagram of which one or both of us are members. We invite you, the reader, to consider your own responses and reactions and notice how components of normative motherhood are carried out at the membership-seeking stage of a digital group or community. Mothers often prove their motherhood (e.g., how many children they have and how old they are). Although this is superficially an attempt to keep nonmothers from joining the group, we notice that these introductory questions serve to reductively enforce norms regarding what types of motherhood are good enough. (We have, for example, observed that it seems rare for digital group membership questions or rules to explicitly comment upon the many different ways in which women become mothers and how providing information, such as birthdays, may be considered invasive—or may be impossible to answer accurately).

We have noticed membership questions geared towards assessing prospective members' reasons for joining such a digital community, which both implicitly and explicitly enforces norms regarding good enough reasons to desire mothering spaces. Although we do not have access to such data, we are curious about the variety of answers (e.g., range of justifications; mothers who are willing to be playful versus those who prioritize seriousness). One of us has previously served as a moderator for one larger digital mothering community and was able to read many hundreds of such responses. Many read like our own. For example, Elizabeth's own responses to this type of question, she has recognized a pressure to prove that her reasons are good enough—that I am thus serious about and committed to my mothering—to be granted access. In the following response, she toys with humorous uses of punctuation or emojis, but she does not risk throwing away the opportunity to be a good mother: "I hope to learn more about other moms' approaches to gentle discipline and screen use! I am excited about the opportunity to connect with other mothers of young kids as we navigate remote learning ☺." Such overtures are certainly ways in which mothers fulfill obligations set out by mothering norms, especially in highly educated, middle-class spaces. Yet of equal interest is how such a seemingly innocuous question ("Why do you want to join this group?") is a site of enacting the norm.

Being a Mother-Member: Enactment and Enforcement of Normative Motherhood

"A Question for The Group"

It has been
[no exaggeration]
a full 4 years since I slept only in adult company.

I know it sounds hyperbolic,
or like I am attempting to gain sympathy from other
Mothers who have decidedly
Had It Much Worse Than Me.

And yet, I have a
real and
valid
question.

It is more a series of questions, if I am being honest;
but I am starting with the one
that I am most assured you will review and
post for the Others to review.

Following a detailed description of my situation,
[leaving out many if not most details]
I wonder
"are there other moms who are co-sleeping and
how do you wean your 42 pound child off of your bed?"

I am asking here because
In addition to my fully competent and very serious attitude towards mothering
You all know full and well that
I cannot ask my pediatrician.

Instead, I come to you,
fellow Mothers.
Please remember that I truly
have nowhere else to ask this question;
be gentle as I have not slept
in a full four years.

Here, Elizabeth considers one of her most recent posts to a digital mother community. We begin our poetic exploration here because this experience speaks to multiple aspects of the norm-enforcement process we described earlier in this chapter. This post, which Elizabeth submitted to a digital space with over ten thousand members, was approved for posting but was immediately met with several comments reminding me of the American Academy of Pediatrics's (AAP) stance on co-sleeping, which they call "bedsharing" to emphasize the dangers of this practice. The AAP advises that to create a safe sleep environment for infants and toddlers, bed sharing is an absolute no. Yet Elizabeth received over twenty private messages on the digital app, commiserating with her experience and secretively speaking to what she quickly realized was a different norm for sleeping behaviour. In fact, more women responded to her privately to admit cosleeping/bedsharing and share their struggles with getting their kids into separate beds than publicly commented on her original post.

Lori's Response

Another mother Elizabeth
        quoted in Valtchanov, Parry, and Glover
sought support from Facebook while sleep training
and

"Forty-five comments later
during the screaming
three-quarters of them told me I was doing child abuse" (136)

It is a radical act
to sleep as a mother

Between Worlds

Hey mamas! Can anyone in here recommend a **daycare**?
I **would never** put my baby in someone else's care.

My **career** would never be more **important** to me than my child.
I'm so **overwhelmed**; I couldn't function without this extra childcare.

I used to say I would never do **screens**, but the pandemic has really shifted—
What kind of mother gives their child a screen?

Mamas! Have you seen the **new story hour** at our library?
Mamas! Does anyone know of a babysitter who can take my kiddo to the **new story hour**?

Here to recommend our **sweet nanny**, who is moving to New Town. If you live there, text her!

Just moved here and I am feeling lonely **at home with my kids**. Any moms who can relate?

This poem, "Between Worlds" composed by Elizabeth, explores the shift that we have experienced—and heard about from other mothers—when moving between distinctly identified digital mothering spaces. As academics and psychologists, we share some overlap in the academic-mother, or mother-scholar, digital groups we frequent; these groups are often dominated by working mother perspectives (e.g., daycare is not demonized; babysitters are essential family members; screen time is understood; and mothers are simply trying to make careers and mothering work). Elizabeth is also an active member of other digital mothering spaces, including but not limited to those geared towards mothers in our shared city (Pittsburgh, PA) as well as those focused on specific parenting-related topics (e.g., gentle parenting and nature-based learning). In these other groups, mother-members occupy much greater diversity in terms of career, which is often the core of the more apparent felt shifts between spaces oriented largely around mothers' career identities versus around mothers' mother identities.

In this piece, we alternate between norms contextualized in our working-mother spaces, shift to norms contextualized in spaces occupied largely by moms who stay home with their child, and then back again. To stay grounded in the felt sense of these different groups, each of these lines is a quote from either a post or a comment in one of these digital mother spaces. When in a single digital group, the strength of the norm-policing can feel overpowering. If everyone in this space would never put their child in daycare, what kind of mother am I to need that help? If everyone in this space thinks screen time is fine, what kind of mother am I to feel wary of it? And so on. The strength of the enforcing becomes necessarily diluted when mothers occupy spaces with disparate perspectives, values, and orientations.

Engaging with Regulatory Bodies: The Mother Who Abides

In this section, we first present a piece, titled "The American Academy of Mothering Practices," in which we explore mothers' relationships to the norm-enforcing purpose of regulatory bodies. We then explore the ways in which medical providers—namely obstetricians, lactation consultants, pediatricians—serve to enforce aspects of normative motherhood in Elizabeth's autoethnographic poem "According to My Expertise."

"The American Academy of Mothering Practices"

A place of study
    Or training in a specific field
    Like artisanal bread baking, or neurosurgery, or fibre arts, or
    Mothering.

I often wonder if
    Anyone else is wondering about
    The very recently-established American Academy of
    Professionals Working with Mothers and Children
    And also the sensorial, terrific, encompassing, ancient academy
    of maternal wisdom
    There is just something about
    "Since the beginning of time..."

And yet
    We
    Mothers
    Are encouraged to look towards
    And evaluated in our adherence to
    The notion of mothering as
    Best practice.

Of the many sites of normative mothering with which mothers routinely engage, the advice and expectations of regulatory bodies—those that guide and inform professionals who work with mothers and children—can at times feel like the most complex to question or challenge. This is not to say that all or even most mothers feel compelled to challenge these entities, and in fact, many may feel more grounded in their mothering by working in dialogue with the guidance of predominant regulatory bodies. These bodies represent, perhaps, more overt ways in which norms are enacted and by which mothering is evaluated. Such enactment and evaluation can then be taken up as comforting, challenging, threatening, or a mixture. For Lori, normative guidance from such regulatory bodies has largely felt, though not entirely, helpful and grounding (e.g., "At least I have some guidelines to consult as needed!"). For Elizabeth, normative guidance from such regulatory bodies has largely felt, though not entirely, stifling and infuriating (e.g., "I wish the American Academy of Pediatrics would shut the f*ck up"). Importantly, as we explore in the next poetic dialogue, engagement with norm enactment from mother/child experts is one way to embody mother-identity and attitudes towards culturally dominant expertise. But we are also careful to avoid enacting a different kind of norm here by inadvertently holding up a particular kind of pushing back on expert opinion as a better or more radical kind of mothering.

"According to My Expertise"

My greatest desire, after a healthy baby (of course—my priorities are in order!)
Is to have an unmedicated birth
Perhaps in a tub of water? (During a full moon? Should I add this to my birth plan?)

> *It is of great importance that you understand that*
> *According to my expertise*
> *There are no medals for feeling pain.*

My baby is this-thing-called-breech
I have learned about this-thing-called-version
I want to try it.

> *It is of great importance that you understand that*
> *According to my expertise*
> *The only option is surgery*
> *If you care about your baby.*

My baby is small but growing
She is breastfeeding so well
I am feeling tentative, sore, swollen... pride?

> *It is of great importance that you understand that*
> *According to my expertise*
> *Your baby must be in the fiftieth percentile*
> *If we are to say that breastfeeding is a success.*

Elizabeth's attitudes towards expert opinions on mothering are largely critical, negative, and at times even defensive. So many aspects of her entry into motherhood have been met with resistance from experts—her obstetrician, who did not support an unmedicated delivery (she then switched to a midwife); her labour and delivery nurse, who laughed when she turned down an epidural and asked for a yoga ball; and her daughter's first pediatrician, who accused her of being selfish in choosing breastfeeding and forced her to breastfeed in front of him. Turns out the baby's latch was fine after all. Yet her towards expert perspectives is grounded in her own situatedness, and many other mothers grapple with expert opinions in a different way:

Lori's Response

Am I allowed to be
    an outlaw mom
        if I trust my pediatrician?

I feel sad about the different experiences that Elizabeth and I have had and am unsure of the cause. I certainly did encounter critical and unhelpful medical professionals throughout pregnancy, birth, and the newborn stage, but they were by far in the minority. Did I luck into kind and competent professionals? Did I just tune out the unsupportive comments and focus on what was helpful? Did they relate to me differently for any number of reasons (e.g., I had both of my children in my thirties and was a professor, whereas Elizabeth was younger and a student)? More importantly, how can we honour both of our experiences?

Concluding Thoughts

In this chapter, we have focused on the sites of, and ways in which, normative mothering is enacted and enforced in our cultural, socioeconomic, and educational milieus via poetry. Although we share many similarities, it is critical to note that we also represent different ways of engaging with mothering wisdom (in-person versus digital, for example); we also represent different responses from mothers on the receiving end of these norms. Differences in our experiences with and attitudes towards norm-enacting sites are part of what make our accounts here especially important in the context of a broader, rich dialogue about what normative motherhood means—and what such norms do for mothers living in relation to them.

Works Cited

Basden Arnold, Lorin, and BettyAnn Martin. "The Digital Maternal: Mothers and Social Media." *Maternal Theory: The Essential Readings*, edited by Andrea O'Reilly. Demeter Press, 2021, pp. 869-82.

Faulkner, Sandra L., editor. *Poetic Inquiry: Craft, Method, and Practice*. 2nd ed. Routledge, 2020.

O'Reilly, Andrea. "Normative Motherhood." *Maternal Theory: The Essential Readings*, edited by Andrea O'Reilly. Demeter Press, 2021, pp. 477-92.

Poulos, Christopher N. *Essentials of Autoethnography*. American Psychological Association, 2021.

Valtchanov, Bronwen L., Diana C. Parry, and Troy D. Glover. "From 'Fakebooking' and 'Flaming' to a 'Mom's Support Network': Reinforcing and Resisting Intensive Mothering Online." *Taking the Village Online: Mothers, Motherhood and Social Media*, edited by Lorin Basden Arnold and BettyAnn Martin. Demeter Press, 2016, pp. 133-52.

Chapter 3.

Social Media and the Management of Normative Motherhood

Megan Marshall

"*April 1965*—Anger, weariness, demoralization. Sudden bouts of weeping. A sense of insufficiency to the moment and to eternity..."
(Rich 30)

"April 2020—Same, same" (Me, marginal notes in *Of Woman Born* 30)

In the introduction to the 1986 reissue of her 1976 book, *Of Woman Born*, Adrienne Rich reminds readers that "Some ideas are not really new but keep having to be reaffirmed from ground up, over and over" (xv). Yet even with this reminder, her theorizing of motherhood as an institution that upholds and reinforces patriarchal society has remained relevant, perhaps chillingly so, close to half a century later. The reasons for this are wide ranging, complex, and inextricably tangled amid the cultural, political, and social institutions that govern human life and are beyond the scope that a single chapter (or my abilities) can deconstruct. Instead, this chapter is an attempt to grab the end of a thread and pull. More specifically, it explores the role of social media in the ongoing preservation of normative (capital M) Motherhood alongside the ways that a crisis—in this case, a worldwide pandemic—exacerbated the requirements of Motherhood not only in the home but across social networks as well. It is widely accepted that these networks sustain and intentionally manage dialogic content across popular platforms, determining the duration and dominance of certain experiences, perspectives, and narratives (Murthy; West). It is harder, though, to measure the potential for mothers to model a resistance to normative motherhood, especially given that the typical mother with a social media account carries little weight when she is alone. Certainly, when we consider a mother in terms of her membership to a larger collective it's logical to assume her concerns would be supported and amplified by others with similar experiences. However, this potential is often diminished when a collective is just one of myriad others all containing multitudes, each kept in place by boundaries they have chosen for themselves.

A Start

I joined Facebook in October of 2008, three days before my first child was born. In fact, thanks to the filter tool, it is easy to locate that first post—"is waiting"—which is still dangling in cyberspace. The post was a cautious and ambiguous signal that marked my status as host to a yet-to-be-born baby who was over a week past the due date. At that point, I was a social media novice and was intrigued by catching glimpses of friends' and past acquaintances' inner lives. At the time, signing up for Facebook quelled my impatience for labour to start. Within a day or so, I had been friended by a host of old classmates and friends who had already begun cultivating the roots of their online personas. I remember being intrigued by how the platform functioned as a seemingly instant series of windows into so many lives, and I was happy to be distracted from the pressing matters of birthing an actual human being and then, somehow, caring for it.

Then my son was born, and it was another two months before I managed a second post—"is dreaming of sleep."

In the months that followed, my online presence was informed by this new life. The sentiments, questions, and photos that peppered my timeline into the first half of 2009 emerged through the lens of early motherhood. Beyond providing a mindless means of escape during that blurred first season of childrearing, it was clear that Facebook was an efficient tool for posting questions or feelings—whether about ear infections, public breastfeeding, Aveeno products, the potential cruelty of the cry-it-out method, or the poetics of *Goodnight Moon*—and then getting a collection of responses in return. Those responses connected me to others beyond my partner and baby, beyond conversations with my aunts and mother, and beyond Dr. Karp's advice for having *The Happiest Baby on the Block* (2002) by using something called a "cuddle cure." In some ways, these connections seemed vital to me. I had moved back to Maine a few months before my son was born and was being rudely reacquainted with a relentless winter. Although my partner worked from home, providing me with his company and a set of arms to hold the baby when I wanted to shower or take the dog for a walk, he was both our sole earner and an introvert struggling to adjust to life in the small New England community I had grown up in—a town that was, in his words, "overrun" with members of my immediate and extended family. And though it went largely unspoken, and though his love for our son was immediate and enormous, it was impossible to forget that my pregnancy had not been planned, that he had left decisions up to me, and that we were now drifting along in the fallout of what I had chosen. This context was amplified not only by the emotional intensity of mothering but also by my problematic aversion to being wrong. At the time, "wrong" translated to appearing needy, confused, or regretful. My gut told me in no uncertain terms that to demonstrate to my partner (and myself) that I had been 100 per cent correct to upend our lives and our nine-year relationship, I would have to learn how to be a good mother.

As luck would have it, message boards, mom bloggers, *AskDr.Sears.com*, and a decent selection of laidback "parentainment" sites, such as *Babble* and *Mamapedia*, offered instant information and advice. The sheer ubiquity of this information made it easy to slip into what Sharon Hays conceptualized as "intensive mothering"—an ideology born from the assumption that optimal child development is dependent upon maternal behaviours that are singularly focused on being a good mother. Her foundational work, *The Cultural Contradictions of Motherhood*, came out in 1996, which was before the internet and social networks offered up at least part of the equation for Hays's framework: expertise and information. Although I had initially sought expert advice in books or independent websites, it was not long before most everything seemed to be integrated into social media. By 2009, Dr. Sears had his own

Facebook page with the (now defunct) *Babble* media/newsgroup following close behind; *Babble* posted its first article on October 20 2009.

By the time *Babble* eventually folded in 2018, I had barely even noticed. By then mom content was everywhere online; it had become integrated into popular web magazines, such as *Huffington Post* and *Slate*, and had been taken up by a slew of mombloggers turned Instagram influencers (who shall be referred to as "momfluencers" from here on out), along with a passel of newer content creators who had skipped the blogging step and built a social media following from scratch. I had by then joined a small handful of mom groups on Facebook, each with its own purpose: one with members who lived in my local community; another small group comprising of a few clusters of intersecting real-life friends, all of us connected by various northeast ties; and yet another group with over one thousand members who identified as academic mothers, which also contained many subgroups addressing specific concerns (such as dealing with migraines).

So, in March of 2020, when the COVID-19 pandemic locked us inside our homes, I was not without a place to vent, ask questions, or share information. In fact, these mom groups felt essential, especially during that first month of lockdown. These were communities I had selected to be a part of and that were comprised of members with whom I shared various frames of reference in a diverse set of contexts. Yet despite these differences, the major topics of concern overlapped across them all—especially regarding homeschooling/e-learning, mitigating the impact of isolation on children, handling health concerns, managing the emotions of children, family members, and ourselves, and finding ways to remain optimistic and energetic through the slog of relentless days of uncertainty. The recurring theme was that we were overwhelmed, exhausted, and grappling with a reality that offered no other option but to manage everything because we were mothers, and that's what mothers do. At first, the uncertainty of what was going to happen seemed to inject us with energy needed to keep our eyes on a mirage of the future, a hazy promise that this was going to end at some point if we could just get through the intensity of right now. But then when the 2020–2021 school year was well underway and the incessant spike of COVID-19 cases and political discord had long become a soundtrack of dismal white noise, mothers became a hot topic in the media. In October of 2020, *The Washington Post* declared that "working moms are not okay" and in February of 2021, *The New York Times* announced that mothers were "in crisis." The premise of these articles, and a slew of others like them, can be distilled into the following refrain: The pandemic has caused mothers to carry enormous and probably inequitable burdens, although to be honest, those burdens have always been there, and as we have done little to address these burdens in the past, it seems like we're set to do more of the same.

At times, these moments of media attention have struck me as trend-driven strategizing, which offers nothing more than a series of perfunctory taps onto the surface of this crisis, when a jackhammer might be a more suitable choice. Yet, casting blame at the headlines for failing to effect actual change was a way to avoid acknowledging that the crisis of Motherhood has no single root, but instead a tangled—and deeply buried—mass of them. Towards the conclusion of her piece in the *New York Times*, "How Society Has Turned its Back on Mothers" Dr. Pooja Lakshmin points out that the struggles mothers experience are not due to failures to achieve balance but instead the result of a systemic, worldwide crisis unfolding in a nation ill-equipped to deal with it. She offers, "In the end, there is no simple solution for the massive societal betrayal working moms have experienced over the past year; to pretend so would add insult to injury." While Lakshmin lets us off the hook from our own expectations, she is also implicitly acknowledging that those other expectations—coming from our children, their teachers, our partners, our colleagues, etc.—are still to be reckoned with.

When entering that watershed moment of locking down in earnest, the circumstances of mothers immediately began to play out online, which, of course, brought into sharp relief the ways social media has long been well situated to reify the conditions of normative motherhood, even while appearing to do the opposite. It also made clear how I had situated myself along those same lines, perhaps unintentionally, perhaps without even paying mind to what I was doing. Certainly, I was aware of how social media perpetuated unrealistic expectations, how it put a filter on reality, and how it offered up various echo chambers to dwell within. Yet it was not until the pandemic had become our all-consuming reality that I started to pick up on the insidious ways that mothering discourses have been mediated. Although social networks operate as polyphonic spaces that encourage the production (and consumption) of new ideas, it is no secret that they do so in the interests of specific stakeholders that have vested interests in maintaining the status quo (West). Although mothers might be afforded space to seek and share resources, form communities, and engage with a wide range of relatable content, the structural mechanisms of these platforms are designed to promote, filter, and redirect content in ways that ultimately sanction and reward normative Motherhood.

Subjects and Positions

My own experiences would be incomplete without getting a sense of what mothers—both within and beyond my circle of friends and acquaintances—have faced. After designing a survey comprised of multiple-choice, scaled, and open-ended questions, I sought participants by posting an explanation of my goals with the link to the survey in a Facebook "mom group" that includes international members, including mothers from Europe, Australia, and North America. Additionally, I asked seven women—friends and former colleagues—who collectively represent the Western, Midwest, Southeast, and Northeastern regions of the United States as well as Toronto, Canada—if they would be willing to share the survey link with mothers that they knew and who met the criteria for participation. The survey was open for ten days and was completed by fifty-five self-identified mothers, a handful of whom indicated they would be open to follow-up questions, thus opting to disclose to me their identities. (This information has remained confidential and deidentified in all documentation.) I did not collect demographic data, such as age, race, or occupation, and I did not ask participants to specify the number or ages of their children (although the survey did indicate that participants must have at least one child eighteen or under living at home during the pandemic). In this chapter, I draw primarily from the open-ended responses to questions about their perceptions of social media, mom/parent-related content, their reasons for engaging with social networks online, and how their online behaviour might have been influenced by the COVID-19 pandemic. At times, participant responses are summarized along common themes; I have edited their quotes for typos and brevity.

Additionally, given that my own experiences are what motivated my thinking and research for this chapter, I make use of first person-plural when warranted. I draw from the work of sociologist Laurel Richardson, who addresses the tensions between academic writing and the self, asking "How does what we write affect who we become?" (295). Reversing this question moves me to consider how who I am informs what (and how) I write. By reflexively acknowledging my position and emotions as a mother, I look to what Richardson calls "feminist-sociological praxis" (303) and pull from the perspectives and experiences of others to enrich and expand my own ways of knowing.

Privileging Normative Motherhood as a Research Objective

Scholars have interrogated social media's impact on parenting for well over a decade, scrutinizing the role of the internet—and then social media more specifically—along with the intersections of social, political, and cultural movements as they pertain to mothering. As is true for many lines of inquiry related to both parenting and social media, the tendency to pathologize is well represented in research and the media, especially when the two subjects are brought together. The addictive nature of social networking and gaming has been seen as a barrier to mother-child interactions, acting as a digital force field that disrupts essential emotional connections between caregivers and their babies (Kostadin and Dunn; Turner) and has also been cited as a reason for childhood injury (Bianchi and Phillips; Christakis; Prokopchap) and most severely, death. These cases tend to generate the most media attention, such as the circumstances surrounding the death of a three-month-old infant in Florida, whose mother admitted that she had shaken him out of frustration when his crying interrupted her game of Farmville on Facebook (Hunt). Additionally, social media is also named as a factor for rising rates of depression and declines in self-confidence in new mothers (Vries and Kuhn; Padoa et al.), and some maintain that it could pose a danger for those who are at risk for postpartum depression (PPD) (Epperson; Paterson). In contrast, a substantial body of literature does counter these arguments and highlights social media as a potential source for support, information, and social connections (Archer; Johnson; Madge and O'Connor; McDaniel). Moreover, social media has served as a site for positive interventions for helping to identify and treat mothers with PPD, especially when measuring its higher rates of consistent attendance against more formal, in-person PPD groups (Boyd et al.).

What stands out about these examinations and others like them is not just that the focus of inquiry is directed at mothers far more than fathers (although that is certainly important to note). But perhaps more intriguing is the implication that, for many, a primary reason to investigate social media's effect on women with children is to use it as a lens to dissect how well (or not) mothers are able perform necessary caregiving tasks. When social media is shown to enhance a mother's shortcomings, the implications of concern look to how her flaws might be to the detriment of her family, even when the focus rests, albeit superficially, on the mother herself. Furthermore, when social media is described as having marked benefits for mothers, the focus on increased knowledge or the cultivation of social relationships that directly supports the intellectual and emotional wellbeing of mothers themselves is seen as secondary to the ways improved mental health bolsters the ability to be a better mother, often without ever having to leave her house (or her children).

Yet in my survey, when mothers shared why and how they interacted with social media during the pandemic—even when they described how social media helped provide them with parenting-specific information—these benefits were often framed as central to their own wellbeing in terms of venting, getting a break from stress and tedium, finding distractions, cultivating new friendships, and being able to actively help other moms. As one participant commented: "It was nice to have a connection during the peak of COVID. It helped me work through the harder moments and helped me be able to support others during their harder moments." In other cases, the affordances extended beyond social connectivity. Some participants cited social media as essential for forging partnerships for collaborative art projects, skill sharing, and strengthening their professional lives:

> Being very active on social media helped me get through the isolation of the pandemic. In terms of mothering, I follow many mother writers on Twitter who write about how the pandemic and unequal distribution of labour in their relationships and/or failure by the govt/society to support working mothers, and

following that discourse, has helped me on a personal level in my own relationship. And my job, like, helped me broach these topics with my partner and boss to try to create more humane and egalitarian conditions for me as a working mother.

Undoubtedly, one might point out that the advantages described above will ultimately serve children and families, but I posit that these benefits should be seen as ancillary. In the majority of studies I reviewed, the research objectives were ultimately invested in the maintenance of normative motherhood, thereby ensuring that children and family unit remained healthy and able to thrive.

Beware the Bubble

Most users of digital media eventually come to recognize, even subconsciously, the ways they must perpetually adapt to the deictic nature of online texts. Since digital communication is in a constant state of flux, social media has been able to leverage trends and cultural moments in ways that expand the definitions and representations of motherhood. Facebook, Instagram, Twitter, Tik Tok, and other platforms contain myriad ideological bubbles in which mothers might situate themselves and offer countless depictions of non-normative family structures that celebrate diversity, choice, imperfection, and/or nonconformity.

Even so, 74.5 per cent of the mothers surveyed for this project stated that they belonged to social media groups that limited membership to mothers (they actively disallowed males and father figures.) Another 14.5 per cent said that they were unsure if the groups in which they members allowed fathers to join; one went on to comment that even if men were allowed, (there were no fathers present in the group). That women dominate these groups is supported by 2019 findings indicating that "81% of U.S. moms on social media use Facebook compared to 61% of the total U.S. population" (Edison Research), which echoes findings from a 2015 Pew Research Report that found mothers' engagement with social media to exceed that of fathers in "statistically significant" ways (Duggan et al.).

Beyond gender and parenting roles, private accounts on Instagram and Facebook Groups are popular for other reasons, as they encourage users to establish themselves as part of communities that share their specific sets of ideals and concerns. As one participant explained: "I'm particular when it comes to FB groups. I choose to be in groups that have people with similar interests and lifestyles. I believe that leads to meaningful interactions." Some participants shared that they belonged to stay-at-home-mom groups, and one mother stated that she belonged to more than one Facebook group that were specifically for mothers with neurodivergent children. Others mentioned finding common ground in groups for working mothers. Some had specific criteria: "The groups I'm part of are specifically for academic mothers so were very helpful in feeling connected to others experiencing the same set of impossible demands."

However, participants did not always describe membership to these tailored communities as helpful or necessary: "I've found supportive interactions with other parents on social media but mostly parents who I have a previous relationship with or who share other interests with me, like writing and politics. 'Mom' focused groups seldom feel welcoming." In some cases, private "mom" Facebook groups or Instagram accounts are seen as sites of drama and negativity: "I often learn about important things in my kid's school and our community, but it's also filled with negative comments. People are rude.... I never comment or post myself because of this." Those who find themselves in groups with members who do not share their views expressed that these instances made them feel isolated and depressed: "Sometimes rants or complaints would leave me feeling less alone, and sometimes they'd just ruin my day.... I think it really depends on the delivery here and the group I'm in. Some people seem to be really great at posting what's bothering them without drawing others into it, and others don't."

Many noted that interactions often turned sour when arguments over politics, vaccines, and school closures were juxtaposed with mothering:

> I live in a conservative and religious part of the country, so the discussions and opinions in [the local mom] group can make me antagonistic if I don't watch myself.... During the pandemic I engaged more negatively than I had previously. But where before I might have just scrolled past comments and posts that I didn't agree with or even found sexist or hateful, I'd comment myself and get caught up in drama. It was never worth it.

Other participants made similar remarks about their interactions in local/community groups. They noted that although these groups were helpful for seeking out logistical information, the dominant conversations and topics tended towards essentialist and idealized versions of motherhood (O'Reilly), leaving little space for non-normative views and topics to gain traction in group discussions. As one participant explained: "No one has ever been rude outright, but the few times I participated in a thread and referenced my sexuality, like when I mention my wife or use the word "queer" it was mostly ignored [and] the conversation would stop, or it would be like I had never posted. I don't even follow it anymore but will check in if I'm looking for something specific." These findings highlight the benefits of groups based on ideology, professions, and shared interests, especially for those who use social media groups to make meaningful connections.

Initially, I found that many of the sentiments and experiences shared by participants were similar to my own, which initially seemed comforting. However, the time I spent mapping connections within and across responses led to another feeling—unease. In ways similar to what many participants described, I have also purposefully used social networks in order to connect with mothers "like me" where political and/or professional similarities promise to neatly correspond to shared concerns about parenting. This is one of the key benefits of social media, especially given the ways that ideological differences can be deeply personal (and political) and seem impossible to resolve. These sorts of divisions caused many mothers (myself included) to limit engagement, respond with negativity and argumentation, or leave certain groups altogether in order to avoid conflict. However, what could these seemingly normative and homogenous groups offer us if we were willing to explore the intersectional potential existing in our local mothering community? Communities, whether online or in real life, are most fruitful when multiple perspectives and ideas are valued in order to create spaces that grow and change. To that end, if we only find value in those digital groups that align with our beliefs and practices, how complicit are we in maintaining the normative ideologies we are trying to disrupt?

Normative Momfluences

Early on in *The Mommy Myth*, readers are asked why "one reactionary, normative [motherhood] ideology, so out of sync with millions of women's lives, seems to be getting the upper hand" (Douglas and Michaels, 24). The authors coined this ideology "new momism," in which mothers maintain traditional normative values while also achieving excellence in their careers (Douglas and Michaels). The authors then go on to illustrate the ways this ideology has always had the upper hand, especially in relation to the various media that have historically positioned motherhood within a patriarchal framework. Social media momfluencers have amplified this largely unattainable ideal via the production of content that is often heavily edited and/or remixed (Chae); they have turned normative motherhood into an aspirational trend, which often results in mothers engaging in negative self-talk after comparing themselves and their families to the filtered version of motherhood they see on the screen.

These comparisons take place in a discursive landscape that has embedded consumerism as an essential mothering practice (O'Reilly), and scrollable media has blurred the line between entertainment and advertisements—often to the degree that viewers are not even aware that they are being pitched a product. As it is the goal of momfluencers to achieve monetary backing from corporate sponsors, they cultivate their online personas to perpetuate a blend of storytelling and salesmanship that has the capacity to strike unexpectedly. For instance, during a random browse through the video reels on Facebook in the spring of 2020, I paused to watch an animated woman who was sitting in the driver's seat of her car, sipping from a mug, and sharing a humorous anecdote about her "absolute panic" when her local library was closed. She then segued into promoting an interactive storytelling app that, apparently, turned her children into geniuses of the narrative form. Her disarming southern lilt drilled directly into my pandemic-induced anxiety about how well (or not) I was maintaining my youngest son's literacy development. This is not to say that this was the first (or last) time I had found myself in the crosshairs of a "momvertisement" (Sorenson), but it made me cognizant of how this sort of content was setting me up to fear that I had dropped the ball on my children's educational enrichment and that I had not been putting enough of my "time, energy, and money" (Hays) into getting my kids through the pandemic with their brains intact.

In the past two decades, the baseline informing Hays's theory of intensive mothering has been distorted by the content put forth on social media. The benchmark for being a good mom keeps changing—to the point meeting normative expectations threatens to exhaust the average woman's emotional and financial resources. Yet the perpetuation of social media content (especially from momfluencers) seems to suggest that we are not trying hard enough:

> I've found on social media (especially on Facebook and especially at the beginning of the pandemic) pressure to embrace this all-in brand of mothering. People sharing craft ideas, snacks, games, toys, etc. People desperate to believe that individual choices, sacrifices, or the stuff we manage to secure for our kids will override the massive structural problems exacerbated by this pandemic.

I contend that this desperation is a symptom of being exposed to the ways that momfluencers have glamorized the trappings of intensive mothering and used them to filter out the unpleasantness of COVID-19. Viewers watch gentle (or gently humorous) interactions with children (and husbands) that are colourful, pleasant, and aspirational—even when what is being performed is the explanation of how to best switch out and display a napping toddler's toys in such a way that he will immediately fall into a frenzy of imaginative play upon waking. The goal, of course, is to motivate viewers to consider buying the artisanal wooden playset with corresponding organizational bins so to make the magic happen at home. She is getting paid to perform normative motherhood to her followers so that they will pay her corporate sponsor for the privilege of being able to enact motherhood themselves. It is a dizzying circle with a number of implications—the most obvious being that motherhood is going to cost you.

Resistance or Reification?

However, there are foils to these pastoral images of motherhood to consider that counter idealized visions of motherhood with texts that suggest there are paths to resisting these norms. Commonly seen in the form of memes or short, humorous videos, these posts often serve as "one offs" that are not usually attributed to a specific person (or momfluencer), depicting mother-child interactions with generic illustrated formats or remixes of popular culture images and narrative trends. In some cases, these dispatches are posted with attribution, yet they often appear to be derivative of similar (usually anonymous) content and revised enough either textually or visually to warrant authorial credit. But are these texts meant to be pointed disruptions to the ongoing narratives of intensive and essentialist motherhood, or are they playful diversions meant to mock their own participation and acceptance of motherhood as relentless (but required) drudgery? In obvious ways, this content extends the same bad mom trope that gained traction in the film franchise of the same name as well as in several mommy blogs, some of which have been sites of controversy and intense mom shaming (Orton-Johnson). Reduced to memes and GIFs, the bad mom archetype has been rendered into a series of bite-sized rejoinders that lean into chicken nuggets shaped like dinosaurs, bottle feeding, messy kitchens, and lots of alcohol (usually wine).

Several survey participants also added additional contact information. After confirming that they were still willing to contribute their perspectives, I distributed a set of Google slides containing a selection of oft-circulated bad mom memes focused on drinking, avoiding one's children, and other declarations of maternal regret. I prompted participants to explain what they noticed about the bad mom trope, especially its presence on social media, as represented in the slides as well as any similar content they may have seen recently. One viewer indicated that they felt these memes were a way to respond to unrealistic expectations of motherhood: "I think some of it is just kind of poking fun at ourselves for pandemic parenting, but some of it is a response to all the mom shaming we were subjected to early on in our parenting." Others found that the memes reflect issues that are more problematic than humorous:

> The impressions I get from mom memes and tropes are that moms are exhausted, angry, and need a lot of alcohol to function.... Some of them are admittedly funny and relatable, but most that I see imply the need for wine in order for mothers to stay sane.
>
> I think it all downplays the very real challenges of being a mother right now; plus it plays into that tired trope that you're supposed

to hate your kids and be sick of being around them. What's happening is, of course, more complicated than that.

I'm certainly guilty of reading (and occasionally sharing) these. But in truth, they all just make me angry and sad for moms—myself included. The perpetuation of this insane idea that moms need to be perfect, and when we're not, we're somehow failing, is so damaging.

Acknowledging the ways these memes minimize the contexts and complications of motherhood and mothering is essential to understanding how they function on social media, given that so many seem to approach the quandary of normative motherhood by suggesting that resistance looks like a lot like failure (or even deviance). What also stands out is the poetic irony of these texts' common anonymity, especially considering that a primary grievance of the bad mom is the loss of her identity. Perhaps a good way to reflect on this trend is to imagine it as a collective of lenticular prints—images that look like one thing until the viewer blinks or tilts her head and finds it has turned into something else. Even when we are granted moments where motherhood is altered in terms of appearance and posture, normative expectations are fixed in place; we blink, and they are back. Yet, however illusory, these are noteworthy texts in the cultural conversations we are having about motherhood, even though they may further problematize, and potentially hinder, advancing a culture of mothering that belongs to itself and is not a series of expectations and archetypes (Rich).

An End?

In closing, I need to return to this chapter's initial goal to figure out the extent of social media's role in maintaining normative motherhood's stronghold in mainstream culture. Although the structural mechanisms (both economic and algorithmic) of social networks are certainly a factor, mothers still choose how they use social media. The practice of selecting bubbles and cultivating echo chambers on Facebook has allowed us to build inestimable discourse communities that provide security and comfort by remaining insulated against unwanted points of view. Moreover, by accepting the framing of opposition to intensive mothering in humorous, potentially problematic, and generally forgettable punchlines, we cope with normative motherhood instead of collectively fighting against it. Although many of us might be altering normative motherhood for ourselves and in the margins, nothing seems to be changing in terms of affecting visible shifts in the social and political institutions that benefit from keeping motherhood as it is. The urgency of headlines that underscore the damage wrought by patriarchal expectations has done little to address the range of concerns, perspectives, and lived experiences of the mothers in the margins; they have instead focused on mother-subjects that sufficiently embody the normative attributes that will make them recognizable to an audience comfortable with mainstream notions of motherhood.

It poses an uncomfortable problem for mothers who want to challenge patriarchal assumptions but would rather quit social media altogether than leave the solace afforded by self-curated social networks. Yes, cutting ties with social media is an option, but doing so is akin to taking a different route towards the same dilemma. A permanent (though evolving) institution in its own right, social networks continue to privilege patriarchal norms by situating Motherhood as the headlining performance on the main stage. If resistance requires claiming a spot on this stage—and perhaps deconstructing the stage altogether—our countless bubbles on the margins need to move towards the center, gather, and break.

Works Cited

Archer, Catherine, and Kai-Ti Kao. "Mother, Baby and Facebook Makes Three: Does Social Media Provide Social Support for New Mothers?" *Media International Australia*, vol. 168, no. 1, Aug. 2018, pp. 122-39.

Boyd, Rhonda C., et al. "Pilot RCT of a Social Media Parenting Intervention for Postpartum Mothers with Depression Symptoms." *Journal of Reproductive and Infant Psychology*, vol. 37, no. 3, 2019, pp. 290-301.

Chae, Jiyoung. "'Am I a Better Mother Than You?': Media and 21st-Century Motherhood in the Context of the Social Comparison Theory." *Communication Research*, vol. 42, no. 4, June 2015, pp. 503–25.

Duggan, M., et al. *Parents and Social Media*. Pew Research Center, July 2015.

Douglas, Susan J., and Meredith W. Michaels. *The Mommy Myth: The Idealization of Motherhood and How It Has Undermined Women.* Free Press, 2004.

Hays, Sharon. *The Cultural Contradictions of Motherhood.* Yale University Press. 1996.

Johnson, Bethany L., and Margaret M. Quinlan. *You're Doing it Wrong: Mothering, Media, and Medical Expertise.* Rutgers University Press, 2019.

Johnson, Sophia A. "'Intimate Mothering Publics': Comparing Face-to-Face Support Groups and Internet Use for Women Seeking Information and Advice in the Transition to First-Time Motherhood." *Culture, Health and Sexuality,* vol. 17, no. 2, 2015, pp. 237-51.

Joyce, Amy, and Ellen McCarthy. "Working Moms are Not Okay: Juggling Careers and Kids was Already a Struggle for Millions of American Women. Then the Pandemic Hit." *The Washington Post,* 2020, www.washingtonpost.com/lifestyle/on-parenting/working-moms-covid-pandemic-jobs/2020/10/29/e76a5ee0-0ef5-11eb-8a35-237ef1eb2ef7_story.html. Accessed 18 Jan. 2023.

Karp, Harvey. *The Happiest Baby on the Block.* Bantam, 2002.

Kushlev, Kostadin, and Elizabeth W. Dunn. "Smartphones Distract Parents from Cultivating Feelings of Connection when Spending Time with Their Children." *Journal of Social and Personal Relationships,* vol. 36, no. 6, 2019, pp. 1619-39.

Lakshmin, Pooja. "How Society Has Turned its Back on Mothers: The Primal Scream." *New York Times,* 2021, www.nytimes.com/2021/02/04/parenting/working-mom-burnout-coronavirus.html. Accessed 18 Jan. 2023.

Madge, Claire, and Henrietta O'Connor. "Parenting Gone Wired: Empowerment of New Mothers on the Internet?" *Social & Cultural Geography,* vol. 7, no. 2, 2006, pp. 199-220.

McDaniel, B.T., S.M. Coyne, and E.K. Holmes. "New Mothers and Media Use: Associations Between Blogging, Social Networking, and Maternal Well-Being." *Maternal and Child Health Journal,* vol. 16, 2012, pp. 1509–17.

Murthy, Dhiraj, et al. "Automation, Algorithms, and Politics | Bots and Political influence: A Sociotechnical Investigation of Social Network

Capital." *International Journal of Communication*, vol. 10, 2016, p. 20.

O'Reilly, Andrea. *Matricentric Feminism: Theory, Activism, and Practice*. Demeter Press, 2016.

Orton-Johnson, Kate. "Mummy Blogs and Representations of Motherhood: 'Bad Mummies' and Their Readers." *Social Media + Society*, vol. 3, no. 2, Apr. 2017, pp. 1-13.

Padoa, Tricia, David Berle, and Lynette Roberts. "Comparative Social Media Use and the Mental Health of Mothers with High Levels of Perfectionism." *Journal of Social and Clinical Psychology*, vol. 37, no. 7, 2018, pp. 514-35.

Rich, Adrienne. *Of Woman Born: Motherhood as Experience and Institution*. Norton, 1986/1976.

Richardson, Laurel. "Skirting a Pleated Text: De-Disciplining an Academic Life." *Qualitative Inquiry*, vol. 3, no. 3, Sept. 1997, pp. 295-303.

Sorenson, Jen. "Momvertising," 2009, JenSorenson.com/momvertising. "Momvertising." Accessed 12 Feb. 2023.

Turner, F. *Social Work Treatment: Interlocking Theoretical Approaches*. Fifth Edition. The Free Press, 2011.

Vries, Diana de A., and Rinaldo Kühne. "Facebook and Self-Perception: Individual Susceptibility to Negative Social Comparison on Facebook." *Personality and Individual Differences*, vol. 86, 2015, pp. 217–21.

West, Sarah Myers. "Raging against the Machine: Network Gatekeeping and Collective Action on Social Media Platforms." *Media and Communication*, vol. 5, no. 3, 2017, pp. 28-36.

Chapter 4.

Social Conditions, Cultural Inheritances, and Normative Motherhoods in Times of COVID-19 in Brazil: Gender Relations and Historical Inequalities

Ana Carolina Eiras Coelho Soares and
Sônia Maria de Magalhães

Introduction

This chapter presents the partial results of a broad investigation. Titled "Social Conditions and Cultural Heritage of Life in Times of COVID-19," the study explored the effects of COVID-19 in the first half of 2020 on the life of the university community of the Federal University of Goiás (UFG). The survey, which was open to the entire community, attracted more women than men respondents, which showed that issues the survey raised affected university students who are mothers more.

The survey questions addressed domestic care and childcare routines, and we noticed that the people who answered the most were cishetero mothers. As a result, the survey, which was initially designed to diagnose the impacts of the pandemic on academic life, led to a discussion about heteronormative motherhood, determined by the parameters of the respondents. The immediate association of domestic care, whether of children or adults, with mothers results in reflections about the idea of the good mother, who should always be the central care provider and expend a huge amount of time and energy on mothering. The mothers' socially mandated tasks in the private sphere, and their additional burdens, cause many in the academic arena to either drop out or become less productive.

Our survey showed the Brazilian society expects women to perform caregiving duties even in the face of a pandemic. Mothers in academe must balance their academic work with their caregiving roles, and if they fail, they are labelled as bad mothers. As Andrea O'Reilly rightly argues in her book *Matricentric Feminism: Theory, Activism, and Practice*, the emergence of motherhood as a patriarchal institution has resulted in discourses and practices that oppress, regulate, and dictate the lives of mothers. With the beginning of the pandemic, state and the measures of sanitary restrictions and social isolation and also seek to understand the strength of cisheteronormative structures that made these mothers feel comfortable to answer the survey, whereas other types of mothers were not interested in the research:

> A few words about motherhood are in order. As a foundational social construct, "motherhood" is invoked whenever we take parenting and reproduction seriously, regardless of whether or not the individuals involved are seen as, or believe themselves to be, "mothers." Even when we consider the practices and perspectives of queer fathers, transgender and transsexual parents, genderqueer parents, intersex parents, or even of queer people who did not ultimately become parents, we grapple with the institution of motherhood. Parenthood, fatherhood, family, and other social constructs may very well be simultaneously queered as we "queer motherhood." Indeed, such further queering is inextricable and inevitable. Further anthologies on queering fatherhood or queering kinship would be welcome contributions. It is also worth noting that the power of "motherhood as an institution" (Rich 34) means that too often *any* alternative versions of motherhood are displaced or dismissed. (Gibson 6)

One of the main goals of the research was to promote debates about maternity issues and gender equity. Social isolation was highlighted, even at the beginning of the pandemic, as a common problem in the domestic area. It is an example of the force of normative motherhood on the everyday actions of women's lives and how women face the burdens of unpaid care work and domestic tasks.

In addition to being primarily responsible for housework and caring for people in the home in general, there is also the emotional work, since mothers are most often responsible for planning and managing the home. For academic mothers, the pandemic has also reduced their production of academic work because most of their time is now dedicated to domestic-related tasks, which has further increased gender inequalities between women and men academics.

UFG is a Brazilian public higher education institution located in the state of Goiás, in the country's Midwest, which is a region highly specialized in the areas of agribusiness and the export of products and, thus, important for the country's economy. The university was founded on December 14, 1960, in Goiânia, during the government of Brazilian President Juscelino Kubitschek (1956–1961). Its history is directly linked to the expansion of higher education in the interior of Brazil as well as to the production of scientific and cultural works in the country.

Since its creation, UFG's main goal has been to spread scientific knowledge to the entire region, enabling improvements in the lives of the citizens around it. It plays an important role for the development of Goiás in terms of its cultural, economic, and social aspects. Currently, UFG is among the best twenty universities in the country. During the pandemic, as with other universities in Brazil, it moved many of its classes online in the format of emergency remote education (ERE). Classes at UFG were officially suspended on March 16, 2020, creating an unprecedented situation in the existence of the institution.

Methodology

This research, based on a descriptive-exploratory methodology, was motivated by the need to understand the different realities and difficulties experienced by the UFG's university staff. It analyzed the quantitative and qualitative data acquired through a survey, which was sent to students, teachers, and technical administrative staff from the entire university. Since the entire survey was conducted remotely, through an online form, and in a social and economic context that favored the portion of the academic community that could afford to maintain and/or acquire adequate electronic devices with internet, it is possible that the survey did not reach those who did not have internet access.

Reports from throughout 2020 showed that in Brazil, entire families were sharing a single cell phone to keep up with online teaching activities. Moreover, many women could not afford to stay at home and needed to keep working, even during the pandemic's peak times, which might have also influenced who could take part in the survey. To help mitigate these problems, we decided to keep the response form open for a long period of time and to periodically send the invitation to complete the survey to all academic units to enable more people to respond. Thus, the survey was open to the entire academic community through an online form from June 3 to August 10, 2020.

The survey was sent out through email, social networks, WhatsApp, and the university's official website. The filling out of the form was optional and open to the entire academic community. The survey aimed to investigate several dimensions of how the pandemic affected university life, and it was well welcomed by the community. Women and student mothers, particularly, responded to the form because they felt they were particularly harmed and overwhelmed by the social isolation and extra work the pandemic forced upon them.

The survey contained forty-five questions. The respondent was first asked to provide demographic information (e.g., gender identity, sexual orientation, and race), and the specific topics were introduced concerning the situations experienced by academics in the context of the pandemic. The pandemic's daily effects were explored, especially in relation to the composition of households and whether their members were socially isolating; the family's monthly income; and the decrease in the family's income, due to the pandemic, resulting in the need for emergency government assistance. The pandemic's negative repercussions on students and academics' health (e.g., anxiety, stress, and the use of medication) due to greater workloads and their implications for meeting research and study deadlines were also explored. Because of the overwhelming response we received, we could address all the data in this chapter. We, thus, intend to address the other questions raised in the questionnaire with more analytical depth in future articles, since it became evident that the women respondents had much to say about the pandemic's negative impact on their wellbeing.

These issues were important even before the pandemic. Silvia Federici has already pointed out that it is necessary and urgent to have a discussion about how women in academe often have more responsibilities in term of domestic care than their male colleagues, leading to more stress and less productivity for them. As a result, we must rethink these relationships:

> Nor is a position in the academic world a path to becoming more accomplished or creative.... It is our relationship with intellectual work and academic institutions that must be changed.... As long as studying is a commodity for which we must pay, or a step in the "job hunt," our relationship with intellectual work cannot be a liberating experience. (Federici 124)

In this sense, our study aims to compare the data and verify how social isolation has highlighted common problems in the domestic environment, where women face the highest burden of unpaid carework and house management tasks. Therefore, we also hope this work may promote debate about gender equity in higher education in Brazil.

A total of 320 responses were obtained from the academic community at UFG, which given the connectivity problems and how the survey was rather extensive can be considered a successful data collection. The exploratory method of the survey allows more space for respondents to respond, since it intends to understand in a representative way the specificities of the academic community. The survey reveals that gender inequalities, and especially maternal overload, reflect the inequalities of a patriarchal social structure that naturalizes domestic work, and romanticizes motherhood. And during the pandemic and its periods of confinement, these structures have increasingly overwhelmed the lives of academic mothers. As a result, data analysis had to focus on gender issues and unequal historical relationships about motherhood and access to academic teaching. And the results showed that during the pandemic, mothers had incorporated some of the tenets of normative motherhood—for example, essentialization, naturalization, idealization, and biologicalization—into their own mothering practices.

This academic research is unprecedented in Brazil, as no other research has explored university communities and the responsibilities regarding the care and maintenance of family routines in such detail. Although we cite research throughout this chapter that focuses on gender inequalities in Brazil and in the academic environment, our intention was to understand how the pandemic affected the ways of living of the academic community during the first semester of 2020.

Other research is being done internationally in a collective effort to understand the effect of the pandemic on women and mothers in academe, such as the *Journal of the Motherhood Initiative*'s edition on academic motherhood and COVID-19, which was released in spring 2021. Our research findings align with many of the conclusions found in that edition—that women, especially mothers, have been the most affected by the pandemic, especially those also marginalized by their gender, race, and class. This research shows that institutional policies that support women and mothers in academe are urgently needed:

> The statement "the staff is political," published in a book by Carol Hanisch (2006 [1970]), has spread internationally and has become an important motto for the feminist struggles, even if it has generated debates and controversies. The idea contained in the statement is that the personal experiences of women were also inserted in a political network, that is, in a network of wider power relations, of which women's experiences were a product and not isolated situations. This conception was indispensable for the reception of women's demands and for the understanding that these demands were common among women and were part of a macro context. (Saldanha and Gonçalves 82)

The objective of the research was to understand the cultural and social heritages of our community as well as the realities of people's experiences and their production in the academic environment in one of the largest and most important universities in West-Central Brazil.

Our research shows that historically rooted ideas about the good mother are still obstacles to the advancement of mothers in academic careers, since one of the central findings of all research on normative motherhood is mothers' fatigue and their immense work overload, which can even be romanticized and seen as natural love. In university life, it also means low productivity, dropping out of higher education courses and master's and doctoral degrees, and failing to advance to the highest management positions within universities. If normative motherhood states so repeatedly that motherhood completes and satisfies the lives of mothers, why should mothers aim for other or more goals in their lives? Fortunately, these same mothers responded to the survey, which means that they are in university and are resisting these discourses.

The questions were designed to understand who takes primary responsibility for domestic work and how this work may affect their mental health, especially women, who have historically been responsible for planning and managing the house. It is therefore necessary, initially, to establish the profile of the respondents and then analyze the results concerning the impact of household work on the daily lives of the academic community affected by the pandemic.

We also mention some current research, such as that published by Parent in Science (Santos Machado et al.), which alarmingly notes that the pandemic is reducing the production of academic papers by women scientists, since the time required to do intellectual work only becomes possible after the domestic work. This situation has only been exacerbated by the pandemic, which the university has done little to address.

The Academic Community

The academic community of UFG is formed by undergraduate and graduate students (specialization, master's, and doctorate), college of application (CEPAE), administrative staff, and professors. The research was done in an exploratory way and sent to all sectors of the community through institutional emails and the pages of the university's websites and internal online communication networks. The responses collected, above all, also demonstrate the respondents' interest in the survey.

From the first question, it is noticeable that the engagement in research was concentrated among students from both undergraduate and graduate courses offered by the university. Most of the answers were provided by students (a total of 73.5 per cent of the answers), as shown in the figure below.

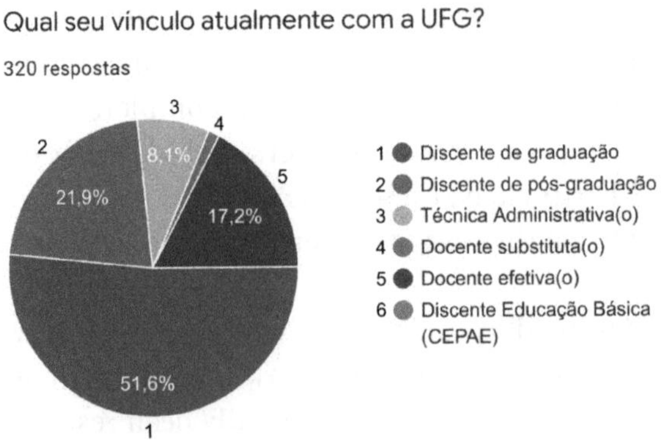

Qual seu vínculo atualmente com a UFG?

320 respostas

1 ● Discente de graduação
2 ● Discente de pós-graduação
3 ● Técnica Administrativa(o)
4 ● Docente substituta(o)
5 ● Docente efetiva(o)
6 ● Discente Educação Básica (CEPAE)

Figure 1. Question: What is your current connection with UFG?

Gender Identification and Sexual Orientation

The profile is important to understand who was interested in answering the questions and whether it identified itself with the research that was being conducted. However, other socio-historical-cultural information was needed for a better understanding of the respondent audience. Therefore, the respondents were asked about their gender, sexual orientation, and race/colour, following the research parameters used by the Brazilian Institute of Geography and Statistics (IBGE), the federal administrative agency responsible for conducting social statistical censuses in Brazil.

Em termos de identidade de gênero, como você se identifica?

320 respostas

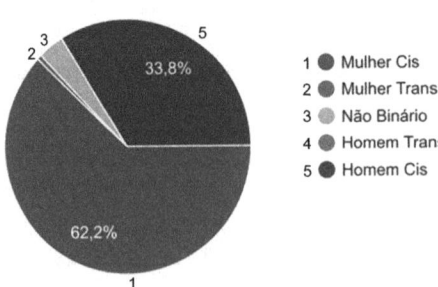

1 ● Mulher Cis
2 ● Mulher Trans
3 ● Não Binário
4 ● Homem Trans
5 ● Homem Cis

Figure 2. Question: In terms of gender identity, how do you identify yourself?

Composed mostly of female students, the following questions sought to better understand the profile of people who were interested in answering the survey and/or had access to the internet and contact with the e-mails sent by UFG, since all the disclosure was done online through institutional e-mails and/or social media linked to UFG.

Figures 2 and 3 show that most students identify themselves in a cisgender manner; only 4 per cent of respondents identified themselves as transgender or nonbinary. It is necessary to emphasize, however, that this survey demonstrates, among other possibilities of analysis, two issues that need to be discussed in the academic environment: access to higher education for the LGBTQ community as well as the precariousness of access to the internet, which many people have experienced throughout the period of social isolation. The latter, however, has primarily affected historically vulnerable populations in Brazilian society:

> The LGBTI+ population in Brazil is distributed among all economic classes, and thus most of this segment lives in situations of poverty or extreme social and economic vulnerability.... What worried us before—violence, discrimination, denial of rights and the poverty situation of the LGBTI population, especially trans and non-binary people—the coronavirus pandemic brought another problem: the economic survival of this population segment, since most of them experience precarious work, informal work and/or have no work at all, doing piecemeal work in various areas or sex work. (IGBE)

In this sense, it is possible to infer that there is a real commitment by UFG to establish policies to help the student population, in which students who experience difficulties can obtain support through various projects and programs:

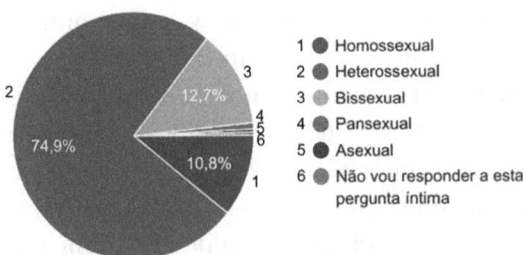

Figure 3. Question: What is your sexual orientation?

This profile, far from being a reflection of academic reality, is actually a rarity in Brazilian universities. After all, if in times of crisis the only people who can remain committed to formal knowledge structures are hetero and cisgender people, is our academic system really as democratic as it is intended to be?

This is not a question that this article intends to answer; instead, it aims to instigate new research and promote full gender and sexual equality.

This discourse of equality, however, tends to reinforce differences of opportunity in academic training and qualification; it pretends to be more egalitarian but hides the historical (and contemporary) reality of racism in the Americas, particularly in Brazilian history, in which universities reflect these racist, homophobic, and patriarchal heritages:

Race or Colour Identification

As seen in figure 4, 53.8 per cent of respondents identify themselves as white, 31.3 per cent as Brown, and 10.3 per cent as Black—a finding that corroborates the outline of this historically privileged profile.

Privilege or nonprivilege is understood as the position occupied by a group or individual throughout their social and historical trajectories. In Brazil, this notion was built on the very foundation of colonization:

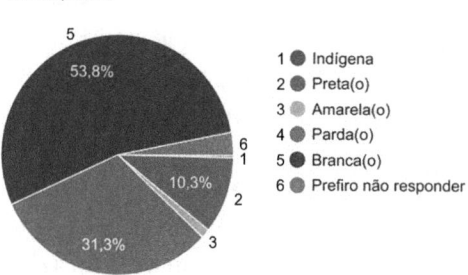

Figure 4. Question: According to the categories of the IBGE census, what race or colour do you identify as?

Although contemporary societies are governed by the principle of equality, by balanced powers and by the distinction between the public and the private, they often disguise their privileges and their social hierarchies. It is necessary, therefore, to be attentive to the transformations of the Modern Age. Differences also in space. In the globalized world, the opportunities for study and access to information cover vast regions in Europe, America, Asia and Africa, parts of the enormous Iberian world between the 16th and 18th centuries. The possibilities of communication and exchange among researchers have also grown. In this context, the paradigm of national histories has been revised, especially in relation to approaches that include the so-called Portuguese or Spanish empires or the Spanish monarchy in its European and plural dimension. Current historical research is more attentive to heterodoxies and cultural mixes, as well as to negotiations around central power. On the other hand, the greater contact with funds from European documents allows us to enrich some of Buarque de Holanda's reflections, for example, regarding "noblemanship" and the logic of personal prestige, which deserve to be contextualized in the context of noble houses, the politics of granting of bounties and prestigious military orders, as well as related to the concepts of honor and reputation. (Monteiro et al. 11-12)

In other words, privilege is a kind of right granted due to its own social existence, advantage, or immunity accessible only to that category. This concept today becomes basic to understanding the historical marks of the powers that are structured to perpetuate inequalities that benefit some groups to the detriment of others, especially those considered in some way less favoured in terms of ethnicity/race, gender, sexual orientation, and/or religion.

Only 4.6 per cent of people identified themselves as Indigenous, East Asian, or preferred not to answer the question. It is necessary to understand this profile of responses within the context of Brazil's historical roots marked by slavery and deep social inequalities:

> Racism—which materializes as racial discrimination—is defined by its systemic character. It is not, therefore, just a discriminatory act or even a set of acts, but a process in which conditions of subordination and privilege that are distributed among racial groups are reproduced in politics, economics, and daily relationships…. Thus the main thesis of those who affirm the existence of institutional racism is that racial conflicts are also part of institutions. Thus, racial inequality is a characteristic of society not only because of the isolated action of racist groups or individuals, but fundamentally because institutions are hegemonized by certain racial groups that use institutional mechanisms to impose their political and economic interests. What can be verified so far is that the institutional conception of racism treats power as a central element of racial relations. In fact, racism is domination. (Almeida 26-32/33)

This initial profile conducted in the survey was fundamental to understanding who the respondent community was. We can affirm that white cishetero mothers were the largest group of respondents, signalling the repeated rewriting of the dominant norm as part of a process of the right to belong. One of the main issues of heterosexism is precisely this notion of the comfort of belonging, and the heteronormative motherhoods that attended the survey empirically demonstrate the strength of this historical, political, and social structure. In this way, it is also understandable that white mothers felt more compelled to respond, since normative intensive motherhood is also a matter of class. Normative motherhood, therefore, is restricted to those who can perform the socially established rules, with other forms of motherhood and people being positioned as bad mothers.

The Behaviour of Families at the Beginning of the COVID-19 Pandemic

In terms of complying with self-isolation policies, only 39.1 per cent of the respondents fully obeyed the social isolation measures, and 60.3 per cent said they only partially followed the restrictive sanitary measures. The justifications given for not complying with social isolation mostly centred on the concept of work. The people with whom they lived still had to go to work, even with the lockdown recommendation. Work was seen as a priority for the maintenance of material living conditions, although it increased the exposure to the virus and the possibility of illness. Even though women themselves also needed to work outside the home, they continued to perform the majority of household and domestic tasks.

Você e as pessoas que moram na sua casa estão em isolamento social?

320 respostas

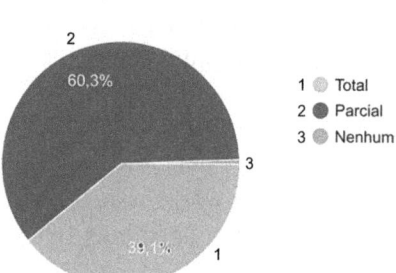

Figure 5. Question: Are you and the people who live in your house in social isolation?

Thus, it is necessary to think about not only how the pandemic has affected society as a whole but also how it has made women's lives even more difficult. Women's domestic work and the greater frequency of women in informal work makes them even more vulnerable from an economic and social point of view, especially during a crisis like the COVID-19 pandemic.

> Women continue to be the most affected by unpaid work, mainly in times of crisis. Due to saturation of health systems and when schools close, the care tasks fall mainly on women, who in general, have the responsibility to take care of sick relatives, elderly people and children.
>
> Employment and care services affect workers in general and, in particular, informal and domestic women workers. The capacity of women to ensure their livelihood is highly affected by the pandemic. Experience has shown that quarantines considerably reduce economic and subsistence activities and affect sectors highly populated by women, such as commerce or tourism.
>
> The reduction in economic activity affects ... informal workers who lose their means of livelihood almost immediately, without any network or possibility to replace the daily income in general. It also affects ... domestic workers who face at least two specific challenges: ... the challenges arising from the greater burden of care due to the increase of unpaid work in the residences and the care of the children during the closing of schools ... [and the] possibility of income loss when, for health reasons, they are requested to stop working because they are considered a risk of contagion for the families they work with. (Onumulheres)

The lack of the possibility of fulfilling social isolation policies highlights economic and social differences: "Confinement is a policy of the rich. It is just one example, among so many others, of a world organization founded on the exploitation and manufacture of superfluous lives" (Vergès 22).

Motherhood is a recurring theme in gender studies and feminist research. In Brazil, research has also been undertaken to examine motherhood in several periods of history. The normativity of maternity in Brazil and its definite link to the structures of patriarchy has its roots prior to World War II and is mixed with such elements as structural racism and a deep social, political, economic and cultural inequality. These elements naturalized motherhood among women, which meant women could only perform two social roles, wife and mother:

> Approaching themes that were supposed to be adequate for the female mind and through the justification of love, the dominant

order in the relationship between the sexes was consolidated showing that, even within the new configuration of public spaces, the woman had the role of guardian of the home and symbol of the family status—through her gestures, attitudes and clothing when in public appearances—and the man the role of provider of the family, husband. (Soares 147)

A number of studies in the areas of gender and feminism have pointed out that women are historically seen as having innate characteristics, so-called femininity, and are, therefore, responsible for taking physical and emotional care of people:

Motherhood is, for most women, one of the most important physical, psychological, intersubjective experiences. We all have mothers, and as women, we have the potential to be mothers; but motherhood is an experience that has been conceptually deformed, avoided, idealized, [and] degraded. Religious, mythological [and] socio-cultural concepts present us with complex connotations, ranging from an almost sickly sentimentalism to a terrified image of a "dark continent" negative, which needs to be controlled, anatomized, sometimes even demonized. (Stevens 17)

In this chapter, we specifically focus on women who are mothers and attend the academic environment. In this section, we also combine issues related to large workloads arising from the extraordinary situation of social isolation caused by the pandemic.

Research on the impact of COVID-19 on maternity and academic production in Brazil has already been done. A book called *Maternidades Plurais: os diferentes oceanos das mães cientistas na pandemia* was published, which has about 140 reports from student mothers and university professors. The word "fatigue" is recurrent in practically all reports. If, as Donna Haraway says in her *A Cyborg Manisfesto*, "Grammar is politics by other means (8)," one must pay attention to the fact that maternal exhaustion has been a recurring factor in the decrease of women's scientific production and even giving up their academic careers. These pioneering studies emerged mainly from political activism within Brazilian universities, such as different mother collectives, Facebook groups, and other social media and research groups led by academic women mothers, such as Parent in Science,

Women in Science at UFF and the Women Scientists and Plural Maternity at UFG. All these groups and collectives are the consequence of the anguish of women who simultaneously perform maternity and academic functions and who understand that it is urgent to create more flexible and welcoming spaces in universities so that women who are mothers can combine work and maternity more completely (Soares).

For example, going back to the research theme of our chapter, when asked who was mainly responsible for the financial provision of the family during the pandemic, of the 320 responses, 62.2 per cent were mothers, whereas fathers were only 20 per cent. The other 17.8 per cent were spread across the other possibilities in figure 6.

In this sense, it is worth pointing out that since this survey was answered mainly by female students, most of them study and work at the same time, balancing their academic responsibilities with their work ones. It is mandatory that we all be the good mothers in our society. The question that remains to be developed is at what cost.

Home Budget and Family Responsibility

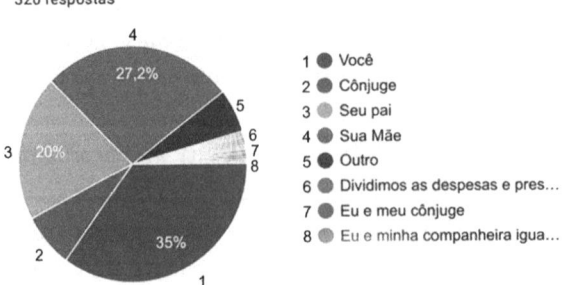

Figure 6. Question: Who is mainly responsible for the financial provision of your family?

The analyzed group, whose profile is heterosexual white cisgender women students, also includes a group that lives with children and adolescents in their homes—more than half of the responses. If we take into account that most of the people who responded as having children and elderly people in their family environment (see figure 7 below), there was intense psychological pressure at the beginning of the pandemic to thoroughly clean everything to stop the spread of the virus.

Among the measures taken by public agencies was the suspension of classes in public and private education in Brazil, which represented an attempt to reduce the spread, but it also resulted in extra work for working women, since schools represent for most mothers the support that allows them to develop their work activities in the public sphere. Initially, the suspension was only to be fifteen days, which could be extended, which in fact occurred.

In private schools, however, the suspension of classes led to remote teaching options, such as recording lessons and making them available online or even returning to class but online. This created a series of adaptations and challenges for the mothers and fathers of these children, who suddenly had to adapt to a new routine (since the suspension of classes was already a first adaptation) by inserting children in virtual environments and in remote classes with teachers who often had never used these technologies:

> With the global crisis of [pandemic], children can no longer attend day care or school. For mothers who have not been able to join teleworking, this is a serious problem, as they do not have the proper structure to leave their children and go to work. Even for those who are in home office, the situation is problematic because bringing more people together at home, caring for their children (and sometimes assisting them in school activities at a distance in the case of those who study in private schools) and the workday is complicated.

> In most homes, [women] do not have a partner or other person with whom they can share chores and relieve the burden of these unpaid activities. Even when there is a spouse in the home, the domestic service burden tends to be concentrated on women. Confinement has put a magnifying glass on gender inequality and the burden on the lives of women workers, mothers, or otherwise. (Rede de Brasil)

There is, therefore, still a long way to go to overcome the effects caused by the pandemic as well as the socially exacerbated gender inequalities in Brazil—a country historically marked by sexism and normative motherhood. The respondent public, mostly white heterosexual cisgender students, who share or are primarily responsible for sustaining their homes, has children in their homes between the ages of zero and nineteen years of age. Some also care for elderly people over the age of sixty who may or may not require additional healthcare. More research is needed to better understand the profiles of current Brazilian students from public universities to better support them.

The mothers' support network in Brazil is primarily private: she must provide, either by enrolling her children in public school or by paying for private school. The closure of schools and introduction of online classes meant a clear disparity of who could afford to provide electronic devices and isolated spaces in the house for classes and who could not. Mothers had more demands on their time, including helping with homework, preparing snacks, making meals, and organizing recreation activities.

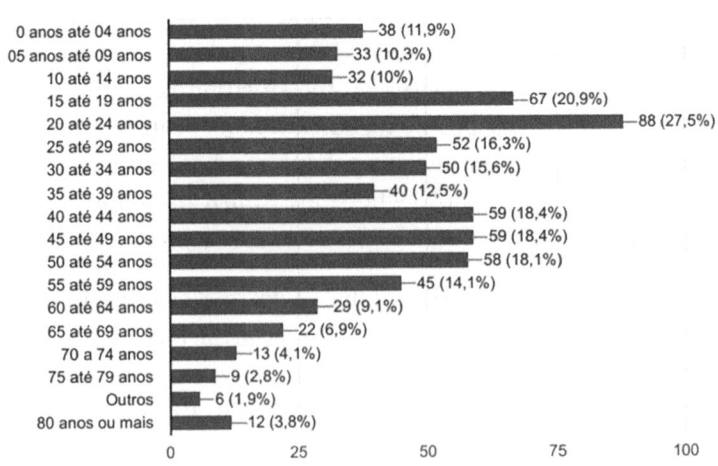

Figure 7. Question: What is the age range of the people who are living with you now?

At the beginning of the social isolation period, the main risk group was the elderly, who in the sampling of this survey lived together in almost one third of the respondents' families (28.6 per cent). In our survey, elderly means over sixty. Other factors contributed to a person being considered in a high-risk group: previous diseases, comorbidities, and poor eating and living habits. According to an April 2020 article published by the Brazilian Ministry of Health:

> People over 60 years of age fall into the risk group, even if they do not have any associated health problems. In addition, people of any age who have comorbidities, such as heart disease, diabetes, pneumopathy, neurological or renal disease, immunodepression, obesity, asthma and puerperal, among others, also need to redouble their care in prevention measures to the coronavirus. (Brazilian Department of Health)

Some additional considerations need to be made, however. The first is that children and adolescents can also contract the disease, though to a lesser degree. But even so, young people become a potential risk to contaminate older people, who are immunocompromised. The impossibility of completely following the measures of social isolation aggravates the risks of contagion and the anxiety of people with older relatives, which affects both their performance in their daily functions and in their work and studies.

The research also sought to understand what the main changes were in terms of cultural habits of living and eating to prevent the spread of COVID-19. Information in media reports insisted on the idea that good eating habits and increased body immunity could help in both the prevention of, and recovery from, COVID-19. It was necessary to investigate what effects this had on cultural practices.

Cultural Heritage and Food

From March 2020 onwards, the search for better culinary practices intensified (Montanari). The research carried out shows that at the beginning of the social isolation period, there was a noticeable improvement in the eating habits of the distinct segments that could work from home. The fear of contagion resulted in families preparing several meals a day, which were healthier in terms of nutritional quality; meals consisted of more fresh vegetables and fruits. 55.9 per cent of respondents said that their meals became healthier (Schieri).

Even rice with beans, which over the decades had lost space on the dinner table, were cooked again during the pandemic (Leme). The closure of restaurants meant that cooking skills had to be put into practice. There was increased motivation to learn how to cook, especially because family members were present: "The act of cooking goes beyond the production of nutritionally balanced (or not!) and sensory attractive (or not!) meals. Cooking favors the family congregation and the transmission of ideas, values, and truths. It promotes a privileged space to share, listen, give way, manage differences and discuss without offense—values so essential (in times of intolerance) that they need to be exercised at home and in the family. In this way, the pandemic resulted in a healthier diet for many.

The data show that most of the respondents prepared about three to five meals a day, which is in line with the current average. Regarding food spending, 6.9 per cent of respondents said there were no changes in spending, 48.4 per cent observed subtle changes in spending, while 44.7 per cent experienced an increase in their food budget.

A comida está sendo prioritariamente preparada em casa ou adquirida em comércios alimentícios (restaurante com sistema de entrega, marmitex e afins)?

320 respostas

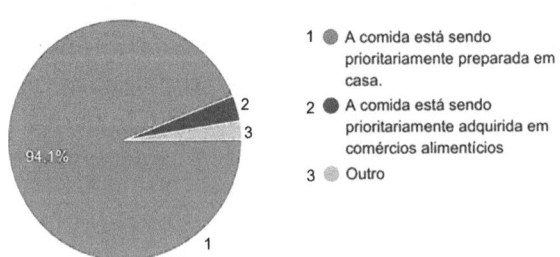

Figure 8. Question: Is food being primarily prepared at home or is it being purchased from stores, including restaurants and home-delivery applications?

With the prolongation of the pandemic and the return to work, cooking one's own food lost priority. As classes returned in the format of emergency remote learning (ERL) work, teachers and students, especially women, also began to do more family and domestic care (such as cleaning, cooking, washing, ironing, and sanitizing), affecting professional activities and inevitably worsening the quality of food intake. Inevitably, there was an increase in the consumption of ultra-processed foods (such as sandwiches, snacks, and pizzas), worsening the quality of health and opening gaps for the development of chronic diseases, such as COVID-19, because healthy foods increase the body's defense mechanisms. Moreover, although there are the arguments that the consumption of "ultra-processed" food moves the economy, there is also the impact on the precariousness of labour relations and the increase in underemployment, showing that the issues of class, race, and gender are interconnected in every way and impact the daily decisions of society.

Academic and Domestic Work

Even when they also work outside the home, women do most of the domestic work. They are also responsible for almost all unpaid care activities, such as the elderly and children, in the family sphere. During the pandemic, the suspension of classes has left many women even more overburdened. For those in the home office, balancing paid work with the thousands of tasks of the so-called second and third shift is no easy task. Even though the survey showed an improvement in the equal division of household chores in the family environment, amounting to 33.4 per cent; 38.7 per cent of the people interviewed said that an unequal division of household chores persists, and 20.9 per cent confirmed that they are the main caregiver of household issues, according to the following chart.

This reality is corroborated by data from IBGE, which confirm that women dedicate almost twice as many hours as men to domestic tasks. In 2019, Brazilians dedicated on average 16.8 hours per week to domestic tasks or caring for people, 21.4 hours per week for women and 11.0 hours for men. From 2016 to 2019, this difference between the hours men and women spent on domestic tasks increased from 9.9 to 10.4 hours per week. It is interesting to observe higher participation among men with higher education (85.7 per cent) and lower participation among those without education or with incomplete elementary education (74.1 per cent) (IBGE).

Como você classificaria as responsabilidades dos cuidados domésticos rotineiros materiais (faxinar, cozinhar, lavar, passar, higienizar) durante a Pandemia?

320 respostas

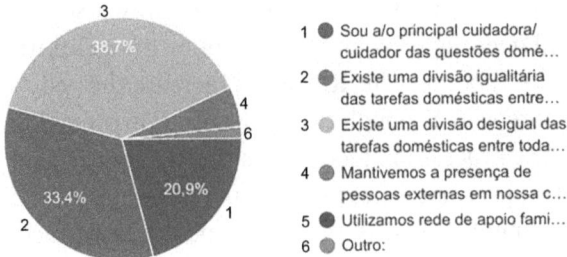

1 ● Sou a/o principal cuidadora/ cuidador das questões domé...
2 ● Existe uma divisão igualitária das tarefas domésticas entre...
3 ● Existe uma divisão desigual das tarefas domésticas entre toda...
4 ● Mantivemos a presença de pessoas externas em nossa c...
5 ● Utilizamos rede de apoio fami...
6 ● Outro:

Figure 9. Question: Who has been most responsible for household duties (such as cleaning, cooking, washing, ironing, and sanitation) during the pandemic?

Moreover, in Brazil, 11 million families are composed of single mothers, who may have no one to share the work with at home. Besides domestic and care work, there is also the mental load of emotional work, which is even more invisible. It is noticeable that most women have not yet been able to share this responsibility, which is not only theirs, with partners and family members. This situation generates intense feelings of anguish. It is the women who, in general, are responsible for planning and managing the home and daily life, trying to anticipate the needs of each member. In this situation, stress is inevitable. We consider it important that mothers can, despite the rules of the normativity of motherhood, respond and express their anxieties, fears, and stress. This is a way to deromanticize motherhood, expressing its difficulties without guilt or judgment. The incorporation of these demands and debates into feminisms is fundamental and urgent for us to have a more just and equitable world in the twenty-first century.

From a professional and performance point of view, there is no unanimity on the effects of COVID-19, since not everyone felt the effects with the same intensity, as shown in figure 10 on the fulfillment of research and study deadlines, which include, for example, submission of articles and reports.

Você tem conseguido cumprir prazos de pesquisa e estudo (submissão de artigos, relatórios e pareceres)?

320 respostas

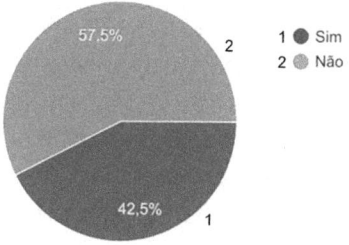

Figure 10. Question: Have you been able to meet research and study deadlines, such as the submission of articles, and reports?

In this research, teaching was not considered, since classes were suspended indefinitely. The resumption of classes took place with the approval of the Normative Instruction no. 01/2020, which established the instructions for ERT on August 31, 2020. It can be seen in the chart that 57.5 per cent of the interviewees were not able to meet the deadlines properly, whereas 42.5 per cent still did not perceive the negative effects.

Discussion

These numbers from Goiás do not reflect the nation as a whole, although they still do raise important points on the structural inequalities that affect academic mothers in universities. Academics with children, (especially up to twelve years old) are the most impacted by the pandemic in terms of academic productivity, according to studies by the Parent in Science group of the Federal University of Rio Grande do Sul. Gender and race are also important factors. According to Rossa Soletti, a researcher at the Federal University of Rio Grande do Sul, "Black women, with and without children, and white women with children have been the most impacted in remote work" (37). They are also the least able to submit their scientific articles for publication. According to Soletti, "While only 50% of women have been able to do this, for men this rate was 70%" (39). She continues: "The age of children is also a very important factor: only 28.8% of researchers who are mothers have been able to do this, while among men with children of the same age, this index is 52.4%" (38). It is noticeable how mothers and Black people are the most impinged upon at the present moment.

This information extracted from the applied research shows the prevalence of patriarchal and normative maternity, extremely oppressive for women, in Brazilian society. O'Reilly conceives the concept of "maternity" as an individual responsibility focused on the figure of the mother. As if these were born naturally for the role of caregiver, without needing specific skills and intelligence for this. From this concept, women are thrown into immense responsibilities and unattainable expectations. Their burden on society is lifted when the nuclear family model is depleted, when in addition to their natural role as mother, wife, and caregiver of children, they find themselves under the inevitable obligation of assuming the role of economic provider for the family, as this research shows.

O'Reilly demonstrates that in the same way that the tenets of normative motherhood (i.e., essentialization, privatization, individualization, naturalization, normalization, idealization, biologization, specialization, intensification, and depoliticization) are culturally constructed, they can be deconstructed. By deconstructing the patriarchal narrative of motherhood, we can destabilize its practices and meanings. This research was initially developed to think about the cultural heritages of Brazilian society in times of COVID-19. The data from the respondents focused on normative motherhood. At the same time, when asked about their mental health, the reports opened the way for a discussion about custodial maternity. As already stated, Brazil has a history full of racism, oppression, and inequality. Overcoming these and building a more equitable society are a fundamental process, especially for maternal feminisms.

These inequalities were worsened by the pandemic. Thus, it is perceived that the experience of remote work has aggravated the gender inequalities in the pandemic. Women's increased domestic responsibilities, worsened by the home office, are also perceived among highly qualified women. Thus, many question the ability to reconcile the roles of mother and academic. Therefore, research of this magnitude is essential to stimulate debate and to mitigate the impacts of social isolation on the careers of academic mothers. There is also an urgent need to implement actions in relation to the differential evaluation of curriculum by academic committees and research promotion agencies.

The pandemic has laid bare the inequalities of Brazilian society. Social isolation is impossible for people experiencing poverty, and food and cleaning conditions are equally marked by the inheritances of colonial inequalities in Brazil. This research shows the urgency of clear public policies of permanence in federal universities and the need to create a more just and equitable society. The burden of unpaid domestic work of women, which the pandemic has worsened, is one of the most obvious challenges that need to be overcome.

Works Cited

Almeida, Silvio. *O que é racismo estrutural?* Letramento, 2018.

Brazilian Department of Health, 2023. www.saude.gov.br/noticias/agencia-saude/46764-coronavirus-43-079-casos-e-2-741-mortes/html. Accessed 15 Feb. 2023.

Butler, Judith. *Vida precária: os poderes da luta e da violência.* Autêntica, 2019.

Federici, Silvia. *O ponto zero da revolução: trabalho doméstico, reprodução e luta feminista.* Elefante, 2019.

Gibson, Margaret F. Queering Motherhood: Narrative and Theoretical Perspectives. Demeter Press, 2014.

Haraway, Donna J. *A Cyborg Manifesto.* Stanford University, 1985.

IBGE, 2023. agenciadenoticias.ibge.gov.br/agencia-sala-de-imprensa/html. Accessed 15 Feb. 2023.

Leme, Adriana Salay. *Feijão, dono das tradições*: representação identitária e consumo efetivo no Brasil. Dissertação de mestrado. Faculdade de Filosofia, Letras e Ciências Humanas, 2015.

Montanari, Massimo. *O mundo na cozinha.* História, identidades, trocas. São Paulo: Estação Liberdade/Senac, 2009.

Monteiro, Rodrigo, et al. *Raízes do privilégio: mobilidade social no mundo ibérico do antigo regime.* Civilização Brasileira, 2011.

O'Reilly, Andrea. *Matricentric Feminism: Theory, Activism, Practice.* Demeter Press, 2021.

Onumulheres Brasil, 2023. www.onumulheres.org.br.html. Accessed

15 Feb. 2023.

Rede Brasil, 2020. www.redebrasilatual.com.br/cidadania/2020/05/pandemia-agrava-vulnerabilidade-da-populacao-trans/.html. Accessed 15 Feb. 2023.

Saldanha, Marinho Paloma Abelin, and Hebe Signorini Gonçalves. "Práticas de empoderamento feminino na América Latina." *Journal of Social Studies*, no. 56, 2016, pp. 80-90.

Santos Machado, L., et al. "Parent in Science: The Impact of Parenthood on the Scientific Career in Brazil." 2019 IEEE/ACM 2nd International Workshop on Gender Equality in Software Engineering (GE), Montreal, Canada, 2019, pp. 37-40, doi: 10.1109/GE.2019.00017.

Soares, Ana Carolina Eiras Coelho. *Moça educada, mulher civilizada, esposa feliz: Relações de gênero e história em José de Alencar*. EDUSC, 2012.

Stevens, Cristina. *Maternidade e feminismo: diálogos interdisciplinares*. Mulheres Press/Edunisc, 2007.

Vergès, Françoise. *Um feminismo decolonial*. UBU, 2020.

Chapter 5.

The Misogyny of Lactivism: Why Breastfeeding Is Central to the Discourse of Normative Motherhood

Karla Knutson

Breastfeeding promotion rhetoric has been extremely successful in the late twentieth and early twenty-first centuries in the United States (US) (Beasley; Copelton et al.; Jung; Knaak, "Problem"). Whether they breastfeed or not, American mothers now live in a cultural context in which they are aware of the expectation that they should breastfeed their infants, given the pervasive, normative rhetoric of "breast is best" and the establishment of breastfeeding as central to the performance of intensive mothering (Jung; Carter; Kukla; Blum). This regulatory discourse is what keeps many women breastfeeding, regardless of inconvenience, discontent, or even pain. Courtney Jung employs the term "lactivism" to describe paternalist, prescriptive breastfeeding advocacy—such as "compulsory breastfeeding, breastfeeding as a moral crusade, and breastfeeding as a means of distinguishing good from bad parents" (7)—and distinguishes it from other types of breastfeeding promotion that champion women making individual decisions about infant-feeding methods. In my contribution to this collection, I analyze the article "Increasing Milk Supply" from the website *Ask Dr. Sears* as an example of lactivism, using philosopher Kate Manne's theory of misogyny. Manne describes misogyny as a system that "polices and enforces" the social relations prescribed through the ideology of sexism (13). In this chapter, I illustrate how lactivism functions as a form of misogyny, imposing a normative version of motherhood, and I argue that it uses shaming misogynist rhetoric to monitor and discipline mothers who do not abide by the normative discourse of "breast is best." After outlining Manne's theory of misogyny and illustrating how lactivist rhetoric draws upon it, I will demonstrate how the article "Increasing Milk Supply" harnesses misogyny through two patriarchal mechanisms articulated by Manne: positioning the reading mother as someone who must identify with the normative social role of the maternal giver and policing women's future behaviour through admonishing and shaming.

Lactivism as Misogyny: A Normative Discourse

Manne suggests a reconceptualization of the working definition of misogyny; no longer should this term be limited to denoting the beliefs of individuals who harbour resentment or hate for women, an understanding she calls "naïve conception" (18-19). Rather, misogyny should be acknowledged to be a system "serving to uphold patriarchal order, understood as one strand among various similar systems of domination.... Misogyny does this by visiting hostile or adverse social consequences on a certain (more or less circumscribed) class of girls or women to enforce and police social norms that are gendered either in theory ... or in practice" (13). Manne distinguishes between misogyny and sexism, clarifying that sexism serves to maintain gendered differences, as "the 'justificatory' branch of a patriarchal order, which consists in ideology that has the overall function of *rationalizing* and *justifying* patriarchal social relations" (79). Misogyny is the system that "polices and enforces" these social relations reified by sexism. She underscores their different utilities: "So sexism is scientific; misogyny is moralistic" (20).

Manne posits that misogyny upholds patriarchal ideology by employing such mechanisms as "women's internalization of the relevant social norms, narratives about women's distinctive proclivities and preferences, and valorizing depictions of the relevant forms of care work as personally rewarding, socially necessary, morally valuable, 'cool,' 'natural,' or healthy" (47). These mechanisms facilitate the appearance of women independently choosing to identify with idealized versions of gendered social roles of mother or wife. If these "coercive" methods fail, then "more or less subtly hostile, threatening, and punitive norm-enforcement mechanisms will be standing at the ready, or operating in the background" (47) and may range from experiencing condemnation in social situations to violence, which Manne terms "'down girl' moves" (68).[1] Through these means, misogyny punishes women who transgress convention (52).

I argue that lactivism is a form of misogyny, as it functions as a normative system to monitor and discipline women who act "out of bounds" by not abiding by the rhetoric of "breast is best"—whether by not breastfeeding or by not breastfeeding for the length of time recommended by leading medical organizations. Lactivism harnesses both patriarchal mechanisms of misogyny articulated by Manne, first by utilizing sexist ideology idealizing the normative version of motherhood performed through "intensive mothering." As Sharon Hays has theorized, this ideology expects a good mother to adopt a stance of selflessness, of thinking first of a child's needs, and of being "responsible for unselfish nurturing while men are responsible for self-interested profit maximization" (175). In this schema, mothers are positioned as what Manne calls a *"human giver,* a woman who is held to owe many if not most of her distinctively human capacities to a suitable boy or man, ideally, and his children, as applicable.... A giver is then obligated to offer love, sex, attention, affection, and admiration, as well as other forms of emotional, social, reproductive and caregiving labor, in accordance with social norms that govern and structure the relevant roles and relations" (301). If women refuse to adhere to these social roles, lactivists employ "down girl moves," primarily those of social disapproval and inducement of shame.

The successful establishment of breastfeeding as a practice of normative motherhood in the US is evident when surveying the increase of breastfeeding initiation rates over the past fifty years. For example, in 1971, the breastfeeding initiation rate was 24 per cent; in 1975, 33 per cent; and in 1980, 54 per cent (Jung 43). According to the United States Centers for Disease Control and Prevention's 2022 Breastfeeding Report Card, 83.2 per cent of US infants born in 2019 began breastfeeding, 55.8 per cent still were breastfeeding at six months, yet only 35.9 per cent were breastfeeding twelve months later (6). The increase in the rate of breastfeeding initiation from 24 per cent in 1971 to 83.2

per cent in 2019 is staggering. Although the Report Card indicates that many infants are breastfed for some length of time, it also points out that breastfeeding mothers in the US do not continue the practice for as long as the leading medical organizations recommend; the American Academy of Pediatrics (AAP) and the World Health Organization (WHO) both advise exclusive breastfeeding for six months and to continue breastfeeding while supplementing with solid foods for at least two years (AAP 1).

However, the mothers who do not breastfeed their infants at all or for the recommended period are not merely unaware of the myriad health and emotional benefits attributed to breastfeeding (Jung 71-95; Wolf). Such scholars as Courtney Jung, Pam Carter, Rebecca Kukla, and Linda M. Blum have established that women know that they are supposed to breastfeed and are not "more easily swayed by advertising and media representations of bottlefeeding, or by a nagging mother-in-law ... or place a lower value on health-promoting behaviors" (Blum 119) as public health campaigns have imagined. Rather, they may not choose to or be able to sustain breastfeeding because they often lack the socioeconomic and emotional resources that make this practice feasible (Blum 120-21; Carter 104). They also may have other personal, political, situational, or health-related reasons to avoid breastfeeding, such as adopting an infant, ongoing medical conditions, occupational structures, or political concerns regarding this practice (Kukla 162-163). Mothers who do sustain breastfeeding in the US are more likely to be middle class, educated, older, and white (Blum; Jung; Carter; Copelton et al.).

The effectiveness of breastfeeding promotion has led to breastfeeding being designated the "moral gold standard for mothering" (Knaak, "Breast-feeding" 197) and a crucial element of normative motherhood. The performance of intensive mothering as a resource-intensive, child-centred form of care provided by mothers prescribes breastfeeding as the appropriate method of infant feeding (Copelton et al. 24), and intensive mothering is embraced, often unconsciously, as the way to parent in this cultural moment for the American middle and upper classes. Both Cindy Stearns and Orit Avishai argue that breastfeeding is labour intensive for these mothers, who conceptualize breastfeeding as "body work" (Stearns 64), a "body-management project" (Avishai 149), as well as "a task to be researched, planned, implemented, and constantly assessed" (Avishai 136). As this practice became vested with "the status of a national standard," those mothers who do not breastfeed, for whatever reason, are now marked as "failing in some important respect" (Jung 11-12) to perform normative motherhood. Breastfeeding advocacy may lead to those mothers who fail experiencing shame (Taylor and Wallace 77).

To illustrate how lactivism functions according to the patriarchal mechanisms of misogyny, my chapter analyzes an example of an important subgenre of the wider category of breastfeeding-advice literature. It examines an online text offering advice for how to increase lactation production, a common area of concern for new mothers.[2] I will look at how the genre of advice for boosting milk supply offers a salient example of misogyny, given its opportunity to offer direction to mothers seeking expert guidance. Rather than encouraging mothers to choose to breastfeed, the subgenre of how to boost breastmilk supply offers lactivists a way to prescribe normative practices—policing the mother who is already invested in breastfeeding.

I chose "Increasing Milk Supply," which was published on the website *Ask Dr. Sears,* as a sample of this genre because of its relevance and its accessibility. As a popular online childcare resource, *Ask Dr. Sears* is a prominent "hit" in the first pages of search engine results and is available when a frantic mother is searching the internet at any hour of the day or night. A well-known name in the parenting-advice world, paediatrician Dr. William (Bill) Sears—in concert with his wife Martha, a registered nurse, and the two of their eight children who are paediatricians—offers a comprehensive website as well as numerous print publications about a variety of childrearing topics. Dr. Sears's name and his ideas are likely to be familiar to American parents, as his championing of attachment parenting in *The Baby Book* helped establish the prevalence of this parenting style in contemporary America (Pickert; Faircloth, *Militant* 96-97; Faircloth, "Is Attachment" 182-84).

This chapter argues that the lactivism of "Increasing Milk Supply" employs shaming misogynist rhetoric. The article relies on sexist ideology, which idealizes a maternal identity as the "human giver" of Manne's theory. Through that idealization, sexism attempts to coerce women to willingly adopt this social role as someone responsible for emotional, reproductive, and domestic labour. Moreover, "Increasing Milk Supply" polices women's future behaviour through encouraging adherence to the social role of maternal caregiver by means of admonishing language designed to induce shame. In the next two sections, I will establish how the text positions the reading mother as a giver and how it shames the mother, as well as how lactivism benefits from the system of misogyny.

The Mother as Giver: Encouraging Identification with Normative Social Roles

Ask Dr. Sears's article "Increasing Milk Supply" offers a list of seventeen recommendations in a recognizable and easily digestible online genre known as a "listicle." The suggestions are presented in bold font and expressed as imperatives, using either a verb phrase, such as "Nurse Longer," or a limiting adjective and noun, as in "No Pacifiers, No Bottles." All the pieces of advice are followed by a brief explication indicating how best to adhere to the command. Unlike other texts on the website, "Increasing Milk Supply" is unsigned, not attributed to any specific author from the Sears organization. However, in *The Baby Book*, a note indicates that the use of a first-person singular pronoun indicates Dr. Bill Sears, and a first-person plural pronoun refers to "the collective Doctors Sears" (Sears 3). Although the article does not use any first-person pronouns to indicate authorship, it does directly address an audience of mothers through the repeated use of second-person pronouns and imperative commands. These stylistic choices position the reader as a mother behaving waywardly, as someone in need of redirection and reminder. The directive style casts the reader as a woman who has failed to give of herself sufficiently.

The article's idealization of mothers as selfless nurturers who must privilege their infants through dedication to lactation over any needs of their own is strategic. Drawing upon a central feature of the ideology of intensive mothering and the expectations of normative motherhood, this tactic construes any questioning of, or resistance to, the advice as the indulgent whims of a self-centred mother, someone who takes rather than gives. As Manne explains, patriarchal relationships are reified through "this uneven, gendered economy of *giving and taking* moral-cum-social goods and services" (107). Givers are "then obligated to offer love, sex, attention, affection, and admiration, as well as other forms of emotional, social, reproductive, and caregiving labor, in accordance with social norms that govern and structure the relevant roles and relations" (301).

Both misogyny and intensive mothering call for most of these goods and services to be given to children by mothers and others engaging in feminine-coded carework. In intensive mothering, the mother, positioned as the primary caregiver, trains her attention on her children to the exclusion of her own needs, engaging in childcare practices that are "*child-centered, expert-guided, emotionally absorbing, labor-intensive,* and *financially expensive*" (Hays 8). The ideological system of intensive mothering "contributes to the continued power and privilege of men by creating a social role for women that marks them, in cultural terms, as ill-prepared and unsuitable participants in the public world and leaves many, in concrete terms, too exhausted to successfully compete for positions of higher authority and prestige in that world" (Hays 175-76).

The parenting philosophy known as attachment parenting also locates primary-care responsibilities with the mother. Maternal attachment and early object relations researchers suggest that an initial strong connection between a mother and an infant is advantageous to a child's development (Rose Ennis 4-5); their research was based on the work of psychiatrist John Bowlby (Blum; Faircloth, *Militant*; Rose Ennis). Building upon these theories, William and Martha Sears's *The Baby Book* introduced the term "attachment parenting" to the wider world (Faircloth, *Militant* 96). This text describes attachment parenting's foundational strategies, which are grounded in the tenets of intensive mothering, as the Doctors Sears encourage mothers to perform three labor- and time-intensive primary practices to create lasting bonds between mother and infant: Mothers are required to breastfeed, to share a bed with, and to wear their babies in a sling (Sears 7-8). As Charlotte Faircloth concludes based on her ethnographic research with mothers attending La Leche League meetings in London, attachment parenting "that validates attentive, embodied care for infants offers women *one* set of norms by which to structure their 'identity work' in congruence with an overarching framework of intensive mothering" ("Is Attachment" 189).

Other scholars studying the institution of motherhood continue to illustrate and challenge the child-focused nature of intensive mothering; for example, Linda Rose Ennis opens her edited collection about the topic by noting the contradictions of the "compartmentalization of children's and mother's needs into two camps that rarely intersected" and her goal to understand these perspectives holistically (4). Furthermore, Andrea O'Reilly issues a call for matricentric feminism—a feminism for those who engage in the work of mothering, with a key characteristic of it being reflective of the perspective of mothers rather than exclusively focusing on the needs of and effects on children (7). Glenda Wall notes that this focus on children's needs pervades discourses of breastfeeding as well—both in terms of health benefits of breastmilk as well as the emotional advantages of an opportunity to develop a close relationship between mother and infant (601-02).

Similarly, reproductive rights advocates have long pointed out that antichoice activists not only ignore but also dismiss concerns about the agency, autonomy, liberty, and safety of women in favour of those concerns regarding the fetus as well as regarding American society (Solinger 232-36). As she surveys the history of reproductive politics in the US, Rickie Solinger illustrates how the approach to reproductive issues reflects not a concern with women's lived experiences, health, needs, and rights but rather a "belief that the social, economic, political, and moral problems that beset our country can be solved best if laws and policies and public opinions press women to reproduce or not in ways that are consistent with a particular version of the country's real needs" (8-9). Manne points to this rhetoric as a representative example of misogyny (120), in which women challenge the social norm of giving feminine-coded goods and services by making a choice that considers and prioritizes their desires, interests, and health. Women embracing choice or pointing out injustice or harm done to them flout the steadiness of the give/take model Manne proposes, leading to misogynist hostility in the form of suspicion: "We tend to suspect [them] of dishonesty and being self-dramatizing—even when there's no evidence of either perfidy" (132).

This suspicion is what I suggest underscores the tone and style of "Increasing Milk Supply"— leading to positioning the reading mothers as givers and to the proactive use of hostile shaming to deter the mother from any resistance to being categorized as a giver. The opening preamble sets the tone, as it uses emphatic language and a second-person address to stress that the mother must discipline herself—mentally, physically, and emotionally—in order to breastfeed successfully:

"Remember the three B's of breastfeeding: the breast, the baby, and the brain. For increasing milk supply, the breast needs more stimulation from the baby and making that happen will require some adjustments in your brain. To increase your milk supply, you have to make breastfeeding a priority." The remainder of the article indicates exactly how a good mother can prioritize breastfeeding: engaging in the childcare strategies of intensive mothering, which are "*child-centered, expert-guided, emotionally absorbing, labor-intensive, and financially expensive*" (Hays 8).

The first nine of the seventeen strategies endorsed are time- and labour-consuming activities: "Increase Feeding Frequency," Don't Wait for Your Breasts to 'Fill Up,'" "Offer the Breast More Often," "Nurse Longer," "Try Switch Nursing," "Increasing Milk Supply by Double-Nursing," "Undress Baby During Feedings," "Nap and Night Nurse," and "Sling Feed." The language used in the explications of how to execute these strategies also makes ample use of the imperative mood; it educates the mother of the necessity of frequent feeding to boost supply, "at least every two hours during the day," in lengthy sessions: "Increasing milk supply will be helped if you don't limit the length of your baby's feedings to a predetermined number of minutes on each side." A repeated refrain throughout these sections is the danger of having a sleepy or relaxed baby, and *Ask Dr. Sears* endorses waking the baby to eat after a two-hour nap during the day as well as for an extra feeding session during the night. The message is clear: If the mother wants "to make breastfeeding a priority," then she must offer the breast as often as possible, privileging this temporally over any other needs (sleep, relaxation, exercise, paid work, household work, etc.) of the infant, the family, and herself.

The advice to "Nap and Night Nurse" is a representative example of the child-centred, not mother-centred, tone. It advocates for the mother to take her "baby to bed and nurse" to "stimulate longer and more frequent nursings." Without providing data to illustrate this claim, the article insists that nursing in bed is "one of the most powerful ways" to boost supply and that it "increases your milk-producing hormones and reminds you that breastfeeding your baby is the most important thing you can do at this stage of your life together." How exactly nursing in bed triggers this reminder is not clear; however, the exhortation serves to remind the mother of the selflessness required by her new role as a mother, and particularly as a successful breastfeeding mother, who must feed, almost continually, from her unrested body.

The mother reading this may start to wonder when she might do something other than breastfeed if she is required to "take the lead and give your baby more frequent opportunities to nurse" through switch nursing, double nursing, nap and night nursing, and wearing her baby for sling feeding. These time-intensive strategies—as well as the admonition to avoid bottles and pacifiers and the conspicuous absence of any mention of using a breast pump (a common suggestion for boosting lactation)—ensure the consistency of the message that "all your baby's sucking should be done at the breast," which offers no physical reprieve from the physical proximity of the mother-infant dyad. Only after reaching the tenth suggestion does the reader encounter an acknowledgment that the mother might have other responsibilities; however, the text presumes that the reader's other concerns are her domestic duties as a giver. She is advised to "get help with laundry, dishes, cooking, and cleaning" and if she has a demanding toddler, "hire a teen to come to your house after school to entertain your older child and give you a few hours or relief so you can sit and relax and nurse your baby." In addition to assuming the mother has multiple children, the article presupposes that the reader has ample socioeconomic resources, such as the ability to access paid help, as well as a partner: "Let go of other responsibilities for a while. Have your partner share in non-feeding infant care, so that you can rest, take a walk, or take a shower." Both passages point to the article's positioning of the reading mother according to normative conventions of gendered labour. She is the person who is primarily responsible for domestic labor and for the reproductive labour of infant care—not only for executing it but for managing it and delegating it to the others she has arranged to help her with her caregiving. In a later edition of *The Baby Book*, the Doctors Sears do acknowledge that these expectations may lead to what they call "mother burnout" (9), but they attempt to reassure the mother that learning to interpret their baby will make it easier to understand the needs of this child as it grows: "True, this style of parenting takes tremendous amounts of patience and stamina, but it's worth it!" (11). This generalization is illustrative of the rhetorical danger facing an exhausted mother reading the Sears's texts: "His homespun language and sometimes vague or contradictory statements can muddy things, leaving mothers to overlook the nuances and take an all-or-nothing approach" (Pickert).

Enforcement by Shaming: Compulsory Adherence to Normative Motherhood

Lactivism attempts to shame women who may transgress and violate normative gendered boundaries by neglecting to breastfeed and to perform the emotional labour of selfless devotion in their reproductive responsibilities. "Increasing Milk Supply" enforces its didactic message instructing women how to become good mothers while breastfeeding using shaming language reflective of the regulatory discourse of normative motherhood. As Manne explains, misogyny operates through the spectre of hostility, serving as "an especially effective deterrent to women who might otherwise ... fail to provide certain feminine-coded goods and services" (84). As the previous section has demonstrated, the ideology of intensive mothering has established breastfeeding as a central component of the reproductive and care-related labour that a mother must provide in order to perform mothering appropriately in the contemporary US. Thus, misogyny requires that the woman who fails to breastfeed must be reminded of her position as giver through hostility in the form of admonishment to induce shame and adherence to normative expectations. As was noted above, the admonishing tone of the article's opening statement exhorting the reader to remember and "to make breastfeeding a priority" shames the audience, which suggests that any mother reading this has somehow neglected her child by not providing enough breastmilk and that her dedication to breastfeeding and to mothering is in question. She must refocus her efforts by adopting the time- and labour-intensive advice immediately to demonstrate that breastfeeding her child is her priority as a central tenet of intensive mothering and normative motherhood.[3]

Whereas the first nine suggestions focus on strategies requiring a mother to give her time and energy, the article's last eight recommendations scold her and advocate for her to adopt a giving-mental perspective. If adjusting breastfeeding technique and duration did not produce the desired effects, then the mother must seek specialized expert interventions, including herbal supplements, lactation consultants and La Leche League leaders, as well as the previously noted household management assistance. *Ask Dr. Sears* positions this reliance on others' expertise and assistance as part of a perspectival shift on the part of the mother, advocated in "Get Focused on Increasing Milk Supply" and "Trust that Nature's System Works." "Get Focused" instigates a reckoning:

> Take inventory of your lifestyle. What activities and worries are draining away energy that could be better spent in caring for yourself and your baby? Are you trying to do too much, so that you're not taking enough time to sit down and feed and enjoy your baby? If you're interested in increasing milk supply for your baby, you have to make breastfeeding and taking care of yourself a priority. Let go of other responsibilities for a while. Have your partner share in non-feeding infant care, so that you can rest, take a walk, or take a shower.

Although the passage contains elements of concern for the mother's personal wellbeing, an overwhelmed, exhausted reader may be induced to feel shame that she has allowed other needs, responsibilities, or desires to interfere with "taking enough time to sit down and feed and enjoy" her child. The under-resourced mother may wonder what it would be like to "let go of other responsibilities" and feel resentment or shame for not performing her role as giver. Similarly, a single mother feels excluded from the advice, as she does not necessarily have a partner to shoulder some duties, as *Ask Dr. Sears* expects. The passage's combination of style—using imperatives like "take inventory," intermingled with questions about personal behaviour—scolds and excludes mothers rather than supports them. Its tone of preemptive rebuke is a classic "down girl" move, an example of the system of enforcement of misogyny.

"Increasing Milk Supply" continues to employ an overtly chiding, hostile tone in the sixteenth suggestion, "Trust that Nature's System Works." After offering fifteen recommendations, the article concludes by doubting the mother's judgment, suggesting that the mother may be overreacting if she expresses concerns about her milk supply. In this section, the article emphasizes that if the mother's technique and frequency are correct, she will "make enough milk," as insufficient supply is "rare." By downplaying the physical and emotional effort required for ample breastmilk production, *Ask Dr. Sears* invokes a discourse of being natural, which may lead women to feel they have failed if they need to seek out breastfeeding resources (Fitzwater Gonzales 301). Moreover, the article rebukes the mother for her concern, the very vigilance the medical establishment has encouraged her to adopt: "And while it may seem that your life is stressful, mothers throughout history have breastfed their babies through war, famine, and personal tragedies." Although it is an ostensible effort to offer solace through context, this line reads as a reproach to any mother anxious about her body's ability to feed her baby. A final reminder attempts to reassure the mother of the importance of trusting the process: "Your body nourished this baby through pregnancy. There's no reason to think that you won't succeed at breastfeeding." However, two sentences of reassurance may not be enough to contradict the elements of misogyny in a text that has repeatedly commanded the reading mother to evaluate her intentions and priorities and to discipline her body to perform her responsibilities as giver. Instead, the effect of the reassurance may be to trivialize her concerns and undermine her trust in herself.

Lactivism Prescribes Normative Motherhood: A Moral Fervor

By conceptualizing mothers as selfless nurturers whose only priority is to feed their children, *Ask Dr. Sears*'s article participates in the regulatory discourse of normative motherhood. It attempts to persuade its readers to accept the social role of giver through preemptive shame and hostility. Its misogyny works in conjunction with the trend to moralize the act of breastfeeding as a practice necessary for the greater public's health, as a civic duty (Knaak, "Contextualizing" 347; Jung 99). Mothers' responsibility to society has been a central tenet of American public life throughout the nation's history (Solinger), and a contemporary manifestation of maternal civic duty is to provide breastmilk—the liquid gold purported to provide a plethora of health benefits for infants. The lactivist discourse of normative mothering requires mothers to be good neoliberal citizens who perform their duties within risk culture, as they are "responsible for ensuring not just the health of their families, but the health of the next generation of citizens" (Kukla 158). To maintain this gendered hierarchy, the misogynistic moral fervour of lactivism is necessary.

Yet lactivists and others attempting to normalize mothering are unlikely to recognize their efforts as indicative of misogyny. For example, the Doctors Sears describe their approach to parenting as "common sense we would all do if left to our healthy resources" (3). And as Manne explains, those performing acts of misogyny in pursuit of normative goals may feel "*righteous*: like standing up for oneself or for morality, or—often combining the two—for the 'little guy'" (20). Jung notes the pervasive public conception of breastfeeding as "so good, and wholesome, and pure" (22)—surely an example of a practice not only worth championing but also worth defending. However, it seems relevant to notice the gender attributed to the baby in "Increasing Milk Supply," the baby who stands to benefit from the emotional and physical advantages conferred by being breastfed. *Ask Dr. Sears* often invites the reading mothers to imagine using the strategies with their babies by using second-person pronouns as limiting adjectives, referring to "your baby." In subsequent references to that imagined baby using gendered third-person pronouns, only once is the baby referred to as "her." Rather, a male baby is invoked with the pronouns "he" and "him" sixteen times. Certainly, there can be little doubt that this example of lactivism reflects a system of misogyny, as the authors imagine the recipient of this increased milk supply to be a male baby, who the system of misogyny indicates is owed nurturing by a female human giver, his mother, according to the prescriptions of normative motherhood.

Endnotes

1. Manne provides a long list of possible "down girl" moves: "As well as infantilizing and belittling, there's ridiculing, humiliating, mocking, slurring, vilifying, demonizing, as well as sexualizing or, alternatively *desexualizing*, silencing, shunning, shaming, blaming, patronizing, condescending, and other forms of treatment that are dismissive and disparaging in specific social contexts. Then there is violence and threatening behavior: including 'punching down'—that is, deferred or displaced aggression" (68).
2. Infant weight gain is one of the first topics to which mothers are particularly attentive because the American Academy of Pediatrics

recommends that medical professionals, who in turn encourage caregivers to act similarly, assess infants' growth according to the WHO Growth Curve Standards to identify infants who are "failing to thrive" (AAP). Insufficient milk supply is cited as the reason most mothers stop breastfeeding earlier than AAP and WHO recommend. Studies indicate great concern over low milk supply in many Western countries (Dykes; Dykes and Williams; Hillervik-Lindquist).

3. In her study of the relationship of infant feeding and maternal identity, Faircloth argues that the imperative to breastfeed may cause some women who do not fulfill this imperative to experience "a moral collapse" (*"Militant"* 4).

Works Cited

American Academy of Pediatrics Section on Breastfeeding. "Policy Statement: Breastfeeding and the Use of Human Milk." *Pediatrics*, vol. 150, no. 1, July 2022, pp. 1-15.

Avishai, Orit. "Managing the Lactating Body: The Breastfeeding Project and Privileged Motherhood." *Qualitative Sociology*, vol. 30, no. 2, 2007, pp. 135-52.

Beasley, Annette. "'Breast is Best' and Other Messages of Breastfeeding Promotion." *Giving Breastmilk: Body Ethics and Contemporary Breastfeeding Practice*, edited by Rhonda Shaw and Alison Bartlett, Demeter Press, 2010, pp. 39-50.

Blum, Linda. *At the Breast: Ideologies of Breastfeeding and Motherhood in the Contemporary United States*. Beacon Press, 1999.

Carter, Pam. *Feminism, Breasts and Breastfeeding*. St. Martin's Press, 1995.

Centers for Disease Control and Prevention. *Breastfeeding Report Card: Progressing toward National Breastfeeding Goals*. GPO, 2020.

Copelton, Denise A., et al. "The Ideological Work of Infant Feeding." *Giving Breastmilk: Body Ethics and Contemporary Breastfeeding Practice*, edited by Rhonda Shaw and Alison Bartlett, Demeter Press, 2010, pp. 24-38.

Dykes, Fiona. "Western Medicine and Marketing: Construction of an Inadequate Milk Syndrome in Lactating Women." *Health Care for*

Women International, vol. 23, no. 5, 2002, pp. 492-502.

Dykes, Fiona, and Catherine Williams. "Falling by the Wayside: A Phenomenological Exploration of Perceived Breast-milk Inadequacy in Lactating Women." *Midwifery*, vol. 15, no. 4, 1999, pp. 232-46.

Ennis, Linda Rose. "Intensive Mothering: Revisiting the Issue Today." *Intensive Mothering: The Cultural Contradictions of Modern Motherhood*, edited by Linda Rose Ennis, Demeter Press, 2014, pp. 1-23.

Faircloth, Charlotte. "Is Attachment Mothering Intensive Mothering?" *Intensive Mothering: The Cultural Contradictions of Modern Motherhood*, edited by Linda Rose Ennis, Demeter Press, 2014, pp. 180-193.

Faircloth, Charlotte. *Militant Lactivism? Attachment Parenting and Intensive Motherhood in the UK and France*. Berghahn Books, 2013.

Gonzales, Laura Fitzwater. "Framing Breastfeeding as 'Natural': Implications for Mothers' Identities." *Breastfeeding and Culture: Discourses and Representations*, edited by Ann Marie A. Short, Abigail L. Palko, and Dionne Irving, Demeter Press, 2018, pp. 285-304.

Hays, Sharon. *The Cultural Contradictions of Motherhood*. Yale University Press, 1996.

Hillervik-Lindquist, Charlotte. "Studies on Perceived Breast Milk Insufficiency: A Prospective Study in a Group of Swedish Women." *Acta Paediatrica Scandinavica*, vol. 376, 1991, pp. 3-27.

"Increasing Milk Supply." *Ask Dr. Sears*, 2020, www.askdrsears.com/topics/feeding-eating/breastfeeding/faqs/increasing-milk-supply/. Accessed 27 Jan. 2023.

Jung, Courtney. *Lactivism: How Feminists and Fundamentalists, Hippies, and Yuppies, and Physicians and Politicians Made Breastfeeding Big Business and Bad Policy*. Basic Books, 2015.

Knaak, Stephanie. "Breast-feeding, Bottle-feeding and Dr. Spock: The Shifting Context of Choice." *Canadian Review of Sociology*, vol. 42, no. 2, 2005, pp. 197-216.

Knaak, Stephanie. "Contextualizing Risk, Constructing Choice: Breastfeeding and Good Mothering in Risk Society." *Health, Risk & Society*, vol. 12, no. 4, 2010, pp. 345-55.

Knaak, Stephanie. "The Problem with Breastfeeding Discourse." *Canadian Journal of Public Health*, vol. 97, no. 5, 2006, pp. 412-14.

Kukla, Rebecca. "Ethics and Ideology in Breastfeeding Advocacy Campaigns." *Hypatia*, vol. 21, no. 1, 2006. 157-181.

Manne, Kate. *Down Girl: The Logic of Misogyny*. Oxford University Press, 2018.

O'Reilly, Andrea. *Matricentric Feminism: Theory, Activism, and Practice*. Demeter Press, 2016.

Pickert, Kate. "The Man Who Remade Motherhood." *Time*, 21 May 2012, time.com/606/the-man-who-remade-motherhood/. Accessed 27 Jan. 2023.

Sears, William, Martha Sears, Robert Sears, and James Sears. *The Baby Book: Everything You Need to Know About Your Baby from Birth to Age Two*. Little, Brown, and Company, 2013.

Solinger, Rickie. Pregnancy and Power: *A Short History of Reproductive Politics in America*. New York University Press, 2005.

Stearns, Cindy. "The Work of Breastfeeding." *WSQ: Women's Studies Quarterly*, vol. 37, nos. 3 & 4, 2009, pp. 63-80.

Taylor, Erin N. and Lora Ebert Wallace. "For Shame: Feminism, Breastfeeding Advocacy, and Maternal Guilt." *Hypatia*, vol. 27, no. 1, 2012, pp. 76-98.

Wall, Glenda. "Moral Constructions of Motherhood in Breastfeeding Discourse." *Gender and Society*, vol. 15, no. 4, 2001, pp. 592-610.

Wolf, Joan B. *Is Breast Best?: Taking on the Breastfeeding Experts and the New High Stakes of Motherhood*. New York University Press, 2011.

World Health Organization. "Breastfeeding." *World Health Organization*, 2021, www.who.int/health-topics/breastfeeding#tab =tab _2. Accessed 27 Jan. 2023.

Part 2.
Representations

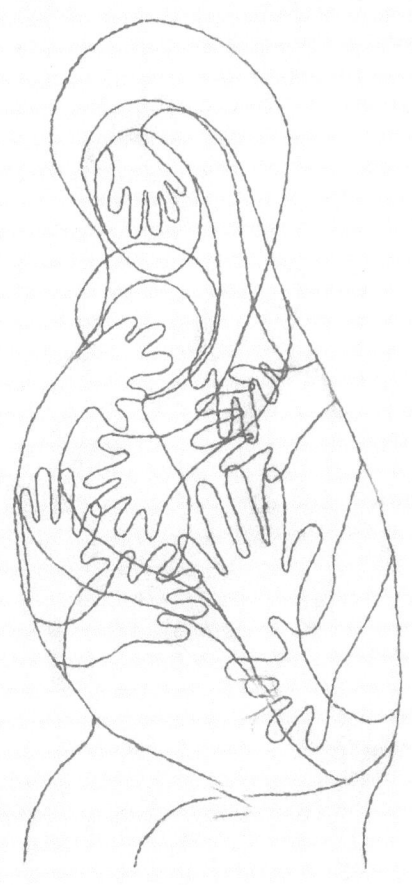

THE SAINTLY MOTHER

Chapter 6.

Upholding the Mother

Vanessa Marr

Vanessa Marr presents three hand-embroidered artworks that visualise subjective ideals of 'normative motherhood', saintly, desirable, and fertile, inspired by art, religion, and iconography. As a mother for four daughters herself, she created these embodiments of motherhood as an autoethnographic visualisation of her own experience and the conflicting, often unrealistic demands made upon mothers today. Her use of embroidery hints at the legacy of stitch that has both empowered and disempowered women, embellished upon a vintage cloth that anchors the mother in the feminine expectations that surround her.

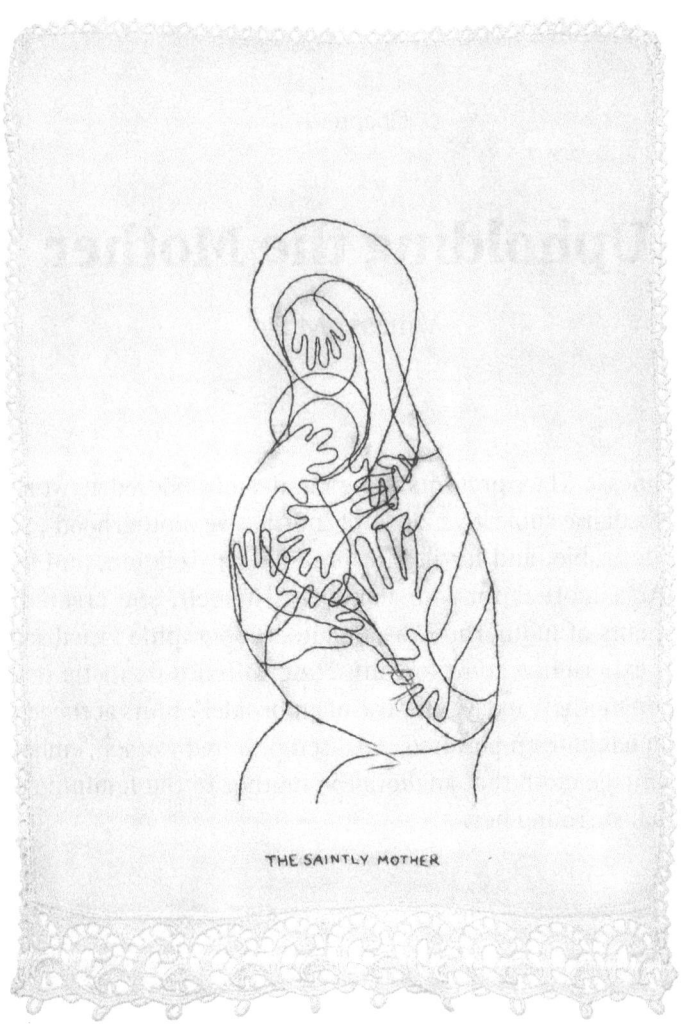

THE SAINTLY MOTHER

The Saintly Mother: Historical religious iconography of the Madonna and Child is suggested by a seated body with babe on lap, cocooned in distorted arms and complete with a halo wrapped around both their heads. The childlike hands that cover this figure converge and grasp towards the child in her arms, who is also the ultimate saintly offspring. Christian ideologies that present the Virgin Mary as the ultimate mother, along with demands for submissiveness and piety, are often at odds with contemporary feminist perspectives on motherhood. Western churches are filled with images of this haloed figure, radiating a sanctity that mortal mothers cannot possibly achieve. By capturing the epitome of saintly motherhood, this piece comments on the unrealistic expectations of patience, kindness, and exceptional virtue that are presented as 'normal' mothering.

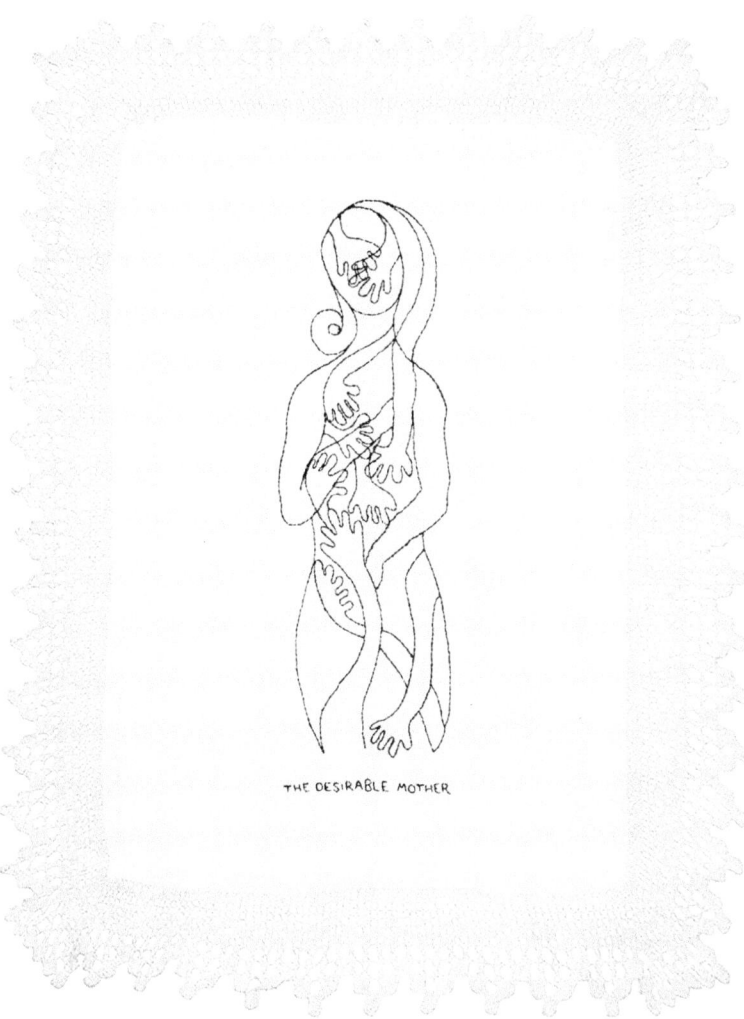

THE DESIRABLE MOTHER

The Desirable Mother: Botticelli's famous painting the Birth of Venus (1485) is suggested by the sweeping gestures of the famous pose, with her face, arms and hips wrapped in childlike clutches; a confusing collision of sexuality and mothering. The combination of sexual desire and mothering is a common social taboo, as female sex and desire is typically presented as most appropriate for those who are young and childless. For mothers themselves, the notion of sexuality is also coupled with her changing body, fatigue, and the expectation that she puts her desires last. The mother figure presented here longs for autonomy; defiantly resisting the normative culture that does not allow her to be desirable and fulfilled.

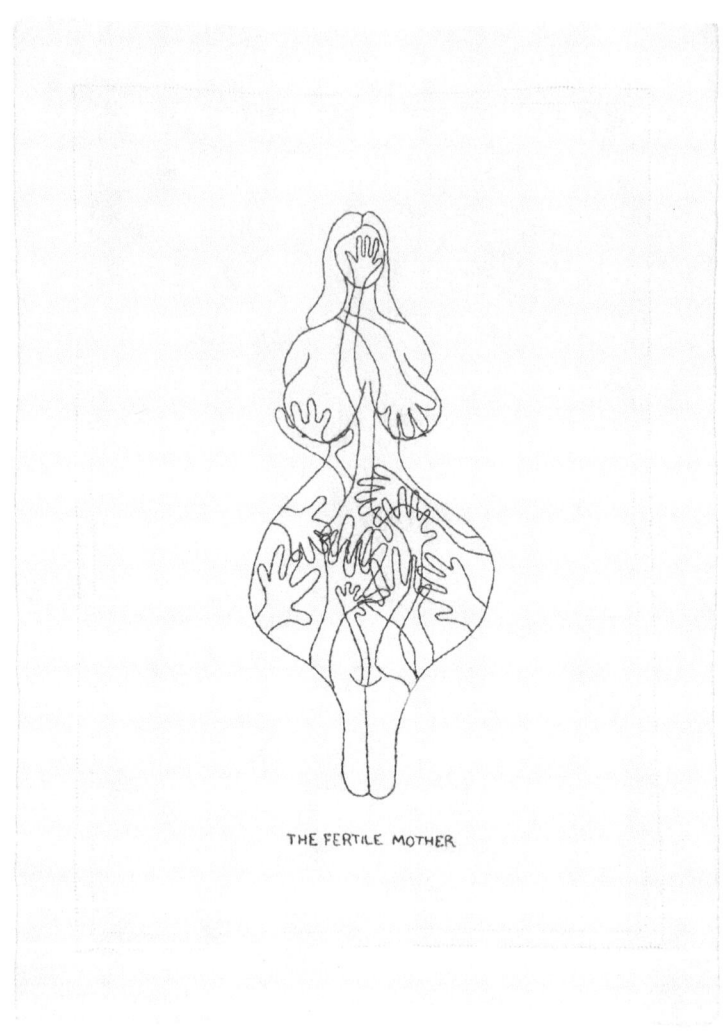

THE FERTILE MOTHER

The Fertile Mother: The ancient Gravettian goddess Venus, an icon of Palaeolithic art c.28,000–19,000 BC, is made contemporary through this image of a fertile woman, with huge breasts and hips, covered in grasping hands. As with the other artworks, the figure's face is covered by the hands that claim her identity; her fertility defines her. Conversely, this artwork also reminds us that some mothers struggle with fertility, not all mothers birth their own children, and that not all mothers are born female.

Chapter 7.

Childrearing by the Book: Motherhood Manuals from Birth to Nineteenth-Century America

Denise Hill

In the bestseller *Little Earthquakes*, Jennifer Weiner's fictional account of four women beginning their journey into motherhood, the character Ayinde is notable for her diligent attention to correctly rearing her new baby. Ayinde carefully follows the advice she received from her mother, but this advice came not in the form of shared personal experience; instead, Ayinde's mother mailed her a parenting guide called *Baby Success!* Weiner depicts Ayinde's attempt to strictly adhere to the *Baby Success!* five-point plan as comical; the reader cannot help but laugh as Ayinde sets an electronic timer to make sure her baby does not nurse longer than the book's prescribed thirty minutes or accosts her sleepy baby with kisses as she fearfully follows the book's mandate of "DO NOT ALLOW DUMPLING TO SLEEP AFTER A FEEDING!" (132).

Although Ayinde's experiences might seem humorous in the pages of a novel, motherhood books have a profound impact on which mothering practices are normalized and which practices are demonized. The powerful role they play can be seen in their sheer numbers: an Amazon search for parenting guides nets over fifty thousand results. These advice books carry mothers through every stage of their parenting—beginning with pregnancy advice from books, such as the ubiquitous *What to Expect When You're Expecting,* and continuing on through empty nest advice from such books as *Letting Go: A Parents' Guide to Understanding the College Years.* Although some of these books are now marketed towards men, women continue to be the primary audience.

But how did this phenomenon come into being? Certainly, we might look back to the debut of Dr. Benjamin Spock's books in the mid-twentieth century as the impetus for the modern fascination with childrearing manuals. However, the history of the genre reaches back much further into the past, with parenting advice appearing in ancient texts. Old Testament writers took up the call to discuss parenting: "Train up a child in the way he should go: and when he is old, he will not depart from it" (Prov. 22:6). Hippocrates and Aristotle wrote about childrearing as well. By the Middle Ages, however, such advice began to be codified into a genre of its own—the motherhood manual—which played a powerful role in prescribing normative mothering practices. According to Stephanie Shields and Beth A. Koster, parenting manuals are inherently ideological: "Child rearing manuals do not reflect the everyday activities of parenting, but they do distill beliefs about parenting" (54). These beliefs serve as normative forces that reify particular childrearing ideologies. Shifts in the genre over time reflect changing norms and who is allowed to shape those norms, vacillating between empowering women and stripping them of authority.

This chapter will trace the historical roots of the contemporary American motherhood manual and the normalizing practices that morphed over time. I will examine four stages of development: conduct manuals of the Middle Ages; manuals for rational mothers during the Enlightenment; Republican motherhood guides of the postcolonial era; and scientific motherhood manuals of the mid-nineteenth century. I argue that these historical texts leave a problematic legacy for contemporary mothers. Although women now have a key role in writing motherhood manuals, giving them agency to shape and enforce normative standards, their compliance to these norms is constantly monitored through a digital panopticon. As advice genre has mushroomed to include magazines, websites, and even TV shows, so too have surveillance technologies, from prenatal ultrasounds to viral mother-shaming memes. This begs the question of whether the development of the motherhood manual genre can in fact be termed "development" at all. Shifts in parenting guides over the centuries do not reflect a linear narrative of progress towards greater agency for women but instead reflect a continuing tug of war for the power to control maternity.

Early Roots: The Conduct Book

The motherhood manual derives from conduct or courtesy literature. Originating in the Middle Ages as a response to the aristocracy's fears that the breakdown of the chivalric system would erode their power and prestige, conduct books served to defend the aristocracy's power "through increasingly elaborate codes of behavior and display" (Batchelor). Early English bestsellers in the courtesy genre include Castiglione's *The Book of the Courtier* (translated from Italian in 1561) and Erasmus's *De Civiltate Morum Puerilium* (1530). Most conduct books focused on educating gentlemen in the manners of behaviour, conversation, and dress that would enable them to command the respect they deserved as aristocrats.

Given this purpose, it is not surprising that most conduct manuals were written by men for men. These texts typically provided counsel from father to son or friend to friend. However, women were not altogether overlooked in early courtesy literature. Some authors addressed women specifically but typically only in so much as the ways women should make themselves appealing to the gentlemen who were the primary audience for courtesy literature. For instance, in a section of *The Book of the Courtier* titled "Of the Chief Conditions and Qualityes in a Waytyng Gentylwoman," Castiglione admonishes gentlewomen "to have the understandinge beinge maried, how to ordre her husbandes substance, her house and children, and to play the good huswyef." For Castiglione, caring for children is merely a part of the gentlewoman performing her role as a good housewife of a gentleman husband. Reifying the norms of the time, women were not afforded agency in childrearing.

Although courtesy literature featured a male voice directing normative practices for women, a shift arose when a subgenre, parental advice books, emerged. Throughout the sixteenth century, such advice books were written almost exclusively by fathers for their sons. However, Nicholas Breton's 1601 book, *The Mother's Blessing,* opened the door for that to change. Although Breton's advice was standard fare, his mode of narration was not: Breton chose to adopt the persona of a mother, the deceased Lady Bartley, to transmit his advice. According to Kristen Poole, Breton's façade of maternity in *The Mothers Blessing* paved the way for women to enter into advice discourse (70). Women readily adopted the genre as an opportunity to share advice with their children in a time period when stark mortality rates (45 per cent of women died before reaching age fifty, more than half from pregnancy complications) often barred mothers from the opportunity to pass on their wisdom to their grown children (Lell). That impending death was a powerful motivator for women to write mothers' advice books is indicated by the titles women chose for their texts, as Susanna Bell's *The Legacy of a Dying Mother to her Mourning Children* (1673) demonstrates. One of the most poignant examples is Elizabeth Brook Joceline's *The Mother's Legacie* (1624), which she wrote out of fear that she would die in childbirth; Joceline would live for only nine days after the birth of her first child, a daughter.

Although these mother's legacy texts were written as general advice books for children, guidance for daughters about how to raise their own children often played a significant role in such works. Mothers began to publish advice about how their children should tend to both the spiritual and physical upbringing of their own children. A notable example is Elizabeth Clinton's 1662 pamphlet, dedicated to her daughter-in-law. Clinton urges mothers to embrace their natural duty to nurse their children rather than employ a wet nurse (as she herself employed for her own children): "Be not so unnatural as to thrust away your own children; be not so hardy as to venture accessory to that disorder of causing a poorer woman to banish her own infant for the entertaining of a richer woman's child, as it were, bidding her to unlove her own to love yours" (qtd. in Prince 284). Thus, through the mother's legacy text, conduct manuals made the turn from general advice texts into early versions of motherhood manuals.

The advent of women publishing motherhood advice is tied to the normalization of the "new mother" in the Early Modern period. During this time, the maternal role gained importance as women developed "increased and clear-cut responsibilities for the raising of her children" (Jones 40). The value placed upon the "new mother" provided mothers with an authority and status not afforded to other women, allowing them to enter the literary world by publishing mother advice books. Although women wrote advice books seemingly directed towards a narrow audience—a child, a daughter-in-law—they also had a larger audience in mind as well, as the publishing of these texts indicates. Through the status they gained as published authors, Susan Staub argues, women were able to enter religious and cultural debates under the guise of maternal advice. Although women maintained their place in a "family-centered, religiously oriented time" as they commented on society, motherhood manuals reflect an important shift in women's agency (Aughterson 72). Not only did these women authors gain the agency to teach others, but their audience also gained access, although limited in scope, to intellectual pursuits. In *The Instruction of a Christian Woman,* a conduct book dedicated to Catharine of Aragon, Juan Luis Vives encourages women's education: "A woman should study ... if nat for her own sake, at the least wyse for her children, that she maye teache and make them good." For the first time, motherhood is constructed as an intellectual pursuit.

Eighteenth-Century Developments: The Emergence of Manuals for Rational Mothers

Whereas in the seventeenth century women claimed literary agency in publishing advice about motherhood for other women, a shift occurred at the beginning of the eighteenth century as men once again took control over defining the acceptable standards of motherhood. As Felicity A. Nussbaum asserts, "Eighteenth-century Englishmen largely defined themselves, sexually and materially, as fully outside the scope of the maternal yet eager to intervene within it" (126). This time, male intervention was not in the form of aristocrats writing to teach women how to be ideal mates for courtiers; instead, it was Enlightenment philosophers and medical experts aiming to teach parents how to raise rational children.

The shift can be marked by the publication of John Locke's *Some Thoughts Concerning Education* in 1699. Locke's stated purpose for writing is to guide the parents (specifically, fathers) who had come to him searching for advice on how to properly rear their children:

> I myself have been consulted of late by so many, who profess themselves at a loss how to breed their children, and the early corruption of youth is now become so general a complaint, that he cannot be thought wholly impertinent, who brings the consideration of this matter on the stage, and offers something, if it be but to excite others, or afford matter for correction; for errors in education should be less indulged than any. These, like faults in the first concoction, that are never mended in the second or third, carry their afterwards-incorrigible taint with them through all the parts and stations of life.

Although he was a bachelor who rarely entered a nursery, Locke embraced the task of advising parents in his book, providing them with a rational and secular approach to childrearing. Locke's advice on feeding, bathing, and toilet training was rather Spartan, as he advised such practices as feeding children only plain food, placing children upon the stool after breakfast, and leaving them there until they had a bowel movement (Cable 53). One of Locke's most lasting contributions to the view of childrearing is his assertion that children are a blank slate onto which parents write. This tabula rasa idea thrusts a great deal of responsibility onto parents—they, rather than nature, are primarily responsible for programming their children's behaviour.

Because of this perception that parents have the great responsibility of writing upon their children's slates, it is no surprise that a flurry of texts were written to teach parents how to approach the task. Childrearing literature of the period was directed towards both men and women but in markedly different ways: Because fathers were thought to possess greater reason than mothers, fathers were taught in ways to educate older children, whereas mothers were guided in the care and feeding of infants (Grant 21). By the 1740s, advice manuals for rational mothers were popular among British women. These texts, typically written by male medical and scientific experts, taught women how to nurse and rear their children. Christine Bolt claims that these texts demonstrate "not only the growing literacy of women but also the increased respect of the work 'that a woman did at home'" (17). However, it is important to clarify that although the task to which women were entrusted might have been respected, that did not mean that mothers themselves were respected by the authors of these motherhood manuals. An abhorrence of women is evident in many texts of the period. One noteworthy example is English physician William Cadogan's *Essay on Nursing* (1749). Cadogan voices distain for women who have followed their great-grandmothers' models rather than nature and reason. He claims, "In my Opinion, this Business has been too long left to the Management of Women, who cannot be supposed to have the proper Knowledge to fit them for such a Task, notwithstanding they look upon it to be their own Province" (qtd. in Grant 20). Cadogan was not alone in his perception of women, for the childrearing literature of this period "rarely paid attention to the audience for whom the works were written . . . and instead restricted itself to narratives in which masculine experts wrested women's authority as mothers away from them" (Grant 5). Whereas the age of the "new mother" valued women's ways of knowing, the eighteenth century saw the denigration of wisdom passed down through generations of women. Instead, the mother is constructed as an imbecile who needs to be guided by a rational man.

If mothers were viewed so negatively by those attempting to train them in the proper strategies for childrearing, why would they read these motherhood manuals? It is likely because of the great sense of strain and anxiety experienced by mothers of the period. In their study of the changes in significant issues in English childrearing literature from the sixteenth through nineteenth centuries, Abigail J. Stewart, David G. Winter, and A. David Jones found that the idea of mother and father as co-rearers encouraged in the sixteenth century was replaced by the idea of the mother as the primary rearer during the eighteenth century (701). As childrearing became "women's work," the anxiety of mothers increased (Grant 2). With so much pressure upon women to adhere to the new normalized role of primary caregiver, it is no wonder that they would turn to books for support, even if those books were demonstrably misogynist.

Post-Revolutionary American Developments in Childrearing Literature

Although early American literature, especially religious texts, emphasized the father's role in childhood education, there was a comparative paucity of information written about mothering infants in colonial America (Bloch 105). According to Bolt, in England "formal attention had been paid to women's traditional duties in literature which advised them on how to nurse and rear their children. There were no equivalent publications in America" (16-17). This did not mean that colonial women were not reading motherhood manuals, however. Mary Cable indicates that although the American colonies contributed little to the literature of childcare, colonial women "paid a great deal of attention to what came to them from abroad" (51). Americans read Locke's *Some Thoughts Concerning Education* as well as other texts popular across the Atlantic.

Yet this lack of American childrearing literature began to shift towards the end of the eighteenth century. The introduction of motherhood manuals published in the United States (US) was, in part, an outgrowth of logistical concerns. As Julia Grant explains:

> Geographic and social mobility were on the rise, especially in New England, where "the stranger became not the exception but the rule." Acquiring information about rearing children could be difficult when word-of-mouth advice from relatives and lifelong friends was not accessible. Literacy afforded parents access to information substantially different from the face-to-face communication that had characterized earlier eras. (15)

Although this practical need to get information after the decline of the close-knit colonial community was certainly an underlying impetus for the growth of advice literature in the US, there was a powerful ideological cause as well: the advent of the new independent nation.

As Anne McClintock asserts, "All nationalisms are gendered, all are invented and all are dangerous" (260). The view of nationalism in the emergent US was inflected with gender, as the patriarchal power structure invented an image of nationhood implicated by a gendered discourse that revealed ideological presumptions about the roles of men and women in the nation. Words commonly associated with homosocial national affinities, such as "fraternity" and "brotherhood," reinforce the role of the boys' club in nation building, for men dominated the public sphere where the growth of nationalism was most visible. Yet women were not absent in the development of nationhood. According to Sylvia Walby's essay "Woman and Nation," women actively participate in national processes, but their contributions are often overlooked because of the "differential integration of women and men into the national project" (235). As familial tropes, such as "motherland" and "mother country" indicate, the feminine contribution to nationalism is generally concentrated upon maternity—both the physical reproduction of the populace and the ideological reproduction of national principles. The task of mothers was to raise strong leaders for the embryonic nation. Benjamin Rush, professor of medicine at the University of Pennsylvania, was among the first to connect republican principles and childrearing. In his *Thoughts upon the Mode of Education Proper in a Republic* (1784), Rush asserts that the patriotic citizens of the Republic would be formed in "nurseries" (qtd. in Reinier 157).

Such a task might seem challenging and daunting for American women living in the post-Revolutionary period. Not only must they face the physical risks of childbirth, but they also must carry the fate of the new nation on their shoulders. Walby asserts that women and men often experience different degrees of enthusiasm for a national project because nationalism does not necessarily support women's goals and claims that "where the national project includes women's interests, then women are more likely to support it" (245). For mothers to feel enthusiasm for their role in shaping the new nation, their maternal contribution needed to be respected and valued. And thus, the idea of the "Republican Mother" began to take shape.

The term "Republican Motherhood," coined by Linda Kerber, relates to a mother's responsibility "to educate her children and guide them in the paths of morality and virtue," thereby creating responsible citizens (283). Although Republican Motherhood preserved traditional gender roles, it simultaneously "carved out a new, political role for women" as mothers became the preservers and advancers of democracy by transmitting national values to their children (Zagarri 192). Republican Motherhood had "acquired unusual forcefulness" by the 1830s; however, women had to overcome decades of negative perceptions about motherhood before Republican Motherhood was granted such status (Kerber 282). According to Ruth Bloch, in the seventeenth and early eighteenth centuries, "motherhood was singularly unidealized, usually disregarded as a subject, and even at times actually denigrated" in American literature (100). Even as cultural perceptions of motherhood experienced a process of making and remaking[1] after the American Revolution, women envisioning a predominant role for motherhood in the new nation faced "severe ridicule, responding both to the anti-intellectual complaint that educating women served no practical purpose and the conservative complaint that women had no political significance" (Kerber 269). Nonetheless, the role of women as Republican Mothers was normalized over time, "aided by the dissemination of an associated rhetoric through the literary marketplace" (Robbins 564).

In the post-Revolutionary literary marketplace, motherhood manuals became available that encouraged women in their roles as Republican Mothers. One of the first and most successful manuals was *The Maternal Physician: A Treatise on the Nurture and Management of Infants, from the Birth until Two Years Old* (1811) by Mary Hunt Palmer Tyler, a well-educated woman who was committed to the ideal of the Republican Mother (Apple 3). Tyler insists that "While forming the future guardians of our beloved country, it is undoubtedly our duty, as *mothers*, to bring up our sons in such a manner as shall render them most useful and happy" (qtd. in Blackwell 31). She believed that childhood illness and death of these future guardians were the result of mothers' lack of education. Rather than encouraging mothers to seek help from the medical profession (although she did say that mothers should consult physicians if their children are very ill), Tyler believed that mothers knew best how to care for their children and sought to give them knowledge to guide them in their task.

Tyler's text is an exception in that most maternal advice books in the post-Revolutionary era, just as in the eighteenth century, were written by male authors. However, unlike the advice books circulating in England since the 1740s, American publications from the early nineteenth century supported and encouraged women's "primacy in the home" (Apple 4). Rather than focusing on practical concerns like bathing and feeding, most of these texts emphasized moral education, continuing the theme of early colonial literature. When authors addressed physical concerns, their approach rarely demonstrated the contempt for women visible in texts like Cadogan's; instead, their texts reflected the belief that women had not been provided with appropriate avenues to access health information. This is seen in the writings of John S. C. Abbott, author of the popular *The Mother at Home; or, The Principles of Maternal Duty* (1833). Abbott asserts that mistakes a mother made "she might have avoided had she consulted the sources of information which are within the reach of all" (qtd. in Apple 4).

The literature of the post-Revolutionary era reflects a culture simultaneously valorizing women's contributions through motherhood while placing greater pressure upon them to perform their task well. While the normalization of the moral mother of the new Republic elevated women's position, their power and agency were limited in that men were still the predominant authors of motherhood manuals and therefore the moderators of women's mothering practices. Not only were men presenting motherhood information, but it also became expected that women read their texts. As Abbott's quote reveals, women were expected to become researchers, consulting the sources of parenting information made available through the literary marketplace. This pressure to learn all they could in order to safeguard their children undoubtedly created anxiety for American mothers, an anxiety that would be developed to a greater extent in the latter half of the nineteenth century.

The Mid-Nineteenth Century: Scientific Motherhood

In the middle of the nineteenth century, several cultural factors coalesced to reshape the ideological construction of mothers and by extension the genre of motherhood advice literature. The first substantial change was industrialization. Because many fathers no longer worked in the home but instead travelled to offices or factories to work, men were even further removed from childcare tasks, placing greater responsibility upon mothers. Tied to industrialization was the shift from rural to urban living. Because most families no longer lived on a family farm and therefore no longer needed a large number of children to maintain an agrarian lifestyle, the pressure for women to produce offspring subsided. More women began to practice contraception, drawing upon information they learned from private letters, public lectures, and medical pamphlets (Scholten 100). By the middle of the nineteenth century, childbearing was no longer a frequent event in women's lives but instead an occasional event as family sizes decreased. During the colonial period, the mothers raised on average seven or eight children to adulthood; this number decreased to three or four by 1900 (Grant 15).

Coinciding with this move towards smaller families was a cultural shift towards individualism. From roughly 1836 to 1860, transcendental philosophy became a powerful influence upon American culture, especially in New England. The transcendental tenet that individual intuition is the highest source of knowledge led to a positive emphasis on individualism. Within families, as most mothers now had a few children rather than a large brood, mothering became focused more upon the individual child. As each child "took on greater significance ... motherhood took on greater importance" (Scholten 98). Because of this added importance, motherhood became something that was no longer a private concern within the home but instead the focus of public planning, study, and control. Parenting transitioned into a specialized occupation, and as such, it became "dependent on information from expert sources, not the least of which are pediatricians, psychologists, and the baby books these professionals produce" (Grant 3).

By the 1840s, a new sort of parenting literature emerged that focused on the physical and health aspects of family life while insisting on the need for expert advice in these areas. Scientific prescriptions for meeting the needs of children as individuals proliferated. Women writers were significant contributors to the genre in this time period, yet their writing served to perpetuate the authority of the male-dominated scientific establishment as authors shifted primacy from maternal instinct to scientific education. Lydia Maria Child, in her *The Mother's Book* (1831), claims that the maternal instinct was fallible and that mothers often "follow impulse, not principle" (qtd in. Grant 23). Likewise, Catherine Beecher claims in her *Treatise on Domestic Economy for the Use of Young Ladies at Home and at School* (1841) that mothers' mistakes in childrearing were due to not having "the knowledge which they have needed" and insisted that all women should receive a domestic education (qtd. in Grant 23). The education that Beecher calls for is rooted in the scientific world. In the childcare section of *The American Woman's Home* (1869), Beecher and co-author Harriet Beecher Stowe quote heavily from medical writers and proudly note that "some of the most distinguished physicians of New-York who have examined this chapter give their full approval of the advice given" (qtd. in Apple 5). Beecher and Stowe do not make any claim for their own expertise—although Beecher's position as a pioneering educator and Stowe's position as a ground-breaking author would in other time periods clearly establish them as trustworthy sources. Instead, the normalization of scientific motherhood rested all authority in male experts from the scientific world.

Although the abundance of scientific information available to women in the nineteenth century certainly had positive benefits —women could access information to improve the health of their children as well as manage their own reproductive health—this information came with a significant psychological cost. The writer of the 1842 text "Anxious Mothers" describes the stress the abundance of information creates for mothers:

> Everywhere we are told of the responsibilities of mothers, the great and arduous duties devolving upon them; and wherever we find a mother alive to these responsibilities, and aware of these high duties, we find also, an anxious, careworn, and dispirited woman.... The excessive interest awakened in behalf of education has produced in the conscientious of our sex a nervous solicitude, totally incompatible with the well discharge of their duties. (qtd. in Grant 2)

The "nervous solicitude" referenced by the writer emphasizes that although women's role as mothers had gained significant importance and public attention in the nineteenth century, such attention did not necessarily translate into greater power for women. Instead, their agency became increasingly restricted as their mothering—previously a private, domestic activity—came under the critical glare of the scientific establishment.

Conclusion: Implications for Contemporary Mothers

The challenges faced by nineteenth-century mothers are eerily similar to those faced by twenty-first-century mothers. In many respects, today's mothers have attained greater power through the fruits of the feminist movement: Mothers can pursue careers more freely, and the definition of who can mother has expanded to include LGBTQ+ parents. Moreover, the roles of fathers have evolved. Like mothering behaviors, "fathering behaviors are culturally influenced and socially constructed," thereby morphing over time (Dick 108). Fathers are now more likely to take on active parenting roles; however, mothers still tend to be the primary parents as only one in five two-parent families have a father as the primary caregiver in the United States.

Nevertheless, for all this progress, today's mothers still face an overwhelming abundance of scientific information about how to fulfill their maternal role. The twenty-first-century mother must contend with more than just motherhood manuals and pamphlets. In the information age, mothers are inundated with parenting advice from parenting books, magazines, the internet, and even TV shows, such as *Super Nanny*. Moreover, a technological panopticon unlike any in history has evolved to enforce parents' adherence to maternal normativity. Surveillance begins prenatally with ultrasounds and diagnostic testing; although these are beneficial for monitoring fetal development, they also surveil the mother's body, limiting her agency. Once the child is born, the mother's adherence to normative standards is policed by the digital horde, which will attack, often viciously, if she deviates from accepted practices.

A notable example of digital policing is the online charge against Mila Kunis. In July of 2021, Kunis and her husband, Ashton Kutcher, appeared on Dax Shepard's podcast, *Armchair Expert*, to discuss cryptocurrency. In a small aside from the main topic, Shepard commented that soaps deplete the body's natural oils. It is important to note that the line of conversation did not originate with Kunis, although in a gendered double-standard, she took the brunt of the digital wrath. Kunis simply agreed with Kutcher and commented, "I wasn't that parent that bathed my newborns, ever." Immediately, the internet was in an uproar, attempting to burn Kunis at the digital stake because she deviated from the accepted practices of scientific motherhood. Major media outlets, from *CNN* to *USA Today* to *People*, ran lead stories about Kunis's mothering habits. Even with the voices of paediatricians stating that it is wise not to overbathe a baby, Kunis was branded the neglectful mom with feral kids.

In light of this inescapable panopticon, we must call into question whether or not the development of the motherhood manual genre can in fact be termed "development" at all. The historical trace presented here demonstrates a tenuous struggle over how much power mothers would be allowed, and although the genre at times afforded women greater power, as when early modern mothers entered spiritual and cultural debates through their motherly advice, it often stripped them of their power. Observing that the twenty-first-century mother has her parenting mandated and monitored through scientific knowledge, it becomes clear that the shifts over the centuries in parenting guides—and the norms they reify—do not reflect a linear narrative of progress towards greater agency for women but instead reflect a continuing battle for the power to define and control maternal normativity.

Endnotes

1. For further discussion of the making and remaking of gender, see Cott, Nancy. *The Bonds of Womanhood: 'Woman's Sphere' in New England, 1780-1835.*

Works Cited

Apple, Rima D. *Perfect Motherhood: Science and Childrearing in America.* Rutgers University Press, 2006.

Aughterson, Kate, ed. *Renaissance Women: A Sourcebook, Constructions of Femininity in England.* Routledge, 1995.

Batchelor, Jennie. "Conduct Book." *The Literary Encyclopedia,* edited by Robert Clark, The Literary Dictionary Company, 9 Jul. 2004, The Literary Dictionary Company, www.litencyc.com/php/stopics.php?rec=true&UID=216. Accessed 10 Feb. 2023.

Bell, Susanna. *The Legacy of a Dying Mother to Her Mourning Children: Being the Experiences of Mrs. Susanna Bell, Who Died March 13, 1672.* John Hancock, Senior and Junior, 1673.

Blackwell, Marilyn S. "The Republican Vision of Mary Palmer Tyler." *Mothers and Motherhood,* edited by Rima D. Apple and Janet Golden, Ohio State University Press, 1997, pp. 31-51.

Bloch, Ruth H. "American Feminine Ideals in Transition: The Rise of the Moral Mother, 1785-1815." *Feminist Studies,* vol. 4, no. 2, 1978, pp. 100-26.

Bolt, Christine. *The Women's Movements in the United States and Britain from the 1790s to the 1920s.* University of Massachusetts Press, 1993.

Cable, Mary. *The Little Darlings: A History of Child Rearing in America.* Charles Scribner's Sons, 1975.

Castiglione, Baldassare. *The Book of the Courtier.* 1561. Translated by Sir Walter Raleigh, University of Oregon, 1997, www.uoregon.edu/~rbear/courtier/courtier.html. Accessed 10 Feb. 2023.

Cott, Nancy. *The Bonds of Womanhood: Woman's Sphere in New England, 1780-1835.* Yale University Press, 1997.

Grant, Julia. *Raising Baby by the Book: The Education of American Mothers.* Yale University Press, 1998.

Dick, Gary L. "The Changing Role of Fatherhood: The Father as a Provider of Selfobject Functions." *Psychoanalytic Social Work*, vol. 18, no. 2, 2001, pp. 107-25.

Holy Bible. Authorized King James Version. Ed. C.I. Scofield. New Scofield Reference Edition. Oxford University Press, 1967.

Jones, Ann Rosalind. "Nets and Bridles: Early Modern Conduct Books and Sixteenth-century Women's Lyrics." *The Ideology of Conduct: Essays on Literature and the History of Sexuality*, edited by Nancy Armstrong and Leonard Tennenhouse. Metheun, 1987, pp. 39-72.

Kerber, Linda K. *Women of the Republic: Intellect and Ideology in Revolutionary America.* University of North Carolina, 1980.

Lell, Erica M. "Mother's Legacy." *Renaissance Motherhood.* 2006, www.users.muohio.edu/mandellc/projects/lellem/birthFla.htm. Accessed 10 Feb. 2023.

Locke, John. *Some Thoughts Concerning Education.* 1699. *Modern History Sourcebook.* Fordham University. 22 Sept. 2001, www.fordham.edu/halsall/mod/1692locke-education.html. Accessed 10 Feb. 2023.

McClintock, Anne. "'No Longer in a Future Heaven': Nationalism, Gender, and Race." *Becoming National: A Reader*, edited by Geoff Eley and Ronald Grigor Suny, Oxford University, 1996, pp. 260-84.

Nussbaum, Felicity A. "'Savage' Mothers: Narratives of Maternity in the Mid-Eighteenth Century." *Cultural Critique*, vol. 20, 1992, pp. 123-51.

Poole, Kristen. "'The Fittest Closet for All Goodness': Authorial Strategies of Jacobean Mothers' Manuals." *Studies in English Literature*, vol. 35, no. 1, 1995, pp. 69-88.

Prince, J. "Infant Feeding through the Ages." *Midwives Chronicle and Nursing Notes*, Dec. 1976, pp. 283-285.

Reinier, Jacqueline S. "Rearing the Republican Child: Attitudes and Practices in Post-Revolutionary Philadelphia." *William and Mary Quarterly*, vol. 39, no. 1, 1982, pp. 150-63.

Robbins, Sarah. "'The Future Good and Great of Our Land': Republican Mothers, Female Authors, and Domesticated Literacy in Antebellum New England." *New England Quarterly*, vol. 75, no. 4, 2002, pp. 562-91.

Scholten, Catherine M. *Childbearing in American Society: 1650–1850*. New York University, 1985.

Sheperd, Dax. "Mila Kunis and Ashton Kutcher." *Armchair Expert*, Simplecast, 19 July 2021, https://armchairexpertpod.com/pods/mila-kunis-ashton-kutcher.

Shields, Stephanie A., and Beth A. Koster. "Emotional Stereotyping of Parents in Child Rearing Manuals, 1915-1980." *Social Psychology Quarterly*, vol. 52, no. 1, 1989, pp. 44-55.

Staub, Susan, ed. *Mother's Advice Books*. Ashgate, 2002.

Stewart, Abigail J., David G. Winter, and A. David Jones. "Coding Categories for the Study of Child-Rearing from Historical Sources." *Journal of Interdisciplinary History*, vol. 5, no. 4, 1975, pp. 687-701.

United States, Department of Health and Human Services. *Charting Parenthood: A Statistical Portrait of Fathers and Mothers in America*. Office of the Assistant Secretary for Planning and Evaluation. Government Printing Office, 2002.

Vives, Juan Luis. *A very Frutefull and Pleasant Boke Called the Instruction of a Christen Woman Made Fyrst in Laten and Dedicated unto the Quenes Good Grace by the Right Famous Clerke Mayster Lewes Vives*. Translated by Rycharde Hyrd. Thomas Berthelet, 1529. *Early English Books Text Creation Partnership*. 2011, quod.lib.umich.edu/cgi/t/text/text-idx?c=eebo2;idno=B00841.0001.001. Accessed 10 Feb. 2023.

Walby, Sylvia. "Woman and Nation." *Mapping the Nation*, edited by Gopal Balakrishnan. Verso, 1996, pp. 235-254.

Weiner, Jennifer. *Little Earthquakes*. Washington Square, 2004.

Zagarri, Rosemarie. "Morals, Manners, and the Republican Mother." *American Quarterly*, vol. 44, no. 2, 1992, pp. 192-215.

Chapter 8.

The Perils of Embracing Respectability Politics: Maternal Conformity and Normativity in Alice Walker's *The Abortion* and Nafissa Thompson-Spires's *Belles Lettres*

Zsuzsanna Lénárt-Muszka

The chapter examines the representations of normative motherhood and respectability politics vis-à-vis Black American motherhood in two contemporary short stories by African American women writers: Alice Walker's "The Abortion" (1981) and Nafissa Thompson-Spires's "Belles Lettres" (2018). After introducing the stories, I briefly establish the historical context of Black American mothers' social position, which I contextualize within the discourses of normative motherhood and respectability politics. Then I examine how the stories affirm or subvert four tenets of normative motherhood—essentialization, normalization, expertization, and intensification—and how the three textual mothers are influenced by the racialized aspects of their motherhoods. The mandates of normative motherhood and respectability politics are intertwined in the stories, leading the protagonists to experience motherhood as a performance done for the sake of an external gaze. I also discuss the narrative ramifications of prioritizing the figure of the ideal mother and reflect on the personal and social implications of adopting or resisting the strategy and imperatives of respectability politics in the texts.

Alice Walker is widely known not only for her novels—chiefly among them *The Color Purple* (1982)—and her womanist essays but also for her short story collections. "The Abortion," published in her 1981 volume, *You Can't Keep a Good Woman Down*, is one short story that has not gained much critical attention despite its rich narrative fabric and nuanced treatment of womanhood and motherhood. Its protagonist, Imani, feels trapped in an emotionally unsatisfying marriage to Clarence, whose political ambitions often eclipse his commitment to his wife. The narrative tracks Imani's journey from getting her first abortion during her college years, then having a daughter, a miscarriage, and another abortion, all during the 1960s' Civil Rights Movement. "Belles Lettres" was published in 2018 in literary up-and-comer Nafissa Thompson-Spires's debut short story collection, *Heads of the Colored People*, a volume which has earned her several awards ("Heads of the Colored People"). The epistolary short story, set over a month in 1991, follows a conflict between two mothers whose daughters attend the same school. The tone of the letters, initially passive aggressive yet polite, escalates to become outright hostile. Even though each story focuses on a different stage of motherhood—pregnancy and taking care of a toddler in Walker and mothering a school-aged child in Thompson-Spires—both feature upper-middle-class women whose options are delineated by several sexist and racist standards they have partially internalized. The characters who populate the worlds of "The Abortion" and "Belles Lettres" are influenced by normative motherhood and womanhood in striving to be the embodiments of respectable, upper-middle-class idea(l)s; thus, both stories echo the expectations of Black respectability politics.

Normative Motherhood and Respectability Politics

Both stories envision motherhood within the bounds of normative idea(l)s underscored by what Andrea O'Reilly terms the "ten dictates of normative motherhood," among them normalization, which cements mothers in the nuclear family; essentialization, which "positions maternity as the basis of female identity;" expertization, which urges mothers to prioritize the advice of experts (medical or otherwise) when it comes to parenting; and intensification, which makes women believe that taking of children should be a complicated, all-consuming endeavour (10–11). The stories thematize how three young Black women grapple with normative motherhood against the backdrop of Black women's history. From colonialism onwards, white American women have been restricted by various patriarchal expectations, but women from various racial minorities, especially Black American women, have suffered under multifaceted manifestations of oppression in the United States. As white racialized identity developed parallel to the spread of the institution of slavery, the (idea of the) white mother became elevated through the denigration of the Black mother (Martinot 86). The nineteenth-century cult of true womanhood and the cult of domesticity are both already restrictive and regulatory discourses, but they took foothold by further restricting and regulating what Black womanhood can mean: White female identity and the construct of white motherhood were cemented through framing Black womanhood as something inherently immoral and debased. As white womanhood's ideological boundaries were drawn to exclude Black women (Carby 38–39), the enslaved woman was "excluded from the mothering realm" (Patton xii), which was the prerogative of white women, resulting in a social order in which the term "mother" itself became paradoxical in the context of slavery (Spillers 76). Stereotypes of greedy, lazy, and pathological Black mothers have permeated American culture ever since. Thus, while the vilification of Black mothers might have changed shape, it has undoubtedly persisted and impacted the maternal identification process of many.

As a response, many Black women have adopted the attitude and discourse of respectability politics in the hope of undermining those stereotypes that seek to cast them as mentally and culturally inferior. Respectability politics is not unique to Black Americans; various marginalized groups have subscribed to it as a way of earning the respect of the majority (Jones), but the term itself was coined in relation to Black women by Evelyn Brooks Higginbotham in 1994. Higginbotham argues that Black Baptist women during the Jim Crow era, in their efforts to organize communities and earn the esteem of the white majority, relied on positioning themselves as respectable: They insisted on conforming to white social norms (185-87). Higginbotham conceives of the Black Baptist women's respectability politics as a form of resistance that ran parallel to nonviolent yet persistent efforts against institutionalized racism (187); however, respectability politics can be a tactic of assimilation and might entail the denial of one's cultural roots as well as excessive self-regulation and self-vigilance (Lee and Hicken 421-22). As a backlash, many Black women and girls are increasingly and unapologetically embracing their "ratchet" identity by adopting an unruly, transgressive persona and proudly presenting themselves as angry and sexually liberated as an antithesis to respectability politics (Payne 6-9). Still, expectations to project a dignified image as a Black woman and mother persist into the twenty-first century.

Essentialized and Normalized Motherhood in "The Abortion"

Influenced by the reverberations of respectability politics, the protagonist of "The Abortion" goes through several life stages. Hints about her premotherhood life reveal that she never intended to marry; rather, she wanted "to take in lovers who could be sent home at dawn, freeing her to work and ramble" (73). Having grown up in the South, she goes to college in New York, where she has her first abortion as a single woman. Far from feeling remorse, she considers the procedure as her initiation into adulthood, a ceremony that ushers in her coming of age (67), but her refusal to remember its painful physicality is a trauma response (Lénárt-Muszka 125). Instead, she reminisces about the abortion, thinking about it in mythical terms as a thrilling, "wonderful" event that enabled her to seize the direction of her life and made her understand that "life—what one saw about one and called Life—was not a façade" (67). This rather cryptic phrase suggests that the procedure was more than a manifestation of her agency—it was an act that was supposed to counteract an earlier feeling of alienation, which Imani does not overtly reflect upon but which might be understood as having its roots in her Southern conservative upbringing that made her feel as if she was behind a façade.

Yet it is exactly this suffocating, alienating environment that Imani goes back to. The next episode from the protagonist's life that the reader is exposed to shows that she has left behind her free, perhaps even bohemian, persona of a New York City college girl and has moved back south, married a so-called good Black man, and had a daughter. Her husband, Clarence, acts as advisor to the small town's first Black mayor, often inviting him for dinner. Supporting the mayor at a racially charged historical moment is of supreme significance to Clarence, which Imani accepts, albeit reluctantly. The husband's allegiance to the mayor stems from his desire to enact meaningful political change in the long run and to avoid the shame and ridicule of having an incompetent and failing Black mayor whom the white supremacist public would surely be eager to point to as the epitome of Black inferiority (67). Yet Imani is quietly indignant, as the mayor "would never look at her directly ... and would instead talk to Clarence as if she were not there [because] he assumed that as a woman she would not be interested in, or even understand, politics" (66). Although Clarence supports Imani's decision to get an abortion, he withdraws emotional support right before Imani flies to New York and instead prioritizes his work with the mayor (67). Not only is she brushed aside by both her husband and the mayor, but she is also indirectly dismissed by the masculinist political concerns prevalent in and around the Civil Rights Movement. Ironically enough, her mother, a schoolteacher, dies from lung cancer caused by the asbestos leaking from the walls of her classroom—contributing to Imani's miscarriage—which is juxtaposed to Clarence and the mayor discussing school desegregation issues while remaining ignorant of Imani's emotional turmoil at the airport (66-67). In Clarence's narrative—and the larger political climate of the Civil Rights Movement—the racial concern of desegregation takes precedence over the importance of the individual Black woman who does the underpaid, pink-collar work of teaching, just as political debates take precedence over Imani's pain, which suggests that Clarence's wish for the whole family to perform the role of respectable Black citizens puts Imani in an always-already inferior position, back behind the façade she wished to escape.

This adherence to normativity and respectability hurts Imani in several ways. The suffocating contrast between the artistic, educated, and urbane woman who prefers an unencumbered lifestyle and the Imani who performs the role of the good, small-town, normative wife and mother is revealed through several images of Clarence's hand resting heavily on her (65), his head pressing against her knees (71), or the discomfort she feels when her daughter, Clarice, is in her lap, pressing down on her abdomen (71). In part, her various health issues, including anemia and dental problems, stem from being or having been pregnant, but her chronic physical discomfort and weakness also testify to how stifling her environment is. Imani repeatedly reflects on how "good" she earlier thought Clarence was, citing it as a reason for why she married him (64-65). Now, she grapples with feeling like a "fraud" because marriage bores her (67), and the breakdowns in their communication and his lack of attention indicate that their relationship is no longer fulfilling. Imani's choice to stay in a marriage that no longer brings her joy hints at her need to cling to the idea of Clarence as an outstanding, worthy man as well as to the notion of the nuclear family, which shows that she has subscribed to the idea of a normative family structure.

More importantly, Imani is unfulfilled in her motherhood. In contrast with the monumental event of the first abortion, she describes becoming a mother in mundane terms: "Having a child is a good experience *to have had*, like graduate school. But if you've had one, you've had the experience and that's enough" (65). Becoming a mother is thus an exercise in gender for her, an item on a list of what a woman does, an essential, unalienable feature of womanhood. The fact that Imani mentions "having"—that is, accumulating—certain experiences, such as becoming a mother or finishing graduate school, together with mentions of having lovers, rambling, and working freely (73), encapsulates her conceptualization of an ideal life: a creative, dynamic one in which one experience follows the other. However, having a child delineates her options, confining her to a lifestyle with a marked contrast to her ideal one.

When Imani gets pregnant amid these circumstances, she realizes that, as she says, "another child would kill me" (65). Her decision to terminate the pregnancy goes in the face of being an obedient, upper-middle-class Black woman and normative mother for several reasons. Prioritizing one's physical and mental health goes directly against the selflessness traditionally imputed to—and expected of—mothers. Furthermore, Imani's small-town, religious community that follows Primitive Baptism—a conservative branch of the religion—would probably disavow of the termination should they know about it. The historical situatedness of abortion discourse in Black American communities adds a further dimension to this problem: A general mistrust of abortion, prevalent until about the mid-1970s, was propagated by, among others, the Nation of Islam and the Black Panther Party and was fuelled by fears of a self-imposed genocide (Nelson 77-85). Imani's decision to terminate her pregnancy, then, seems to contradict several, overlapping, and culturally embedded imperatives.

A closer examination of her drive to, as she puts it, "choose herself" (70) reveals that the act of the termination becomes an antidote to her situation. Getting the second abortion is an attempt to improve her marriage. Seeing that her mother's working conditions are considered unimportant and she herself is expected to be a mute accessory to her husband's ambitions, Imani is desperate to provoke Clarence into prioritizing her worries and helping her make the decision of whether to keep the baby (64-65). The abortion also signals her yearning for control over her body (69). More significantly, the termination is an act of rebellion against her oppressive circumstances. Insofar as the first abortion's relevance lies in teaching Imani that life is not a façade, she hopes the second one will be the remedy to her increasingly empty life—a life in which she has learned that she is confined to the sidelines, that is, put behind a façade. The narrator explains: "She felt the two of them, Clarence and Clarice, clinging to her, using her. And that the only way she could claim herself, free herself distinct from them, was by doing something painful, self-defining but self-destructive" (71). I would therefore argue that the second abortion can be read not merely as an act of gaining agency and establishing bodily autonomy but as a tool of resisting the respectable, normative life Imani has crafted for herself.

This reading is also supported by an instance of linguistic ambiguity in the text. A focal point in the story is the church memorial service in honour of Holly Monroe, a Black girl who became the victim of racially motivated police brutality on the day of her high school graduation five years before the main events of the plot. Even though Imani finds her family suffocating, she enjoys being part of the small-town Baptist community and makes a point of attending these annual memorials out of solidarity. A few days after the second abortion, she performs physically draining tasks, including bathing and dressing Clarice, then goes to the service in an emotionally heightened state. There, after observing that the murdered girl's classmates all resemble Holly, Imani reflects: "Every black girl of a certain vulnerable age *was* Holly Monroe. And an even deeper truth was that Holly Monroe was herself. Herself shot down, aborted on the eve of becoming herself" (73). The associative link between Holly and being aborted hints at Imani's repressed grief and remorse about terminating her pregnancies, implying that Holly symbolizes the aborted fetus(es). Yet Holly being "herself" could refer to her (i.e., Holly) not standing in for anyone, not being a proxy for any Black girl, but having her own personal, not necessarily politicized story. The structure of the sentence, however, allows for another interpretation as well: Holly Monroe symbolizes Imani, who was "aborted on the eve of becoming herself." Here, the abortion does not refer to the procedure but to Imani's lost potential: She "aborted" herself by trading a free, unencumbered life for becoming a traditional wife and mother.

Imani identifies with Holly to such an extent that when Clarence and the mayor choose to continue a conversation about the city's new charter instead of joining the memorial, Imani is furious and feels personally slighted; she later points to that moment as the one that marks her uncoupling from her husband. The story concludes on an optimistic note: Even though she cries as she packs her bags, there is a sense of relief, much of the anxiety has dissipated, and Imani has regained her health. The reader has no information about how their separation will impact the family, but the fact that it is Imani who packs might mean that she leaves Clarice behind as well. Imani's tragedy lies in the fact that she turns away from a lifestyle that she knows would suit her and instead runs towards a respectable life of normative comfort and acquiesces to the expectation to have a child. With the abortion and the subsequent dissolution of her marriage, she rebels against the quotidian racism and sexism of her environment. Whether this includes the radical and taboo act of moving on alone, without Clarice, is unclear, but even if she takes her daughter with her, Imani unequivocally closes a chapter of her life and presumably at least partially breaks away from the yoke of normalized, essentialized motherhood.

Expertization and Intensification in "Belles Lettres"

Whereas Imani lives in a predominantly Black milieu, Monica and Lucinda in "Belles Lettres" are in a unique position within their community. For a while, Lucinda's daughter, Christina, is the only Black girl in her school in an affluent California neighborhood, which changes with the arrival of Fatima, Monica's daughter. Lucinda reaches out to Monica in the hope of quashing the rivalry between the two girls, who appear to bully each other. As the reader is only exposed to the letters with no information about the girls' behaviour, it is unclear how the conflict started. It is implied, though, that Christinia feels that she has established her position as the only Black girl in class and now feels that she is in competition with the newcomer. Thus, the friction between the girls, and hence between the mothers, stems from clinging or aspiring to a status of being exceptional. While the girls prank each other and spread rumors about each other in order to stand out in their social group, the mothers do the same: They are desperate to fulfill the role of a respectable Black person in a predominantly white community. Monica remarks, "I'm not of the mind that the only two black children in the class should be enemies, nor do I like the attention it draws to them (or their parents) when they're already in a difficult position" (37), but Lucinda seems to pride herself on their singularity: "We are not self-conscious about Christinia's blackness. I attended Westwood myself as a child and was very happy there, even though at the time I was the only black child in the entire K–6 division" (38). One way or the other, trying to conform to an affluent, suburban, and white space puts pressure on both the mothers and the daughters, causing their misguided attempts to fit in.

What makes the mothers' situation even more complicated is that both are professional women with high-status careers: Lucinda is a family therapist with a PsyD (Doctor of Psychology) degree, whereas Monica is a college professor of education with a PhD. Lucinda makes it clear that she is a licensed therapist in her first letter's signature, and whereas she signs it as "Dr. Lucinda Johnston, PsyD," she addresses the other woman with a casual "Hello Monica" (34). In response, Monica uses a letterhead that clarifies her institutional affiliation and credentials, and from then on, the letterheads and the signatures only get more informative and sprawling while the greetings get more aggressive. The sarcastic "Dear Lucinda, or should I say Dr. Johnston"

(37) soon deteriorates into a curt "Lucinda" (38). These paratextual devices—along with less subtle digs such as "Isn't your degree, by the way, an EdD?" (38)—evince that the mothers rely on their qualifications to garner some respect when they feel attacked. During their correspondence, they hurl accusations towards each other's daughter and, by implication, towards each other as well, trying to undermine the others' professional credentials. They feel that their children's potential shortcomings betray their own weaknesses as mothers, making them resort to using their careers—thus, their respectability—as shields.

Significantly, both Monica's and Lucinda's degrees are related to children's development. They make overt references to their own supposed professional superiority. Lucinda attacks both Monica and Fatima by writing: "You are, unfortunately, enabling your child's arrogance and stifling her growth even at this young age. I write about this very thing in chapter three of my first book, *Caution with Coddling*" (39). Monica calls Lucinda's qualifications into question (38) and remarks "how lucky" it is for Christinia to have access to psychotherapy through Lucinda's practice (35). Gradually, they resort to insulting each other by referring to the other's supposed marital infidelity (40), and, finally, they outright mock and threaten each other (43). Both mothers are supposed to be childrearing experts on paper, yet they are depicted as increasingly petty and hectic. The authorial choice to represent these educated women this way reveals a critique of expertization. It suggests that even though Monica and Lucinda might be competent at their job and might be compassionate, fierce mothers bent on defending their daughters, their expert status is not their redeeming quality, and it certainly does not help them convince the other. The two spheres—the professional one and that of mothering—do not, cannot, interact. Therefore, the fact that they cannot use their expertise in this setting implies that this knowledge is not transferable and not applicable in real-life parenting situations, calling into question the legitimacy of expert knowledge in childrearing itself.

Apart from expertization, another tenet of normative motherhood that features strongly in Thompson-Spires's story is intensification. Even though Lucinda claims that "here [in our community] we try to help the children work through their problems without getting too involved" (36), both women make a point of participating in the daughter's school life: Lucinda works with the school's Jack and Jill of America chapter, an organization aimed at fostering the leadership skills of Black children (36); Monica donates a substantial amount of money to the school and joins its welcoming committee (45), and they both chaperone the class field trip (34). The mothers' investment in their daughter's school life, the frequency of their correspondence, and the intensity of their feelings, evident in the escalation of their conflict, bespeaks their wish to be good mothers—an ideal to which they wholeheartedly subscribe. Monica's remark about Lucinda needing to spend more time with Christinia (37) underscores that she views intense parenting as a virtue by insinuating that Lucinda is a neglectful parent. Furthermore, their repeated references to Fatima's and Christinia's academic success and social popularity are underpinned by the mothers' hope that their intense mothering efforts will result in exceptional children, through whom they can live vicariously. Intensification, much like expertization, is an avenue of the respectability that Monica and Lucinda hope to attain through their daughters. "Belles Lettres" exposes that the intensification of mothering leads to a hyperalert state in which the mothers assume the worst about each other's parenting abilities; furthermore, it criticizes the idea of expertization by throwing its inadequacy into sharp relief.

The extent to which Lucinda and Monica are influenced by the dictates of normative motherhood is closely intertwined with Blackness: They undermine each other by using insults inflected by race. Lucinda's attempt to shame Monica by mentioning Fatima's backpack smelling of rotten eggs (36) evokes the centuries-old notion of olfactory racism used to justify Atlantic slavery (Kettler xi), now internalized by Lucinda. Monica takes aim at Christinia's body by mentioning her "size" (39) and "girth" (37), echoing those phobias rooted in white supremacy that have historically posited the Black female body as excessive and hyperembodied while suturing obesity to immorality (Strings, "Introduction"). Insults about hair (42), wearing "seventies-style caftans" (40), "bourgieness" (41) and being "ghetto" and "uppity" (41) are similarly racialized, as is the mothers' repeated insinuations that the other child cannot read (38-39). The latter might seem like a simple accusation serving to highlight one child's superiority over the other, but enduring claims of Black Americans' mental inferiority as well as their historic quest for literacy make these insults more pronounced. Clothing choices, hair styling, language use, and many other, seemingly trivial aspects of everyday life thus become targets that both mothers exploit in order to appear more respectable as a woman and mother than the other.

Crucially, the story's conclusion suggests that the status quo will be upheld indefinitely. The news of Monica and Lucinda's conflict reaches the school management, but after a meeting with the principal, Monica makes a "generous donation," which miraculously results in the "sharp improvement" of her daughter's behaviour (45-46). In the last letter, Monica thanks Lucinda for inviting Fatima to their party and refers to other future social plans (46). Whereas Imani changes directions, Monica and Lucinda seem to get even more involved in the children's lives. Instead of berating each other, they now seem to be on cordial terms; nevertheless, their communication still revolves around how they and their children are perceived, which reveals their worries about staying respectable. The dictates of normative motherhood clearly coalesce with the tenets of respectability politics in these Black mothers' desperation to counter those stereotypes that have long depicted them as inadequate, careless mothers.

Motherhood as Performance

Indeed, all the mothers live under an external but internalized gaze, so much so that motherhood becomes a performance—something to do, a respectable role to enact. At the intersection of her Blackness, womanhood, motherhood, and class, Imani is driven by a need to cling to normative notions of what a proper Black wife should do. She repeatedly holds her daughter in her arms, bathes and dresses her to take her to church, and hosts the mayor for dinner despite her inner turmoil, without ever directly talking about her concerns. Comparably, Monica and Lucinda are portrayed as mothers who perform rather than feel and do rather than are. The significance of being the only Black student and the only Black mom with a high-status job weighs heavily on both mothers. Their feud reveals that they want to seem better not only in the eyes of their white peers but also in each other's eyes. They long for validation from each other, but instead of mutual celebration, they attempt to one up the other. They defend their daughters, but what the narration withholds is how they actually treat them away from the public eye and how they feel about motherhood. Whereas Fatima's and Christinia's mothers insist that their own daughter is smarter, kinder, and more well-adjusted than the other girl, it is not yet the daughter's success that Imani craves and lives vicariously through. Rather, it is the daughter's mere existence, presence, and even appearance that she hopes to get validation from. The process through which she scrubs her and dresses her nicely before church is detailed meticulously in the narrative (72), which can be interpreted in multiple ways: as an act that pays respect to God or Holly or one of those quotidian acts of care that mothers routinely perform. However, the economy of the text also signifies that the child becomes an accessory, a status symbol for Imani, just as Fatima and Christinia do for their respective mothers.

Narrative Ramifications

A motive for portraying Imani as a mute mother and putting the emphasis on what Monica and Lucinda write—but not on how they feel—could be to illustrate the degree to which these mothers are impacted by respectability politics. The narrative gaps discussed above imply the mothers' disconnection to what they want as individuals and underscore their wish to adhere to the norms expected of them as Black women, Black mothers, and prominent Black members of their communities. The relative silence of these mothers raises the question of which character is the protagonist in each story. Much of Black women's fiction has tackled the issue of motherhood through the daughter's lens or relied on the figure of the mother as merely a symbol of the past, often effacing the lived experience of being a mother (see the importance of the matrilineal tradition, Sadoff 12, Dubey 245-48); in contrast, "The Abortion" and "Belles Lettres" seem to offer a maternal perspective by focusing on the experiences of flesh-and-blood mothers. However, I argue that "The Abortion" and "Belles Lettres" are matrifocal narratives only to a degree: The actual perspective and the subjectivity of the mother remain hidden behind a façade used to uphold the status quo. The texts are preoccupied with how the mothers behave exactly because the mothers are preoccupied by how they themselves behave, meaning that a wish to adhere to respectability politics permeates the texts and guides their very narrative design just as it guides the mothers' lives. The central character seems to be the elusive, looming figure of the ideal mother, not the mothers themselves.

Even though the texts feature individual women, they expose the underlying structures that frame Imani's, Lucinda's, and Monica's lives, without indicting the mothers themselves. The context and the primary cause of how all three women relate to themselves (and each other) is white supremacist patriarchal expectations. In "The Abortion," Imani feels the added responsibility of shaping local politics in the hope of racial uplift, whereas Holly's memorials act as reminders of the presence of systemic racism. In "Belles Lettres," the additional pressure to perform the role of the Black academic (child development expert, to boot) drives the mothers to compete with each other. All mothers thus subscribe to an ideal they cannot reach, but the texts portray these reactions sympathetically—it is understandable that they want validation and even a semblance of power as they exist in the intersection of being a woman, a mother, and a Black American. Even though "Belles Lettres" satirizes the two competing women, it extends them a certain amount of sympathy in not depicting them as villains but as women trapped in their rivalry, which stems from trying to enact the script of respectable motherhood. Similarly, "The Abortion" positions Imani as the one who is wronged and dismissed and whose ensuing rebellion makes complete sense.

Conclusion

In both Alice Walker's and Nafissa Thompson-Spires's story, then, the issue of normative motherhood and respectability politics are intertwined: They have a multiplying effect. In both texts, the pressure to conform to respectability politics and normative motherhood proves to navigate the mothers into a cul-de-sac. Having structured her life in accordance with the ideological mandates of essentialization and naturalization of motherhood, Imani finds herself unable to enjoy being a mother. Written and set during the second wave of feminism, "The Abortion" revolves around the questions of bodily autonomy and choice, whereas "Belles Lettres," set just before the rise of third-wave feminism, reflects on the contemporary phenomenon of the intensification of motherhood. The mothers in Thompson-Spires's story fall victim to intensification to such a degree that it becomes comical, and the notion of expertization is subverted through the figures of two professionals who are satirized for behaving in a very much unprofessional manner. While Imani makes a decision that ultimately results in her relief, Lucinda and Monica cannot extricate themselves from the bounds of what they perceive to be good mothers. The texts thus expose that if the only avenue society leaves open for mothers is to live in accordance with outside norms under the gaze of the white supremacist patriarchy, then mothering can only be lived in a way that leads to dissatisfaction. I argue therefore that in both stories, the strictures imposed by the wider social context and as well as the historical reverberations of Black motherhood compel these women to define themselves as "good," "normal" mothers, but it is exactly this context that eventually sabotages their attempts while racialized and gendered injunctions remain in place.

Works Cited

"Heads of the Colored People." *Simon&Schuster*, www.simonandschuster.com/books/Heads-of-the-Colored-People/Nafissa-Thompson-Spires/9781501168000. Accessed 10 Feb. 2023.

Carby, Hazel V. *Reconstructing Womanhood: The Emergence of the Afro-American Woman Novelist*. Oxford University Press, 1987.

Dubey, Madhu. "Gayl Jones and the Matrilineal Metaphor of Tradition." *Signs*, vol. 20, no. 2, 1955, pp. 245-67. *JSTOR*, www.jstor.org/stable/3174949. Accessed 15 May 2016.

Higginbotham, Evelyn B. *Righteous Discontent: The Women's Movement in the Black Baptist Church, 1880-1920*. Harvard University Press, 1994.

Jones, Philip Edward. "Respectability Politics and Straight Support for LGB Rights." *Political Research Quarterly*, vol. 75, no. 4, 2021, pp. 935-49. *SAGE*, https://doi.org/10.1177/10659129211035834. Accessed 10 Feb. 2023.

Kettler, Andrew. *The Smell of Slavery: Olfactory Racism and the Atlantic World*. Cambridge University Press, 2020.

Lee, Hedwig, and Margaret Takako Hicken. "Death by a Thousand Cuts: The Health Implications of Black Respectability Politics." *Souls: A Critical Journal of Black Politics, Culture, and Society*, vol. 18, no. 2-4, 2016, pp. 421-45. *NCBI*, https://doi.org/10.1080%2F1099

9949.2016.1230828. Accessed 10 Feb. 2023.

Lénárt-Muszka, Zsuzsanna. "The Subjectivity of Pregnancy and the Trauma of Abortion in Alice Walker's 'The Abortion.'" *Watermark: A Scholarly Journal*, vol. 12, 2018, pp. 121-30.

Martinot, Steven. "Motherhood and the Invention of Race." *Hypatia*, vol. 22, no. 2, 2007, pp. 79-97. *JSTOR*, www.jstor.org/stable/4640063. Accessed 10 Feb. 2023.

Nelson, Jennifer. *Women of Color and the Reproductive Rights Movement*. New York University Press, 2003.

O'Reilly, Andrea. *Matricentric Feminism: Theory, Activism, Practice*. 2nd ed., Demeter Press, 2021.

Patton, Venetria K. *Women in Chains: The Legacy of Slavery in Black Women's Fiction*. State U of New York, 2000.

Payne, Ashley N. "The Cardi B–Beyoncé Complex: Ratchet Respectability and Black Adolescent Girlhood." *Journal of Hip Hop Studies*, vol. 7, no. 1, 2020, pp. 26-43. *VCU Scholars Compass*, scholarscompass.vcu.edu/jhhs/vol7/iss1/5. Accessed 10 Feb. 2023.

Sadoff, Diane. "Black Matrilineage: The Case of Alice Walker and Zora Neale Hurston." *Signs*, vol. 11, no. 1, 1985, pp. 4-26. *JSTOR*, www.jstor.org/stable/3174284. Accessed 10 Feb. 2023.

Spillers, Hortense J. "Mama's Baby, Papa's Maybe: An American Grammar Book." *Diacritics*, vol. 17, no. 2, 1987, pp. 64-81. *JSTOR*, www.jstor.org/stable/464747. Accessed 10 Feb. 2023.

Strings, Sabrina. *Fearing the Black Body: The Racial Origins of Fat Phobia*. New York UP, 2019.

Thompson-Spires, Nafissa. "Belles Lettres." *Heads of the Colored People*, 37 Ink, 2018, pp. 34-46.

Thompson-Spires, Nafissa. "The Body's Defenses against Itself." *Heads of the Colored People*, 37 Ink, 2018, pp. 47-58.

Walker, Alice. "The Abortion." *You Can't Keep a Good Woman Down*. Women's Press, 1981, pp. 64-76.

Walker, Alice. *The Color Purple*. Harcourt, 1982.

Chapter 9.

"What Finally Dragged Her under the Water and Who Carried the Spark": The Intergenerational Trauma of Normative Motherhood in Celeste Ng's *Everything I Never Told You* and *Little Fires Everywhere*

Andrea O'Reilly

In a 2017 interview, Celeste Ng commented: "The truth is that many women—myself included—have complicated and even contradictory feelings about motherhood…. When we try to turn a concept as huge and multifaceted into an ideal, we lose sight of the complexities of what being a mother actually means" (qtd. in Selvin). In contemporary patriarchal culture, this ideal refers to normative motherhood, which defines mothering as natural to women and essential to their being, positions the mother as the central caregiver of her biological children, and assumes that children require full-time mothering. This good mother is nurturing, altruistic, patient, devoted, loving, and selfless; she always puts the needs of her children before her own and is available to her children whenever needed. Children are the centre of her life. Susan Douglas and Meredith Michaels coined the term "new momism" to define normative motherhood and describe it as the following:

> The insistence that no woman is truly complete or fulfilled unless she has kids, that women remain the best primary caretakers of children, and that to be a remotely decent mother, a woman has to devote her entire physical, psychological, emotional, intellectual being, 24/7, to her children. The new momism is a highly romanticized view of motherhood in which the standards for success are impossible to meet. (4)

Feminist scholars argue that normative motherhood is disempowering if not oppressive for a multitude of reasons—including, the societal devaluation of motherwork, the endless tasks of privatized mothering, the incompatibility of waged work and motherwork, and the impossible standards of idealized motherhood

Celeste Ng's two novels *Everything I Never Told You* (2014) and *Little Fires Everywhere* (2018) incisively contribute to this critique of normative motherhood in their portrayal of the frustrated ambitions, forsaken dreams, and lost selves of the white middle-class mothers in the two novels. However, I argue that the novels do more than just detail and document what sociologists term "the motherhood penalty"; they also perceptively and uniquely show the cost of this for the daughters of these mothers. The original and significant insight of Ng's two novels is their understanding and renderings of the intergenerational effects of normative motherhood—how the mothers' experiences in and with normative motherhood are transmitted and transferred to the daughter and give rise to the disempowerment of the daughter and estrangement between mother and daughter. In *Everything I Never Told You*, Marilyn's discontent in normative motherhood results in pressuring her daughter Lydia to live the life she was denied, which causes Lydia to lose her own life both metaphorically and literally. In *Little Fires Everywhere,* Elena resents her daughter Izzy because she reminds her of the life she once had; this resentment causes Elena to rebuke her "wayward and wild" Izzy (89), leading to mother-daughter estrangement and ending with Izzy's repudiation of her mother and the eradication of what she represents. Although the intergenerational enactments may differ—in *Everything I Never Told You*, the mother seeks to save her daughter from normative motherhood, whereas in *Little Fires Everywhere*, it is imposed on the daughter—each novel shows how the harms and hurts of normative motherhood extend beyond the mother to determine the way she mothers her daughter and result in troubled daughters and damaged mother-daughter relationships.

The unique and important insight of Ng's two novels is how normative motherhood thwarts reciprocal mother-daughter empowerment and causes mother-daughter estrangement. Through what I have termed "the intergenerational trauma of normative motherhood," mothers transmit to their daughters their own unresolved conciliations and compromises with becoming and being the ideal mother of normative motherhood. In *Everything I Never Told You*, this is enacted in Marilyn's resistance to normative motherhood, whereas in *Little Fires Everywhere*, it is done in Elena's compliance with it. More specifically, in *Everything I Never Told You*, it is Marilyn's desire for her daughter to have the life denied to her as a normative mother that causes mother-daughter estrangement and results in the disempowerment and eventual death of her daughter. In *Little Fires Everywhere*, in contrast, it is Elena's repression of the self she was once, to become a normative mother, that causes her to resent her daughter Izzy, who manifests this denied self. This leads to the daughter's repudiation of her mother by setting ablaze the family home, which signifies the spurned values of her mother's life. Indeed, as both mothers come to understand at the conclusion of the novels, it was their own unresolved traumas of being and becoming a normative mother—transferred and transmitted to their daughters—that caused the disempowerment of their daughters and the estrangement in their relationship.

"What I Wanted for My Daughter, but She Never Embraced": *Everything I Never Told You*

In an interview with Anne Stameshkin, Ng explains why she opens *Everything I Never Told You* with Lydia's death: "I never wanted to write a whodunit, and "putting 'what' out there" right away signals readers to focus on the 'why'—the family dynamics that lead to this tragedy." Indeed, as Karissa Chen notes, "Even though Ng books start out feeling like a mystery of what happened, as we go through them, they become less about what happened and become more about why."

Following the death of her daughter, Marilyn makes herself a promise: "She will figure out what happened to Lydia. She will find out who is responsible. She will find out what went wrong" (76). What "went wrong" is normative motherhood: Marilyn's losses and longings are imparted and transferred to Lydia; the life denied to Marilyn as a white middle-class woman becomes a life imposed on her biracial daughter. In losing her self in normative motherhood, Marilyn paradoxically causes the same in her daughter. In making this argument, I am not suggesting that other factors—such as the racism experienced by Lydia, the Lee's separateness from the community as an interracial family, and the father's expectations of Lydia to be liked and popular— are incon-sequential or extraneous but rather that they, in making Lydia so solitary and vulnerable, render her even more susceptible to inter-nalizing and acting out the intergenerational trauma of normative motherhood. Nor am I suggesting that the mother is responsible but rather it is Marilyn's unhappiness caused by normative motherhood and continued in the mothering of Lydia that causes the death of her daughter. The question is not "who is responsible" but "how did it happen?" To this discussion, I now turn.

A pivotal metaphor of the novel is a physics lesson learned and remembered by Lydia: "*For every action, there is an equal and opposite reaction. One went up and the other went down. One gained, the other lost. One escaped, the other was trapped, forever*" (225). I suggest that Marilyn's longing to live a life beyond that dictated by normative motherhood, and then seeking to achieve this for her daughter, is the action, whereas Lydia's loss of identity caused by her mother's transferred hopes and dreams is the reaction. However, and significantly, these actions and reactions are created from a larger web of familial relations and the interfaces between past and present. Lydia wonders:

> How had it begun? Like, everything: with mothers and fathers. Because of Lydia's mother and father, because of her mother's and father's mothers and fathers. Because long ago her mother had gone missing, and her father brought her home. Because more than anything, her mother had wanted to stand out; because more than anything, her father had wanted to blend in. Because those things had been impossible (25).

Significantly, Lydia's reflections occur at the opening of Chapter

Two, just after her death is confirmed and just before the mother's own history is narrated, suggesting a correlation between the two.

In the novel, there are two timelines, both moving forwards: The present timeline starts with Lydia's death and goes on to show its aftermath, whereas the past timeline starts when Lydia's parents meet, then moves through her childhood, and up to her death. There is, as Ng explains, "a clear pattern—present, past, present, past—and at each 'handoff' there's a reason for switching from past to present" (qtd. in Stamesh-kin). Chapter Three ends with Marilyn searching Lydia's diary for clues about her death, and Chapter Four begins with five-year-old Lydia getting her first diary. Similarly, Chapter Two concludes with Marilyn seeing her mother for the last time, and Chapter Three opens with Marilyn reflecting that she had never thought about her daughter's death. This narrative structure, interweaving the past with the present and linking them through a shared event or emotion, conceives, conveys, and confirms the interconnectedness of past sufferings with those of the present, particularly as they are experienced by mothers and daughters through the intergenerational trauma of normative motherhood. As Marilyn is resolved to "find out everything she doesn't know ... to understand her daughter completely" (120), the novel suggests that this answer for her daughter in the present is to be found in the mother's past—particularly in how Marilyn's resistance to and compliance with normative motherhood shaped the mothering of her daughter Lydia.

Significantly, the actions and reactions of the intergenerational trauma of normative motherhood examined in the novel begin with Marilyn as a daughter. Marilyn is resolved to live a life different from her mother, Doris, the home economics teacher at Lydia's high school, who had been raising Lydia as a single mother since her husband abandoned the family when Lydia was three. In the opening speech of her class each year, Doris, or Mrs. Walker, promises "to teach [the girls] everything a *young lady* needed to keep a house" (28). Reflecting on her mother's words, Marilyn thinks "so they called it *keeping house* for a reason.... Sometimes it did run away" (28). Although she no longer had a husband to impress, Doris still insisted on changing clothes before dinner, powdering her nose after cooking, and putting on fresh lipstick before coming down for breakfast (28). When Doris learns of Marilyn's scholarship to Radcliffe, her exclamations of pride are quickly followed by the comment: "You will meet a lot of Harvard men" (29). However, Marilyn's dream is to become a doctor: "The furthest thing she could imagine from her mother's life where sewing a neat hem was a laudable accomplishment and removing beet stains from a blouse was a cause for celebration. Instead, she would blunt pain and staunch bleeding and set bones. She would save lives" (30). Yet in the end, as Marilyn reflects, "It happened just as her mother predicated: she met a man ... and it would bother Marilyn for the rest of her life that her mother had been right" (30).

In her junior year at Radcliffe, Marilyn meets James, the professor of the new course "The Cowboy in American Culture." With his last name Lee and being from Virginia, Marilyn expected the professor to be "someone in a sand-colored blazar, someone with a slight drawl and a Southern pedigree" (31); instead, he was *"An Oriental ... she had never seen one in person before"* (31). After Marilyn impulsively kisses him during office hours, she realizes "that it was right, that she wanted this man in her life. Something inside her said, *He understands. What's it like to be different*" (36). As someone who "always liked surprising people" (27) and who imagined a life different from that of her mother and most women in the 1950s, Marilyn believes that James accepts and appreciates her uniqueness. However, James who "never felt he belonged" fell in love with Marilyn specifically because "she blended in so perfectly, because she had seemed so completely and utterly at home" (38). Within a year of dating, James learns he has not been chosen for the position at Harvard, and Marilyn discovers she is pregnant: "Instead of Boston, small-town Ohio: instead of medical school, a wedding. Nothing quite as planned" (50). Not surprisingly when Doris learns her daughter Marilyn is marrying an Asian man, a marriage that would be illegal in many states, she tells her daughter that "it's not right; you will regret it later" (54). Although Marilyn retorts "This is my life," Doris's plea "think about the children" and her worry "You won't fit in anywhere" (54) do anticipate the discrimination and segregation their interracial family will experience, which contributed to Lydia's death. Indeed, years later when Lydia's death is ruled a suicide, James says to Marilyn "If she were a white girl, none of this would have happened" (202).

Although the wedding is the last time Marilyn will see her mother, the significance of their relationship, particularly as it relates to the intergenerational trauma of normative motherhood, is denoted by the narrative commentary on the resemblance of mother and daughter and symbolically marked by a lipstick stain. Looking at her mother, Lydia notices "a tiny wrinkle creased her mother's eyebrows ... years later, her daughter Hannah would spy this same mark of deep worry on her mother's face, though she would not know its source and Marilyn would never have admitted the resemblance" (53). The chapter ends with Marilyn observing the lipstick stain on her mother's sleeve, which was created when Marilyn jerked free from her mother, causing the lipstick to somehow make a long red streak down her mother's sleeve. Although Doris "blotted her sleeve again and again ... the red mark still showed beneath ... like an old bloodstain" (55). The moment Marilyn noticed this, she wiped a smudge of lipstick from James's upper lip (56). I suggest that the resemblance noted between mother and daughter and the shared lipstick stain signify that although Marilyn and James had made "a pact; to let the past drift away ... to look forward from then on, never back" (49), this past, particularly in relation to Marilyn's resistance to and then acceptance of normative motherhood, determines the mothering of Lydia in the present.

In 1957, when Marilyn takes a leave of absence from university for marriage and motherhood, "she was certain that everything she had dreamed for herself—medical school, doctorhood, that new and important life—sat poised for her return, like a well-trained dog awaiting its master" (50). However, it would be, "almost eight years before school would seem real and possible and tangible again, but Marilyn didn't know that" (50). Significantly, it is the death of her mother that provokes and compels Marilyn to return to school and seek to realize her deferred dream of becoming a doctor. At twenty-nine, with their son, Nathan in grade one and Lydia in nursery school, Marilyn finds herself "unoccupied" and thinks "of her mother and the life her mother wanted for her and the life she had hoped to lead" and realizes "there was nothing more her mother could have wished for her. The thought did not put her in a festive mood" (78). Later that evening at a Christmas party when Tom, a colleague of James, tells Marilyn about his research, she with breathless earnestness expresses her interest, and he agrees to her working for him—"if her husband didn't mind, that is" (79). And while James does not allow Marilyn to work, Marilyn keeps Tom's phone number and finally does call him after the death of her mother.

The death of her mother marks a crucial and transformative moment in Marilyn's negotiations with normative motherhood. Marilyn arrives to her mother's home following her death to sort through her possessions, but she finds nothing she wants to keep and wonders, "How could she miss her mother, when her mother was nowhere to be found?" (82). Upon seeing her mother's beloved Betty Crocker cookbook, she thinks, "with sharp and painful pity of her mother, who had planned on a golden, vanilla-scented life but ended up alone, trapped like a fly in this small and sad and empty life" (83). Marilyn realizes that she is not sad but "furious at the smallness of her mother's life" (83). As she holds the cookbook, she thinks: "*This is all I need to remember about her. This is all I want to keep*" (83). Later as she is driving home, Marilyn realizes that in the end, the only thing worth remembering about her mother's life is that she cooked, and then she thinks uneasily about her own life—the hours spent making breakfast, serving dinners, and packing lunches. Twice repeated in italics Marilyn tells herself: "*Never.... I will never end up like that*" (86). Significantly, this promise is made as Marilyn is standing outside her car in torrential rain and again in the car after she strips herself naked and catches a glimpse of her reflection and thinks, "Instead of being embarrassed to see herself stripped so naked and vulnerable, she admired the pale gleam of her own skin" (86). The rain and her nakedness symbolize rebirth, which signifies Marilyn's transition from accepting normative motherhood to once again challenging it. Marilyn's rebirth in the rainwater likewise foreshadows Lydia's later death by drowning in a lake, which emphasizes the interconnectedness of their lives, as each is determined by the intergenerational trauma of normative motherhood.

Upon her return home, Marilyn phones Tom about the job to discover that he had offered the position to an undergrad because, as he explains, "I had no idea you were actually serious about that. With your children and your husband and all" (93). Following the phone call, she drives aimlessly, and significantly twice around the lake where Lydia will later drown, recalling his words "*with your children and husband and all*," and finds herself at the hospital where she sees Dr. Wolff, the mother of Jack, who lives on her street. Mesmerized and astonished by the respect this woman doctor commands, Marilyn wonders: "How was it possible? How had she managed it?" She then remembers the words in her mother's cookbook: "*Make somebody happy today—bake a cake to take to a party ... is there anything that gives you a deeper sense of satisfaction?"* (96). The woman doctor symbolizes resistance to normative motherhood while the cookbook's words signify compliance with it. Marilyn initially thinks: "Of course it was possible for her; she had no husband. She let her son run wild. Without a husband, without children perhaps it would have been possible. *I could have done that"* (96). But then with tears running down her face, she corrects "the hypothetical past perfect, the tense of missed chances" and realizes "*I could do that*" (96). The following evening, Marilyn resolves that there is more to life than this and decides to leave her family to finish her college degree and apply for medical school eight years later than she had planned. In the weeks before leaving, Marilyn cooks lavish meals with a fake smile as she packs her old college textbooks in the quiet dark and takes with her a trinket from each child to remember them by. Significantly, this chapter that describes the mother leaving concludes with Lydia's perspective as she reflects, "How to explain what had happened.... how someone she loved so dearly could be there one minute, and the next minute *gone*" (101), which suggests once again how the lives of mothers and daughters intertwine in the intergenerational trauma of normative motherhood.

The chapter concerned with the summer "their mother was gone" confirms the cause and effect of the intergenerational trauma of normative motherhood. The chapter opens: "The summer Lydia fell into the lake, the summer Marilyn went missing all of them tried to forget it. They did not talk about it; they never mentioned it" (124). Lydia's falling into the lake during the mother's absence foreshadows Lydia's drowning in the same lake many years later and establishes a connection between Lydia's suicide and her mother's absence when she was a young girl. And the lasting impact of the mother's absence is described as a bad smell that lingers: "It had suffused them so deeply it could never wash out" (124). The only comfort Lydia finds during her mother's absence is, significantly, her cookbook: "Lydia knew [it] was her mother's favorite book, and she leafed through it with the adoration of a devotee touching a Bible" (187). As Lydia reads the words in the cookbook "*And what little girl doesn't love learning with Mom?*" she realizes, as she cries onto the page, that the bumps in the cookbook are the markings of her mother's tears—"Her mother must have cried over this page, too" (137). However, young Lydia does not understand that for her mother, the tears were shed in anger at the life denied to her by the expectations of normative motherhood, whereas for Lydia, they are shed in longing for her mother who left her to create this life beyond normative motherhood. Believing it is her fault that her mother left, Lydia resolves that if her mother every came home, "She would do everything her mother told her. Everything her mother wanted" (187).

The next section of the chapter significantly shifts to the mother's perspective with the words "Marilyn did not hear the silent promise her young daughter was making" (137). However, Marilyn does return nine weeks later after discovering she is pregnant: "Everything she had dreamed for herself faded away, like fine mist on a breeze. She could not remember now why she thought it had been possible" (144). For Lydia, her mother's return "was nothing short of a miracle" (146). Believing that her mother had heard her promise and come home, Lydia makes the decision to hide the cookbook she believes caused her mother's sadness. However, for Marilyn, her daughter's loss of the cookbook is seen as a "sign [that] for her it was too late. But it wasn't too late for Lydia" (147). Marilyn resolves: "She would not be like her own mother, shunting her daughter toward husband and home. She would help Lydia do everything she was capable of" (147). As her daughter's silent promise was to be good so that her mother would never leave again, Marilyn's silent promise is to "never to suggest that there were jobs or lives or worlds not meant for [Lydia] ... to encourage her, for the rest of her life, to do more than her mother had" (147). These silent promises, I suggest, are created from the intergenerational trauma of normative motherhood. Marilyn leaves her family seeking to become the woman she had always dreamed of being but was denied by the institution of motherhood. However, upon realizing that it was too late for her, Marilyn transfers her dreams and desires to her daughter so she may become this woman. Lydia says, "*yes, yes, yes*" (150) to her mother's aspirations but not because she wants this life beyond normative motherhood that her mother has planned for her, but simply to please her mother so she will never leave again. As Marilyn dreams of Lydia "in high heels and a white coat, a stethoscope around her neck," Lydia studies algebra in the summer and enrolls in biology at the college "to make her mother smile" (165). With "her mother's heart drumming one beat 'doctor, doctor, doctor,'" Lydia "could not imagine another future, another life" (163).

In the months before her death, with her science grade plummeting and with her brother soon leaving for university, Lydia becomes friends with Jack, the son of the doctor. On the day of her death, Jack reveals to Lydia that he is gay and that his affections are not for her but for her brother, Nathan. He then says to her: "At least I don't let other people tell me what I want. At least I know who I am. What I want. He then asks Lydia: What about you? What do you want?" (269). Lydia thinks, "*Of course I know what I want*," but "when she opened her mouth, she found it was empty" (269). In her mind, "words ricocheted like glass marbles—doctor, popular, happy—and scattered into silence" (269). Significantly, the last words Jack says to her are "At least I'm not afraid" (269). The night of her death as she stands by the shore of the lake Lydia makes a different promise: "She will stop pretending to be someone she is not. From now on, she will do what she wants" (274-75); she "will start everything over again. So, she would never again be afraid to be alone" (275). Though terrified of water and unable to swim, Lydia takes the boat onto the lake "to seal her promises, to make them real" (275). She looks up at the sky "believing that anything was possible" (275) and steps out of the boat into the water. Earlier her mother had pleaded with Lydia to not let her life slip away. In drowning, I suggest, Lydia does let the life her mother planned for her slip away, as she was certain she could swim to shore.

Lydia's intent that night remains ambiguous: She steps into the water believing that everything would be alright but also knowing she cannot swim. The police rule her death a suicide, yet at the moment of her death, Lydia describes the universe as "glittering with possibilities" (275). Whether Lydia fully understood that by stepping into the water she would die by drowning remains unclear. What is certain is that by stepping into the water Lydia seals the promises she made to herself to begin again. Significantly, the first thing she promises to do is take down the posters and put away the books her mother gave her, knowing that if she never becomes a doctor, "it will be alright" (274). After Lydia's death, it is the mother who tears the posters from the wall and scatters all the books she had bought for her as they "reminded her of Lydia and all she could have been" (246). In so doing, she finds the cookbook that Lydia years ago said she had lost, and Marilyn realizes that her daughter hid the book so that she would never have to see it again. This realization leads to another. Every time Lydia had said

"Show me again" had not been about science but about love. At this moment, among the rubble of shredded posters and discarded books, Marilyn understands "that everything that she had wanted for Lydia, which Lydia had never wanted but had embraced anyway" is what "had dragged Lydia underwater at last" (247). She realizes that in imposing the life normative motherhood denied to her upon her daughter she caused Lydia to lose her own life both metaphorically and literally.

"The Child Who She Thought Had Been Her Opposite but Who Had Inherited Her Spark": *Little Fires Everywhere*

Celeste Ng's second novel, *Little Fires Everywhere*, similarly explores the intergenerational trauma of normative motherhood through the relationship of Mrs. Richardson and her lastborn child, Izzy. Just as *Everything I Never Told You* begins with the death of Lydia by drowning, *Little Fires Everywhere* opens with the Richardson's home smouldering in flames from the fire Izzy set. And like the first novel, *Little Fires Everywhere* opens with the ending of the story to compel readers to ask, "How did it happen?" As Ng explains in an interview, "I start my novels with a bang because I want the readers to know that we're going somewhere, and it's going to be interesting" (qtd. in Martin). *Little Fires Everywhere* opens with its ending to explore and explain how we got to Izzy setting her family home on fire.

I suggest that as with Lydia's drowning, Izzy's setting her home ablaze is caused by the intergenerational trauma of normative motherhood. Whereas in *Everything I Never Told You* the mother seeks to save her daughter from normative motherhood, in *Little Fires Everywhere*, Mrs. Richardson imposes it on her daughter to legitimate her own life as a normative mother. And as Lydia's rejection of the life her mother chose for her is enacted through drowning, Izzy does so by burning down the family home, which symbolizes all her mother demanded of her. Significantly in *Little Fires Everywhere*, this cause and effect of the trauma of normative motherhood is enacted less through intergenerational relations, as in *Everything I Never Told You*, but through the relationship between two mothers in the novel, Mrs. Richardson and Mia Warren—the single Chinese artist mother who embodies the empowered female selfhood that Izzy desires and Mrs. Richardson denies.

Mrs. Richardson is described as the "human embodiment of Shaker Heights," the community where she and her family live. Celeste Ng moved to Shaker Heights in the early 1990s: It was one of the first planned communities owned by the Shakers, a utopian religious group, intended to be a kind of suburban utopia. This community outside of Cleveland was known for being racially diverse (at least in terms of Black and white), progressive, and affluent. If Shaker Heights was a high school, Ng explains, "its goal would be the pretty, straight-A honor roll student who is also Homecoming queen and co-captain of the field hockey team, who is also well-liked and totally down to earth and volunteers at food banks on the weekends" (qtd. in Chung). Perfection was the goal of Shaker Heights to be achieved through order and regulation: "They had regulated everything: the proper time for rising in the morning, the proper color window curtains, the proper length of man's hair, the proper way to fold one's hands in prayer" (23). As with her community, Mrs. Richardson "had her entire existence lived an orderly and regimented life"; she weighed herself once a week, ate exactly a half cup of Cheerios for breakfast, and allowed herself one glass of red wine in the evening. She had been brought up to follow the rules. She had a plan from girlhood on (high school, college, boyfriend, marriage, job, mortgage, and children) and followed it scrupulously. She had done everything right and had built a good life—"the kind of life she wanted, the kind of life everyone wanted" (69). The mother is called Mrs. Richardson except on the few occasions when the narrative point of view is from her perspective or that of her husband, signifying her identity as a devoted wife and mother. When Pearl, Mia's daughter, first meets Mrs. Richardson, she is making cookies, and Pearl describes their home "as a tableau of domestic perfection" (33). With her "perfect life in a perfect place" (158), Mrs. Richardson is the ideal mother of normative motherhood.

However, Mrs. Richardson, unlike Marilyn in *Everything I Never Told You*, graduated from university and has a job as a reporter for her local newspaper. She graduated second in her class and had her choice of colleges but chose Denison rather than Oberlin, her mother's preference, because Oberlin, with its student activism, felt like "a foreign country where rules did not reach" (102). On her second day at university, she meets Bill Richardson and together they "chastely made plans for the future" (102)—a white wedding, lots of children, law school for him, and reporting for her. It was "a plan they followed meticulously" (102). And while young Elena once dreamed of being a journalist at a major newspaper, she stayed at the local Sun Press, writing "feel good stories" that were "*nice* and correspondingly dull" (103). As a young girl and woman Elena was an "ardent idealist" (72). As a child, she attended the great March on Washington with her mother, and as a young woman of fifteen, she watched news coverage about the assassination of Martin Luther King Jr. and the student revolts with concern and compassion. As Elena watches "the chaos flaring up across the country like a bush fire," "deep inside her a spark kindled, a spark that would flare in Izzy years later" (159). However, as the narrator explains: "Three generations of Shaker reverence for order and rules and decorum would stay with Elena and she would never quite be able to bring those two ideas into balance" (159). When the antiwar protests start out, Elena does not join them but instead writes impassioned letters and signs petitions. In her senior year at high school, Jamie, a boy she likes, tells her he is dropping out of school and asks her to go with him to California. Though wanting "badly to go with him," Elena does not because she worries about what her parents, the neighbors, teachers, and friends [would] say" (150). Elena reflects that she has no regrets: "She'd been crazy to have considered it; what she felt for Jamie back then had been just a tiny passing flame" (161). The language used here—flaring, bush fire, spark, flame—signify passion which for Elena "was like a fire, a dangerous thing" (161). Elena reflects: "It so easily went out of control. It scaled walls and jumped over trenches.... Better to control that spark and pass it carefully from one generation to the next, like an Olympic torch. Or perhaps, to tend it carefully like an eternal flame: a reminder of light and goodness that would never—could never—set anything ablaze. Carefully controlled" (161). This philosophy carries Elena through her life: "Rules existed for a reason: if you followed them, you would succeed; if you didn't you might burn the world to the ground" (161).

The repeated references to fire foreshadow Izzy's burning down of the family home many years later and signify the passion Elena has repressed to become the ideal mother of normative motherhood and acquire the "beautiful house, steady job, a loving husband and a brood of healthy and happy children" (161)—a passion that would resurface in her "fiery" daughter Izzy (89). As Elena asks, "Do you have to burn down the old to make way for the new," Izzy realizes she must do so to eradicate the life her mother has planned for her. Izzy is the outcast of the perfect Richardson family—the one who took everything seriously, who is impulsive, and who is the crazy one. After Mrs. Richardson's difficult pregnancy, Izzy is born eleven-weeks premature, with the doctor warning that she could suffer from a range of illnesses. With an anxiety and fear "at a cellular level," Mrs. Richardson scrutinizes and monitors her daughter's every behaviour, but the more her mother watches her, "the more Izzy [is] chafed at the attention" (11). With Izzy's birth, Mrs. Richardson learns "how ... life could trundle along on its safe little track and then, with no warning, skid spectacularly off course" (110), and every time she looks at Izzy a feeling "of things spiraling out of control coil[s] around her again" (110). I suggest that Izzy is "a particular disappointment" (111) and is resented by Mrs. Richardson because the circumstances of her birth and her defiant personality attest that all cannot be planned or be under one's control as Mrs. Richardson so fervently believes. Mr. Richardson, in contrast, is delighted by Izzy's intelligence and her spirit, and significantly *"she reminded him of her mother, when she'd been younger"* (emphasis added, 112). Mother and daughter both share the same spark, the certainty of purpose, and are deeply concerned with right versus wrong, although with Mrs. Richardson "the fiery side of her after so many safe years in the suburbs had cooled to embers" (112). Mrs. Richardson cannot let Izzy be and is constantly asking what is wrong with her, precisely because Izzy signifies and enacts the passion that Mrs. Richardson has repressed to achieve her perfect ordered life—which she cannot domesticate in her daughter.

The spark that Mrs. Richardson refutes and seeks to subdue in Izzy is kindled and cultivated by Mia Warren. Whereas Mrs. Richardson embodies normative motherhood, Mia enacts empowered mothering: Mia is a single mother and artist who does "not like to be tied down" (30). Pearl, her daughter, does not mind their life of "thrift-store clothes, their salvaged beds, and chairs, the shifting precariousness of it all because she knew that everyone would see her mother's brilliance and she would be famous one day" (29). For Moody, one of Mrs. Richardson's sons, "this kind of existence was all but unfathomable" —one he was "fascinated by" (29). When Mrs. Richardson first meets Mia, thinking of her own "right and good life" (69), she reflects:

"Here was a completely different kind of woman leading a completely different life, who seemed to make her own rules with no apologies" (69). Mrs. Richardson finds this "perturbing but strangely compelling," and a part of her is uneasy, "wanting to keep an eye on Mia, as you might keep an eye on a dangerous beast" (69). Mia, as Mrs. Richardson later reflects, takes "an almost perverse pleasure in flouting the normal order" (138).

It is Mia who sees and responds to Izzy's "mute, futile fury" (79). When Izzy tells Mia about her unfair suspension from school after standing up to a teacher for her racist behaviour, Mia asks her, "Well? What are going to do about it?" (79). Izzy thinks: "It was not a question she had been asked before" (79). Later when Izzy asks Mia if she could be her assistant, Mia recognizes herself in Izzy at that age—"single minded almost to an excess" and "something in Izzy reached out to her and caught fire" (89). Izzy spends her afternoons with Mia at her apartment imagining that Pearl, Mia's daughter, does not exist and spinning dreams that Mia is her real mother and that her parents are not her real parents, explaining "why no one in her family understood her and why she seemed so different from them" (91). With Mia, as Izzy reflects at the end of the novel, "she'd been different, in a way she hadn't known she could be" and realizes that she could never go back to life as it had been before in "their beautiful, perfectly ordered city, where everyone got along and everyone followed the rules and everything had to be beautiful and perfect on the outside, no matter what mess lay within" (323). Remembering the first time she met Mia when she asked Izzy "what are you going to do about it?" Izzy realizes that "Mia had opened a door in her that could not be shut again" (323). And while her mother always believed that you do not have to burn down the old to make way for the new, Izzy remembers Mia's words: "*Sometimes you need to scorch everything to the ground and start over*" (324).

The normative motherhood that Mrs. Richardson represents, and which Izzy refuses, is further contrasted to the empowered mothering of Mia through the two mothers' divergent views on the custody court case of baby Ling/Mirabelle. Bebe, the mother of Ling, is a single Chinese woman who after being abandoned by the baby's father, losing her job, and experiencing postpartum depression leaves her baby girl on the doorsteps of a fire station. The baby girl is adopted by an affluent white family, who are friends of the Richardsons, and renamed

Mirabelle. Mia who works with Bebe tells her of this adoption, and Bebe is determined to get her daughter back, and a custody court case ensues. Everyone, as the text tells us, has an opinion: "A mother deserved to raise her child. A mother who abandoned her child did not deserve a second chance. A white family would separate a Chinese child from her culture. A loving family should matter more than the color of the parents. Ling had a right to know her own mother. The McCulloughs were the only family Mirabelle had ever known" (151-52). Mrs. Richardson, not surprisingly, believes that the baby should stay with the adopted family because no one "deserves a child more than Mrs. McCullough does," whereas Mia, who kept her baby Pearl after breaking her agreement with the surrogate parents, asserts: "It's not a question of deserving. I just think a mother has the right to raise her own child" (302). When Mrs. Richardson learns that it was Mia who informed Bebe of the adoption—"stirring up trouble, heedlessly throwing sparks" (162)— she seethes and "the hot speck of fury that had been carefully banked within her burst[s] into flames" (162). Mrs. Richardson tells herself that it is loyalty to her friend Linda McCullough that causes her to investigate the truth of Mia's past, as she could never "admit even to herself that it hadn't been about the baby at all" (139). She continues: "It had been some complicated thing about Mia herself, the dark discomfort this woman stirred up that Mrs. Richardson would have much preferred to keep in its box" (139).

Mia elicits discomfort and ignites fury in Mrs. Richardson because Mia lives her own life by her own beliefs and passions—precisely what Mrs. Richardson has denied and repressed to achieve the life of normative motherhood. For Mrs. Richardson—who "had been brought up to follow rules, and to believe that the proper functioning of the world depended on her compliance" (69)—Mia represents someone who has broken the rules and got away with it. As Mrs. Richardson reflects: "You can't just do what you want. Why should Mia get to do so when no one else did?" (162). When Mrs. Richardson learns of Mia's plan to give her baby away to the surrogate parents, she feels a tinge of unexpected sympathy but then thinks: "*I would never have let myself get into that situation. I would have made better choices along the way*" (239). Again, for Mrs. Richardson, Mia's predicament is of her own making; if she had followed the rules, she would have made the right choices. However, as Mr. Richardson reflects after hearing the court's decision to award Mirabelle to the McCulloughs:

> "Bebe Chow had been a poor mother: Linda McCullough has been a good one. One had followed the rules, and one had not. But the problem with rules was that they implied a right way and wrong way to do things. When, in fact, most of the time there were simply *ways*, none of them quite wrong or quite right" (269).

However, for Mrs. Richardson of Shaker Heights, there is only one right way—that of "her perfect life in this perfect place." Near the end of the novel, Mia asks Mrs. Richardson: "It bothers you, doesn't it? ...I think you can't imagine. Why anyone might choose a different life from the one you've got. Why anyone might want something other than a big house with a big lawn, a fancy car, a job in an office" (302). Mia then says: "It terrifies you. That you missed out on something. That you gave up something you didn't know you wanted.... What was it? Was it a boy? Was it a vocation? Or was it a whole life?" (303). I suggest that indeed Mrs. Richardson has "missed out on a whole life" by extinguishing the spark of fiery Elena to become and be the ideal mother of normative motherhood.

Her daughter Izzy refuses to extinguish that spark demanded by normative motherhood and symbolically enacts this refusal by setting the family home ablaze. Remembering Mia's words Izzy understands that after scorching everything to the ground, the soil is richer, and new things can grow (324) and leaves Shaker Heights in search of Pearl and Mia. Like the conclusion of *Everything I Never Told You*, *Little Fires Everywhere* ends with the daughter gone and the mother finally understanding the inter-generational trauma of motherhood which caused the estrangement of mother and daughter. She reflects: "That child who she thought had been her opposite but who had deep inside her, inherited and carried and nursed that spark her mother had long ago tampered down" " (336). The novel ends with Mrs. Richardson resolved to find her daughter, knowing that "she was sure she would still know her own child, just as she would know herself" (336).

Conclusion

The Seattle Times calls *Little Fires Everywhere* a "haunting, layered story of mothers and daughters, and how they attract and repel each other," while *Refinery29* describes the novel as "a meditation on the unspoken pains and contradictions of motherhood" (Ng, 2018). I have argued that these unspoken pains are specifically the intergenerational trauma of normative motherhood that indeed haunt and layer the mother and daughter relationships in *Everything I Never Told You* and *Little Fires Everywhere*. In *Everything I Never Told You*, the intergenerational trauma is enacted in Marilyn's resistance to normative motherhood, whereas in *Little Fires Everywhere*, it is done in Elena's compliance with it. However, although the intergenerational enactments may differ in each novel, both show how the harms and hurts of normative motherhood extend beyond the mother to determine the way she mothers her daughter and can result in troubled daughters and damaged mother-daughter relationships. In conclusion, I suggest, paraphrasing the titles of Ng's two novels, that the intergenerational trauma of normative motherhood is the "everything never told" that causes the "little fires everywhere."

Works Cited

Arcana, Judith. *Our Mother's Daughters*. Shameless Hussy Press, 1979.

Bernard, Jesse. "Letter to Her Daughter." *Between Ourselves: Letters between Mothers and Daughters*, edited by Karen Payne, Houghton Mifflin Company, 1983, pp. 271-272.

Chen, Karissa. "'I Didn't Want There to Be a Clear Hero or Villain Side'—A conversation with Celeste Ng." *Hyphen Asia America Unabridged*, 8 Sept. 2017, hyphenmagazine.com/blog/2017/09/i-didn%E2%80%99t-want-there-be-clear-hero-or-villain-side-%E2%80%94-conversation-celeste-ng. Accessed 1 Feb. 2023.

Chung, Nicole. "'I've Always Been Political': Celeste Ng and Nicole Chung in Conversation on Transracial Adoption, Social Media, and *Little Fires Everywhere*." *Literary Hub*, 12 Sept., 2014, lithub.com/ive-always-been-political-celeste-ng-and-nicole-chung-in-conversation/. Accessed 1 Feb. 2023.

Debold, Elizabeth, et al. *The Mother Daughter Revolution*. Addison-Wesley, 1993.

Douglas, Susan J., and Meredith Michaels. *The Mommy Myth: The Idealization of Motherhood and How It Has Undermined Women*. Free

Press, 2004.

Gilligan, Carol. *In a Different Voice: Psychological Theory and Women's Development*. Harvard University Press, 1982.

Johnson, Miriam. *Strong Mothers, Weak Wives: The Search for Gender Equality*. University of California Press, 1988.

Martin, Emily. "An Interview with Celeste Ng, The 2018 Independent Bookstore Day Ambassador." *BookRiot*, 27 Apr. 2018, bookriot.com/celeste-ng-interview/. Accessed 1 Feb. 2023.

Ng, Celeste. *Everything I Never Told You*. Penguin Books, 2014.

Ng, Celeste. *Little Fires Everywhere*. Penguin Books, 2018.

Payne, Karen. *Between Ourselves: Letters Between Mothers and Daughters 1750-1982*. Mariner Books, 1984.

Pipher, Mary. *Reviving Ophelia: Saving the Selves of Adolescent Girls*. G.P. Putman's Sons, 1994.

Rich, Adrienne. *Of Woman Born: Motherhood as Experience and Institution*. 2nd ed., W.W. Norton, 1986.

Rutter, Virginia Beanne. *Celebrating Girls*. Conari Press, 1996.

Selvin, Rachel, "This Novel Promises There's No Wrong Way to Mother." *Yahoo*, 27 Sept. 2017, www.yahoo.com/entertainment/novel-promises-apos-no-wrong-212000508.html. Accessed 1 Feb. 2023.

Stameshkin, Anne. "Sometimes Taking Things Out Counts as Writing: An Interview with Celeste Ng." *Fiction Writer Review*, 30 June 2014, fictionwritersreview.com/interview/sometimes-taking-things-out-counts-as-writing-an-interview-with-celeste-ng/. Accessed 1 Feb. 2023.

Chapter 10.

Buzz Kill and Eye Candy: Normative Motherhood Disrupted and Matricritics in Courtney Kessel and Chloé Clevenger's *In Balance With*

Natalie Bruvels

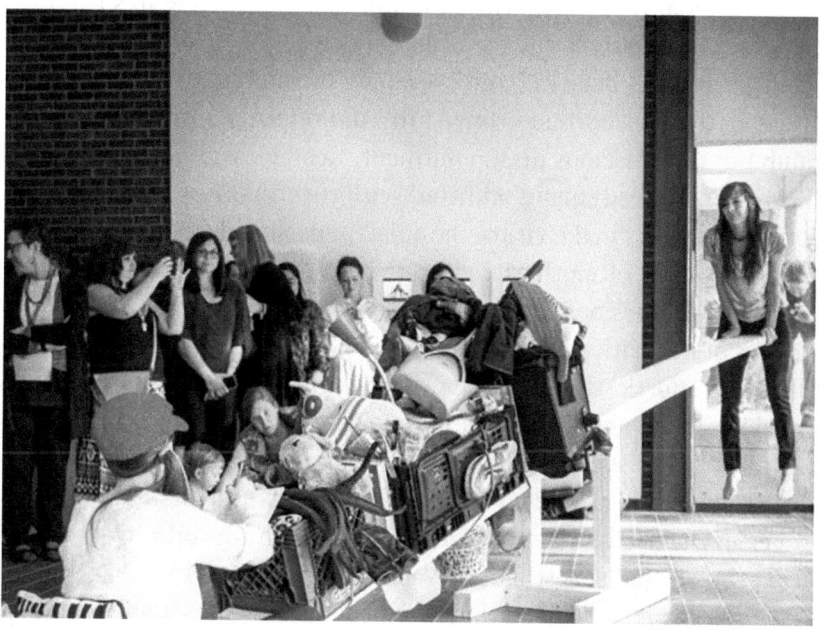

Figure 1. Courtney Kessel and Chloé Clevenger, *In Balance With*, FAB Gallery, Edmonton, Canada, 2016. Photo credit: Michael J.H. Woolley.

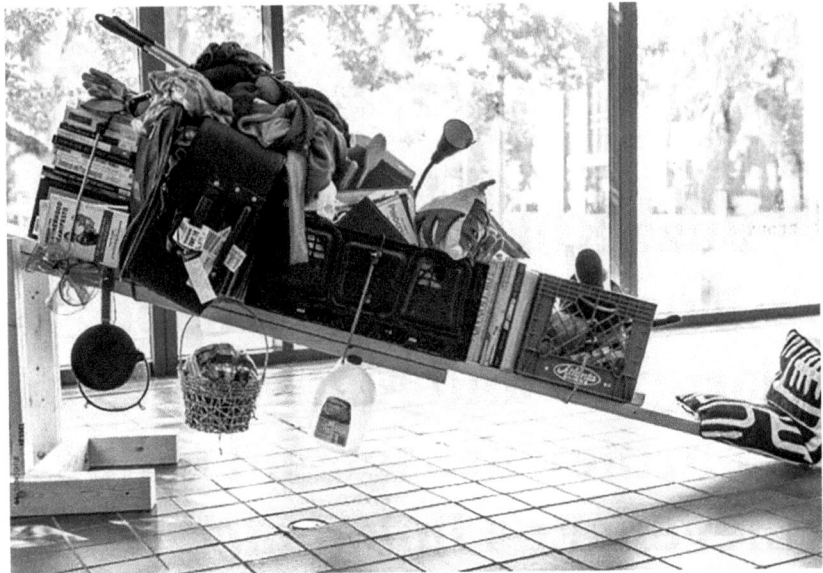

Figure 2. Courtney Kessel and Chloé Clevenger, *In Balance With*, FAB Gallery, Edmonton, Canada, 2016. Photo credit: Michael J.H. Woolley.

This chapter argues that in their work *In Balance With* [Figures 1 and 2], visual artists Courtney Kessel and Chloé Clevenger employ an aesthetic strategy of buzz kill and eye candy by interrupting the dictates of normative motherhood (buzz kill) and offering a distraction (eye candy) to subconscious disappointment. Kessel involves her daughter Clevenger in readymade additive sculpture making and body art performances to "make visible the quiet, understated, and often unseen love and labour of motherhood" (Loveless). This visualization of the maternal operates outside the bounds of normative motherhood. The dictates of normative motherhood position mother as a dedicated, fulfilled, and effortlessly sacrificial primary caregiver, particularly as signified in the archetypal Madonna and Child. Many artists engaging in the maternal resist the representational logic of normative motherhood, opting not to idealize maternal experiences and instead employ strategies that foster maternal subjectivity, which are collectively called the new maternalist aesthetics (Wade 282). Still, many mother-artists have reported having their work deemed less critically significant and belittled (Judah 14) when operating outside the bounds of normative motherhood. This resistance to maternal subjectivity is a normativizing process in action. To counter this dilemma, this chapter first suggests interrupting the dictates of normative motherhood to foster an unidealized maternal artistic subjectivity. It then offers a distraction to the viewer's subconscious disappointment by not representing normative motherhood. Feminist philosopher Julia Kristeva articulates expectations in viewer encounters with idealized representations of motherhood (61). For Kristeva, when encountering the Madonna and Child form, the viewer does not identify with the mother but the child and is transported to an "idealization of primary narcissism" (Wade 283)—a time during infancy where the nondifferentiated mother-child bond becomes an object of fantasy in adult life. Kristeva's reflection gives insight into this impasse in the act of viewing unidealized depictions of the maternal. Kessel and Clevenger's *In Balance With* negotiates this epistemological crisis.

In Balance With is an iterative art project that Courtney Kessel and Chloé Clevenger have performed about once a year since 2010, when Clevenger was six years old (Donoghue 43). In an art gallery setting, Clevenger sits at one end of a wooden seesaw occupying herself with a book, a device, or grabbing a snack from her lunch kit while her mother, Kessel, adds items to Clevenger's end of the seesaw. They are objects from their daily life—books, toys and other domestic items. Kessel places, knots, tucks in, or hangs the items. Once the manual labour is completed, Kessel walks to the vacant end of the seesaw, lifts one of her legs up, and sits astride the plank. The approximately thirty-minute performance is over when young Clevenger declares it to be (Loveless 481).

I analyze the problem of resistance to maternal artistic subjectivity in a three-fold manner. First, this chapter traces what is at stake in normative representations of the maternal from the archetype of Madonna and Child to a newer neoliberal archetype of the juggling mother, as conceptualized by sociologist Amanda Watson. Motherhood scholar Andrea O'Reilly's dictates of normative motherhood and Kristeva's feminist psychoanalytic observation of primary narcissism in the Marian form together reveal that the expectation in the visualization of normative motherhood is both instructive and disciplinary.

Second, this chapter articulates the artwork's disruptions to normative motherhood by visualizing the labour that the Marian form occludes. Additionally, Kessel's prioritization of manual domestic labour over conspicuous affective care and her positioning of motherhood as political challenges the intensification and depoliticization of the juggling mother. This section follows artist-writer Eti Wade's assertion that unidealized maternal art is integral to generating maternal subjectivity. However, by disallowing the primary narcissism that the idealized maternal form provides, *In Balance With*, along with other nonidealized maternal art projects, results in subconscious disappointment—a buzz kill for the viewer. This subconscious disappointment offers insight into the resistance to the art of the maternal.

Third, this chapter offers a way to forget this disappointment by presenting the viewer with much eye candy—a copious number of colourful everyday objects inserted into the additive sculptural-performative piece. Using Oliva Heal's theory of matricritics, which is thematically aligned with Elaine Showalter's feminist poetics, this final section begins with a matricritcal reading of *In Balance With*. It then concludes with charting the structural mechanics of Heal's matricritical framework, emphasizing description over interpretation and vulnerability, in place of categorizing and analysing the form. By consciously trying to bypass categorization and the subsequent expectations of the maternal form, Heal's postcritical cocktail can function as a way to reroute a powerful subconscious mechanism and facilitate encounters with maternal artistic subjectivity.

A Warm Buzz: Primary Narcissism in Representations of Normative Motherhood

Adrienne Rich made the distinction between mothering (a potential relationship) and motherhood (an oppressive institution) (13). Motherhood as institution is a social construction responsive to and fundamentally in service of economic and social shifts (O'Reilly xi). O'Reilly theorizes a matricentric feminism and asserts that one's relationship and role in reproductive labour are critical sites of research (2). The patriarchal version of motherhood articulated in matricentric feminism's dictates of normative motherhood provides a framework for how artworks and art practices subvert or reiterate oppressive representations of motherhood, providing the conceptual tools for a matricentric feminist critique. In other words, the dictates of normative motherhood enable a systematic analysis of the objectification of motherhood in visual culture. Feminists have long understood the political significance of images. We need a feminist critique to identify "woman as signifier of sexuality" (Mulvey 37) and therefore also need a matricentric feminist critique to appreciate mother as a signifier of unconditional love and the weighty expectations that converge on those bodies as a result.

Thinking about the Judeo-Christian art historical archetype of the Madonna and Child may seem like an archaic endeavour in a constitutionally secular late-capitalist context. This two-thousand-year-old motif, however, has endured and persists in neoliberal visual culture from celebrity moms in various media to the sanctification of suffering and sacrifice of single mothers in charity poster campaigns. This symbolic representation facilitates the Madonna-whore dichotomy (Bareket et al.), which is refurbished into the powerful tropes of "good" mother and "bad" mother.

The pervasive and loving image of the Madonna and Child provides a flexible visual distillation of the dictates of normative motherhood. A mother is by herself (essentialization, individualization) and needs no outside help (privatization) because she is both a natural and an expert (naturalization, expertization). She makes no political claim or comment on her working conditions other than her selfless offering of nurturance because motherhood is the full expression of her womanhood (depoliticization, idealization, and intensification). It is assumed, though not visualized, that she is the biological mother (biologicalization) and part of a heteronormative, nuclear family structure (normalization). The Marian form is ideologically malleable and can capture the shifting valuations of motherhood, such as the intensification of motherhood, which will be discussed below. In effect, the communicative strength of the Madonna and Child is in what it both shows and what it hides. It shows affective care, to be done by that one body, while hiding everything else. In *In Balance With*, Kessel's prioritizing of the puttering motions of domestic labour over displays of child-oriented nurturance flips these dictates on their head.

Watson has conceptualized a newer, and still normativizing, archetype of the juggling mother (Watson 900). The juggling mother, highly prevalent in advertising campaigns and television programming, is the mother that does too much and is expected to do too much; she fits with a neoliberal intensification of the experience of motherhood. Unlike the

Madonna, the juggling mother shows the work associated with her disciplinary aims, prioritizing the child's enrichment over domestic labour (although the housework still needs to get done) or turning domestic labour into a pedagogical adventure (Wade 282). To be a good mother within this ideology is to have an all-in commitment physically, emotionally, and psychologically with her children and to be fundamentally accepting of this situation. Watson points out that although the labour is visualized, the juggling mother is not a radical figure because of her fundamental acceptance of her situation. The juggling mother is a visualization of the intensification of motherhood while still inhabiting the normativizing dictates of motherhood. In *In Balance With*, Kessel shows the work that the Madonna and Child hides and the unsmiling fatigue that the juggling mother disallows.

Wade, drawing from writer Andrea Liss, asserts that uncritical maternal representations that reiterate dictates of normative motherhood supress maternal subjectivity by silencing and distorting the maternal experience. In addition to the suppression of maternal subjectivity, there are expectations as to what maternal representations should provide. Wade cites Kristeva's psychoanalytic interpretation of audience experiences with the Madonna and Child that inhibit identification with the maternal:

> We live in a civilization where the consecrated (religious or secular) representation of femininity is absorbed by motherhood. If, however, one looks at it more closely, this motherhood is the fantasy that is nurtured by the adult, man or woman, of a lost territory: what is more, it involves less an idealized archaic mother than the idealization of the relationship that bounds us to her, one that cannot be localized—an idealization of primary narcissism (Kristeva qtd. in Wade 283)

Audience encounters with the Madonna and Child reveal a subconscious desire to reinhabit a place and a time of unidirectional affective and preservative care. In this dyadic composition, the viewer is equipped to see themselves via the child and daydream of nurturance or mourn an idyllic pre-mirror phase. Not only it is unlikely for viewers to relate to the maternal figure, regardless of their own gender expression, but there are also poignant subconscious emotional expectations of primary narcissism from this form. Therefore, any artist working against the representations of normative motherhood is disrupting this subconscious expectation.

Buzz Kill: *In Balance With*'s Interruptions to the Representation of Normative Motherhood's Primary Narcissism

Kessel and Clevenger enact an aesthetic strategy that Wade terms "performance of the raw everyday," as a taxonomical distinction of new maternalist aesthetic forms (275). These are aesthetic strategies that artists dealing with the maternal employ to offer nonidealized and non-normativizing representations of the maternal. Matricentric feminism and new maternalist aesthetic strategies are aligned in activist and epistemological aims. *In Balance With* critiques many of the dictates of normative motherhood.

By blurring the line between domestic and public spaces (Donoghue 199), *In Balance With* critiques privatization and individualization. As a single mother, Kessel has little time for a studio practice. By engaging in both childcare and performance with her daughter in a gallery setting, Kessel combines her two work worlds of childcare and art. The work is an institutional critique of not viewing childcare as critical infrastructure and of historically prioritizing the perspectives of those not engaged in these disciplinary aims because the work is expected to be individualized onto the maternal body. Here, Kessel is occupied with moving and organizing objects while refraining from posing with Clevenger or engaging in conspicuous displays of love and affective care. By not engaging in affective care or turning the domestic labour into a pedagogical activity for her child's intellectual benefit, *In Balance With* critiques the intensified and idealized requirements to be a good mother.

The objects that Kessel positions also offer a critique of normative motherhood. The seesaw is strewn with books on parenting, which engages the contradictory aims of naturalization and expertization. The good mother is expected to be a natural at mothering while conversant with all the latest child-centric parenting ideologies. If it were possible to be a natural at childrearing, there would be no need to refer to knowledge amassed in books. Kessel ironically shows that all this knowledge accumulated and transferred vis à vis the parenting books still cannot make her workload tenable. *In Balance With* contains Kessel's own schoolbooks running counter to essentialization and depoliticization. If motherhood is Kessel's full expression of womanhood, she would not feel the need to attend grad school and immerse herself in writing about art or feminist and matricentric feminist activist methods.

Normative motherhood's dictate of normalization assumes that maternal practices are performed within the context of a nuclear family. With Kessel as a single mother, she disrupts this cultural construction. In fact, *In Balance With* collapses the distinctions between mother and child and the family portrait. Interestingly, this information is only obtainable by Kessel's disclosure, not visualized through this art piece. A line of inquiry that develops from this artistic collapse of the maternal and family portrait is beyond the scope of this chapter but would make for a site of future inquiry with emphasis on the implications of that collapse for the bodies of single mothers.

After Kessel has loaded all the items and placed herself at one end of the seesaw, the performance is over when Clevenger says it is (Loveless 481), which explores the phenomenology of maternal time and calls into question maternal agency. Kessel is responsive to her daughter's needs and desires. Interestingly, when Kessel and Clevenger performed *In Balance With* in the early years, Kessel would offer sufficient counterweight to have the seesaw balance with her one side and Clevenger with the items on the other. With the 2016 iteration of *In Balance With*, discussed in this chapter, Kessel is unable to offer a counterweight for her daughter and the assemblage of items. The cumulative effect of Kessel's workload and responsibilities are unmanageable. The idea of balance, however, is called into question throughout the iterations of the performance as Kessel's legs dangle from the seesaw. With a play device that no longer works, play itself is interrogated, as it is experienced differently for the mother and the child. The child plays, and the mother putters. When the puttering is over, the mother watches the daughter with tired eyes.

By disrupting dictates of normative motherhood, *In Balance With* counters objectifying practices that converge in the Madonna as well as the juggling mother. Her work is soundly positioned in a realm of critically informed maternal subjectivity. Kessel, however, has lamented that although her practice has received international attention, her work is being siloed thematically into shows dealing with the maternal, family, and feminist concerns (Kashef 163). Thus remains the predicament.

Wade contends that art is "a significant social tool" (274) and that the maternal experience is "failed by dominant language" (281), resulting in epistemological crises. She contends that visual arts offer a way to communicate the maternal and bridge this gap in communication. Taking this assertion of art as a political tool along with the limitations of dominant language, a subsequent line of questioning surrounding the appraisal of the hospitality of aesthetics, which are also rooted in patriarchal viewpoints and objectives regarding the subject of motherhood is required.

Kessel and Clevenger's, along with many other artists', clear engagement with new materialist aesthetic strategies, disrupt the visuals of normative motherhood. They operate outside patriarchal requirements, showing both elements of work and subjectivity, and they use art as the political tool that Wade and many other artist and writers claim it to be. Yet considering Kristeva's observation of the mourning of primary narcissism, which results in the strong unlikeliness of being able to identify with the maternal figure, can the viewer identify with any maternal subjective expression? Has this objectification via the centuries-old Marian form set parameters for future conceptual engagement that are hard to shake? Does it matter to show the work of childcare, the associated aching fatigue, the crazy-making frustration, the effects of the weight of expectations, the potential and often permanent transformations to a maternal body—the sagging, stretchmarks etc.—if viewers, including even mothers, are so well trained to have emotional expectations from the artistic maternal form while disregarding maternal subjectivity? Olivia Heal, drawing from Showalter, offers a matricritics, which can be mobilized to disrupt this sticking point.

Eye Candy: Matricritics in *In Balance With*

The following description, using Heal's matricritics, of *In Balance With* (Figs. 1 and 2) is based on photo documentation of Kessel and Clevenger's performance at FAB Gallery, Edmonton, Canada, 2016, curated by Natalie Loveless.

There are panes of large floor-to-ceiling windows with rolling blinds resting at the top of the windows. They reveal a summer exterior with a few shrubby trees, brown bark, and green leaves. A white interior wall covers a portion of a brick wall in the gallery space. There are square terracotta floor tiles and a drain in the floor. Nearby, people are talking to one another and looking at the mother and child. A lot of the people are wearing glasses. I think almost everyone has pale skin. I think almost everyone has dark hair. Rough-cut planks make a seesaw. Clevenger is at one end of the seesaw sitting cross-legged on a pillow. The rough-cut seesaw plank touches the terracotta square tiles. Clevenger is wearing dark blue jeans, a long-sleeved white shirt, and a brown cap. She two long brown pigtails. She is writing in a book with her right hand using a pencil. Behind her hangs a bag of lemons. She has a back rest; her mother does not. Attached to the backrest is another plastic bag, in it, maybe fruit, or maybe bread. In front of Clevenger are black milk crates holding toys, books, and other things I cannot identify as well as a red reading lamp. Also in front of Clevenger are a brown plush toy and a chartreuse pillow with a hot pink/magenta spikey fringe; a book that says *Feminist Art* on the spine and another saying *Dictionary* are squeezed between two of the milk crates. Two other books are in the group, but I cannot make out the letters. There is a closed black suitcase with airport tags on the handle. Piled on top are three fabrics: One is jewel-tone cerulean blue, one is hottish pink, and the other is burnt sienna. Now I see purple too. And there is a wooden spoon sticking out. Pressed up against the suitcase is a pile of books secured with a bungee cord. Gardening work gloves—red and white—are on top of the pile of books. I think they are a little dirty. Hanging from the bungee cord is a small pink net, maybe for catching bugs. Next to that is something that might be a net or something that might be a frying pan. Next to the thing that might be a net or might be a frying pan is a basket made of thin woven wire. The edge of the basket, where the opening is, is decorated with wire Easter eggs that look like they are leaning on each other, and maybe laughing to each other, maybe whispering. There is a smaller wire egg leaning towards and touching a larger wire egg. The larger wire egg is leaning towards and touching the smaller wire egg. There looks to be a used bag of potting soil in the basket. The colour of the crumpled plastic bag is mostly blue and yellow. There is one fibre that hangs low from the basket's bottom. The milk crates are all tied down with a bungee cord. Kessel is at the other end of the seesaw. In jeans and a t-shirt, her feet dangle. Both hands grasp the plank of the seesaw. She is leaning slightly forwards, looking at the child. Kessel's legs drape over the edge of the seesaw. We used to call it a teeter-totter. Her feet are not touching the floor. Is she barefoot? From one end to the other of the seesaw, descending to ascending, it goes: food, backrest, pillow, daughter, stuff, books, space, and then mother. There is a slight bend in the wood from the weight.

By attending to the many objects in *In Balance With* difference narratives emerge that draw the focus away from traditional expectations of the maternal form in art. Drawing from Showalter's essay "Towards a Feminist Poetics," which calls for a method of engagement with creative works made by women, Heal has offered a schematic matricritical framework. Even though feminist and matricentric feminist critiques remain essential in illuminating objectification, the lack of female subjectivity, and oppressive stereotypes, Heal shares Showalter's desire for shifting critical engagement so that it moves beyond revealing the ethical and intellectual limitations of male-oriented impressions of the maternal experience. Showalter explains: "If we study stereotypes of women, the sexism of male critics, and the limited role women play in literary history, we are not learning what women have felt and experienced, but only what men have thought what women should be" (216).

Heal offers experimental strategies that are drawn from various sources: positioning oneself beside to allow for reparative reading, emphasizing first person while inhabiting ethical and political positions, description over interpretation, listening to lesser beats, and acknowledging vulnerability, with the aim of promoting maternal subjectivity while avoiding recreating oppressive imaginaries of a good mother (123-24).

Positioning Oneself Beside

In advocating for positioning oneself beside the work, as opposed to above it or below it, Heal is drawing from Eve Kosofsky Sedgwick's *Touching Feeling Affect*. "Without attempting to devalue such critical practices," Sedgwick has, "tried in this project to explore some ways around the topos of depth of hiddenness, typically followed by a drama of exposure, that has been such a staple of critical work of the last four decades" (Sedgwick 8). It is the critical ethos of a "hermeneutics of suspicion" (Sedgwick 124) that matricentric feminism necessarily subscribes to. Although matricentric feminism may be late to the critical party, when delivering a matricentric feminist critique by using the dictates of normative motherhood as a framework, there is a feeling of satisfaction, even an impression of finality, a sense of righting a perceived wrong, of giving a critical spanking in the name of mothers. Shaking a work through a matricentric feminist sieve to see how it fares is a radical and vital step towards representations of empowered mothering. Watching television and seeing advertisements at commercial breaks featuring a juggling mother, critically informed viewers can critically evaluate the representation as having a disciplinary and normativizing function as opposed to depicting an example of a good mother. As a critical grid, O'Reilly's dictates of normative motherhood serve an epistemological purpose that allows for the appreciation of how Kessel and Clevenger visually repudiate the dictates of normative motherhood. Postcritical strategies, such as matricritics, with different aims than those of matricentric feminism, do not deliver the same cathartic conclusion. At this juncture, the search for knowledge is not about exposure or judgment; it is about relationality and hanging in the balance. Heal's matricritics encourage encounters with *In Balance With* exterior to taxonomical parameters established by idealized representations of the maternal.

Speaking in First Person While Considering One's Political and Ethical Position

Speaking in first person acknowledges and probes authority of experience. The insertion of two maternal subjectivities—artist and viewer—allows for an artistic conversation to combat othering by "social, patriarchal, psychoanalytic, and even feminist frameworks" (Heal 118). Courtney Kessel is a white single mother who was pursuing grad studies in art school when she began this project. These are all criteria to which I personally relate: the social protection of whiteness for both mother and child as well as the challenging and perhaps impossible balancing act of childcare, grad school, and an art practice as a single mother. However, the prescription need not be that of similar life experiences to engage with the artwork, as this would enact a critical siloing along the same lines as the curatorial siloing Kessel identified. Speaking in first person does, however, invite the contemplation of the spectrum of experiential congruencies and their impact on the act of looking and engaging.

Describing over Interpretating

In *In Balance With*, Kessel and Clevenger disrupt normative representational logic of the maternal. Recalling Kristeva, there are long-held expectations as to what the form of mother and child should provide for the viewer. Whether one consciously associates positive emotions with a maternal figure or not, the mind is transported into a daydream of unconditional love. This observation is not a sarcastic repudiation of the power of love. On the contrary, it is to acknowledge the power of that aesthetic form and the psycho-emotional fantasies and subsequent expectations it can elicit. When I encounter the form, my response is Pavlovian. I prefer if there is a bench upon which to sit. It is better to be able to relax when one's eyes are taking in the drug of unconditional love. For a moment, I imagine being in the care of the one who takes the pain away, the one who nourishes. It likely slows the heartrate and opens the floodgates of oxytocin. I imagine the oxytocin squealing "yay" down their favourite waterslide. With *In Balance With*, it is like our favourite ride at the amusement park is closed for repairs. With Kessel's domestic labour predominating the work and Clevenger's being entertained by Auntie Apple or Uncle Samsung, the viewer is denied that pleasure—the visualization of attentive and affective care. Krisetva reminds us that in encounters with the Marian form, the viewer becomes the child. Kessel is so busy with the stuff that she has no time for us.

What to do at this psycho-aesthetic impasse? Can a strategy of description in place of categorizing function as a subconscious re-routing? This was my aim in my description of *In Balance With* at the beginning of this chapter. By using Heal and Sedgwick's postcritical strategies, I aimed to offer a distraction from the disappointment that Kessel and Clevenger provide with the interruptions and expectations of primary narcissism. Kessel and Clevenger engage Laura Mulvey's concept of the destruction of pleasure as a radical weapon, and it is all the viewer's subconscious can do not to pout. With an object-oriented description, can the viewer get caught up in the sensorial eros of the objects and in the description of them? Can the mind go on a different walk? Can this strategy take the viewer's attention elsewhere, like distracting a child with candy? And in Kessel and Clevenger's art piece, there are many optic sweets.

As previously mentioned, my analysis of *In Balance With* is performed by referencing images and writings about the work. Art theorist Amelia Jones cautions against the belief in privileging access to the truth from experiencing a performance *in situ* versus photographic and textual traces (Jones 11). In this sense, where a semiotic retraining is required, might there be an advantage to not experiencing the performance in person? Not that I would deny the opportunity to see the performance live, but my experience would have been different had I not seen it live. I would have been able to appreciate the nuance of each facial expression, likely performing a comparative analysis between mother and daughter. I imagine my eyes would have followed Kessel's actions. By studying the images of *In Balance With* and consciously employing Heal's matricritics I can think beyond categorization, beyond what the representation of the maternal should provide, and beyond what the real-life mother should provide. Instead, it is as though I am looking at domestic panoply in an *I Spy Book*—a much-loved children's book series that invites treasure seeking and making little discoveries. By employing a matricritical method, I am taking my time and allowing the potential for an object-oriented narrative to develop, which is at times still narratively rooted in the maternal: *There is a smaller wire egg leaning towards a larger wire egg. The larger wire egg is leaning towards the smaller wire egg.*

Acknowledge Our Own Vulnerability

For Heal, and drawing from sociologist Tiffany Page, acknowledging our own vulnerability encourages us, as omniscient critics and researchers, to "question assumptions and forms of certitude, to return to materials and change our minds" (Page 16). In the description I provided of Kessel and Clevenger's *In Balance With*, there were many instances where I could not identify the objects with certainty. Thinking along the same lines as Page's vulnerable writing methodology, I opted to not occlude the lack of certainty. Vulnerability can be defined as "The quality or state of being exposed to the possibility of being attacked or harmed, either physically or emotionally" (Lexico Dictionaries English).

The concept of exposure is crucial for two reasons. First, it is an epistemological break with the "drama of exposure" (Sedgwick 8). The possibility of exposure comes not from an exterior framework but from an interior locus of experience. Second, many mothers have reported the difficulties of speaking openly and honestly about their maternal experiences. Writer Susan Maushart describes the "values of a culture that glorifies the ideal of motherhood but takes for granted the work of motherhood and ignores the experience of motherhood" (274) as the "mask of motherhood." The fact that the realities of motherhood come as a shock to so many—coupled with mothers feeling difficulty in being able to speak openly about the experience—indicates something is awry in the knowledge-making practices of the maternal order. As a knowledge-sharing species, concealing the plethora of maternal experiences seems decidedly antievolutionary. Put differently, it is the effective operationalizing of the regulatory discourse and practice of patriarchal motherhood that seeks to fundamentally disempower mothers. Thus, because of the social stigma attached to operating outside the dictates of normative motherhood, acknowledging vulnerability is a strategy of resistance and potential kinship building.

The idea of vulnerability can be taken much further than acknowledging a lack of certainty to include the emotional experience of the viewer. What does it feel like to look at Kessel and Clevenger's *In Balance With*? With the pressure to conform and the expectation of sacrifice bearing down on a maternal viewer, it is unlikely to be an entirely placid experience. Is there judgment of Kessel's parenting skills or the judgment of one's own? Is there jealousy? Does the mind turn to childcare? The viewer is invited to probe their interior life of thoughts, memories, fears, comparisons, and affects. In this way, channels open, allowing for the communicative potential of varied maternal experiences.

Conclusion

There is a cartoon from the *New Yorker* by Caitlin Cass that features two women in an art gallery looking at paintings. One says to the other, "It's all significantly less impressive once you realize these guys had free childcare" (Cass 2021). There are memes online that go something like:

Mom: Ok, I definitely need help.

World: Look at you go, girl, you're killing it!
Mom: No, you're not understanding. This is unsustainable, I'm breaking down.
World: You're a superhero and we love you!!!!

Taken together, the cartoon and composite meme represent a crisis of an enduring nature that Kessel and Clevenger's work engages: the invisibilization of domestic labour and the inability to process and/or the ease of disregarding (artistic) maternal subjectivity. With annual iterations showing the passing of time through the growth of both child and mother, *In Balance With* asks what will it take to listen?

When looking at *In Balance With* in terms of bodies in the artwork, it is a mom and her daughter. The Western art canon is replete with representations of mother and child that are influenced heavily by the Judeo-Christian archetype Madonna and Child, which seeks to idealize and normativize the maternal. Many mother-artists have reported intergenerationally that their own expressions of motherhood in the arts are fraught with marginalization and are even identified as taboo (Judah 14). This reality speaks to the need for both critically informed subjectivities as well as accommodating frameworks. In other words, there is a need to produce work that is not in the image of patriarchal maternal representations and to have strategies for interaction with these types of works. Matricentric feminist critiques and matricritics are divergent strategies. A matricentric feminist critique, à la O'Reilly's dictates of normative motherhood, is situated within a hermeneutics of suspicion with the aim of exposing power structures. Heal's matricritics, in contrast, draws on Sedgwick's desire to move beyond a hermeneutics of suspicion and a "drama of exposure" and Love's desire for a descriptive (as opposed to interpretive) turn in order to better attend to previously ignored qualities in a work. Facing the art historical and contemporary visual context, matricentric feminism and matricritics function in a complementary manner. Matricentric feminism can be mobilized to better understand how normative motherhood can be upheld (i.e., Madonna and Child and the juggling mother) or can be subverted and even taken into new directions (Kessel and Clevenger's *In Balance With*).

Recalling Kristeva, there are high subconscious emotional expectations from the Marian form that are disrupted in *In Balance With*. By not visualizing the demands of normative motherhood, Kessel and

Clevenger create a buzz kill. Matricritical strategies offer a way to engage with art that bypasses categorization. They offer a way to let go of thinking, relying instead on visual, emotional, affective experiences—that is, falling for Kessel and Clevenger's eye candy and maybe even appreciating the tenuousness (or aspiration) of being *In Balance With*.

Works Cited

Barekey, Kahalon R., P. Shnabel, and P. Glick. "The Madonna-Whore Dichotomy: Men Who Perceive Women's Nurturance and Sexuality as Mutually Exclusive Endorse Patriarchy and Show Lower Relationship Satisfaction." *Sex Roles*, vol. 79, no. 9-10, 2018, pp. 519-32.

Cass, Caitlin. Free Child Care, New Yorker Cartoons, *New Yorker*, 4. Oct. 2021, www.newyorker.com/cartoons/issue-cartoons/cartoons-from-the-october-4-2021-issue. Accessed 11 Feb. 2023.

Donoghue, Deirdre M. "Entre Nous: Moments, Holes and Stuff. On the Maternal Aesthetics of Courtney Kessel," *New Maternalisms: Redux*, edited by Natalie Loveless, Department of Art and Design, University of Alberta, 2018, pp. 32-54.

Heal, Olivia. "Towards a Matricentric Feminist Poetics." *Journal of the Motherhood Initiative*, vol. 10, no 1- 2, Spring/Fall, 2019, pp. 117-129.

Jones, Amelia. "'Presence' in Absentia. Experiencing Performance as Documentation." *Art Journal*, New York, vol. 56, no. 4, 1997, pp. 11–18.

Judah, Hettie. "Fully, Messy and Beautiful." *Report on the Representations of Female Artists in Britain During 2019*, edited by Kate McMillan, Freelands Foundation, 2019, pp. 14-20.

Kashef, Niku. "The Durational Performance of the Parent-Artist and other Subversive Acts." *Inappropriate Bodies: Art, Design and Maternity*, edited by Rachel Epp Buller and Charles Reeve, Demeter Press, 2019, pp. 155-76.

Kristeva, Julia. "Stabat Mater." *The Kristeva Reader*, edited by Toril Moi, Columbia University Press, 1986, pp. 160-86.

Love, Heather. "Close but not Deep: Literary Ethics and the Descriptive Turn." *New Literary History*, vol. 41, no.2, 2010, pp. 371-91.

Loveless, Natalie. "Maternal Mattering: The Performance and Politics of the Maternal in Contemporary Art." *A Companion to Feminist Art*, edited by Hilary Robinson and Maria Elena Buszek, John Wiley & Sons, 2019, pp. 75-491.

Loveless, Natalie, et al. *New Maternalisms: Maternidades y Nuevos Feminismos*. Santiago de Chile: Museo de Arts Contemporaneo MAC, 2014.

Maushart, Susan. "Faking Motherhood: The Mask Revealed." *Maternal Theory: Essential Readings*, edited by Andrea O'Reilly, Demeter Press, 2021, pp. 273-294.

Mulvey, Laura. "Visual Pleasure and Narrative Cinema." *Visual and Other Pleasures*. Palgrave MacMillan, 1975.

Nochlin, Linda. "Why Have There Been No Great Women Artists?" *Feminism-Art-Theory: An Anthology 1968-2014*, Second Edition. Edited by Hilary Robinson. John Wiley & Sons, Ltd, 2016.

O'Reilly, Andrea. *Matricentric Feminism: Theory, Activism and Practice*. Demeter Press, 2020.

Page, Tiffany. "Vulnerable Writing as a Feminist Methodological Practice." *Feminist Review*, vol. 115, no. 1, 2017, pp. 13-29.

Rich, Adrienne. *Of Woman Born: Motherhood as Experience and Institution*. W.W. Norton and Company, 1976.

Showalter, Elaine. "Towards a Feminist Poetics." *Twentieth-Century Literary Theory*, edited by K.M. Newton, MacMillan Publishers Limited, 1998, pp. 216-19.

Stephens, Julie. *Confronting Postmaternal Thinking: Feminism, Memory, and Care*. Columbia University Press, 2011.

Thurer, Shari L. *The Myths of Motherhood: How Culture Reinvents the Good Mother*. Penguin, 1994.

Sedgwick, Eve Kosofsky. *Touching, Feeling: Affect, Pedagogy, Performativity*. Duke University Press, 2002.

"Vulnerability–English Definition and Meaning" *Lexico Dictionaries English*, web.archive.org/web/20210118111731/https://www.lexico.com/en/definition/vulnerability Accessed 11 Feb. 2023.

Wade, Eti. "Maternal Art Practices: In Support of New Maternalist Aesthetic Forms." *New Maternalisms: Tales of Motherwork (Dislodging the Unthinkable),* edited by Roksana Badruddoja and Maki Motapanyane, Demeter Press, 2016, pp. 274-93.

Watson, Amanda. "The Juggling Mother." *Maternal Theory: Essential Readings,* edited by Andrea O'Reilly, Demeter Press, 2021, pp. 915-28.

Part 3.
Reclamations

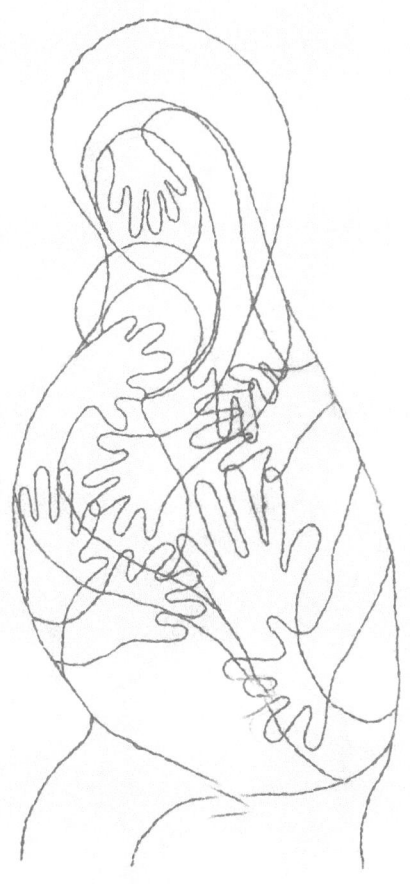

THE SAINTLY MOTHER

Chapter 11.

The Death of the God Mother: Deconstructing Normative Motherhood and Its Resistance

Isabelle Portelinha

Common representations revolving around gender equality often go hand in hand with a general sense that most feminist battles have been won (Criado-Perez; Crittenden; Hank and Steinbach). In contrast to these beliefs, however, women, and particularly mothers, remain trapped under a vigorous patriarchal hold. The invisibility and weight of reproductive labour done within the confines of the nuclear family, given its alienation from the valuation sphere, are as painful and intractable as ever. Normative motherhood, as the hegemonic representation of mothering work, is but a critical pillar of the oppressive apparatus (O'Reilly, *Matricentric Feminism*).

From a sociopsychological perspective, normative motherhood can be understood as a set of beliefs evolving in a sociopolitical and historically situated context. These representations consist in assumptions regarding how relevant others understand motherhood and what they deem as good practice. In other words, normative beliefs refer to standards of values and behaviours perceived as used and/or abided by others. Such representations, regardless of their objectivity, can have significant repercussions—that is, silencing any counter-narratives and maintaining the representational status quo. Whereas normative beliefs can be extremely malleable, those associated with motherhood, though potentially diverse, tend to remain relatively stable. It is precisely this feature that is the focus of this chapter. In particular, I consider the processes that diffuse beliefs contributing to the desolidarization of women and the silencing of alternative representations of motherhood. The invisibility of daily acts of resistance is examined as well as the neoliberal socio-cognitive and practical processes affecting our ways of relating to one another and to mothers in particular.

The present chapter intends to shed light on the diffusion of, and resistance to, normative motherhood. Moreover, it proposes a conceptual clarification of the term to further separate the experiential dimension of normative motherhood from its institutional one (see Rich). In particular, the analogy drawn between the figure of the good mother, on the one hand, and that of the god mother, on the other, illuminates different sociopsychological processes at play in the maintenance of normative motherhood. The death of the god mother is ultimately considered in response to the desolidarizing neoliberal context at the source of the pervasive silencing of the mother's voice.

Normative Motherhood, Its Diffusion, and Maintenance

From a sociopsychological perspective, normative motherhood refers to a set of behaviours, experiences, and beliefs socially associated with prototypical mothers. For theorists then, normative motherhood and its study fall into the realm of social influence, a vast and ever-developing field of inquiry in psychology. Social influence refers to the processes through which people's thoughts, behaviours, and feelings are affected by others, be they real or imagined. Research in this domain has emphasized that individuals tend to compare themselves with other beings and behave according to what people they identify with—that is, in-group members—value or do. With motherhood, mothers are likely to compare themselves with friends, family members, neighbours, contacts on social media, etc.

When engaging in social comparisons (beyond the interpersonal sphere), two types of influence can be at work: normative and informational influence. The former refers to cases where individuals conform to what they perceive as being the perspective of many. For mothers immersed in an environment where intensive parenting[1] seems to be the norm (Belsky, Lerner, and Spanier; Hays; for assumptions of parental determinism see Wall), influence could take the form of not raising their voice when frustrated or striving to respond to their children's anticipated needs. Interestingly, normative influence does not require private acceptance of said behaviour. The performance is predominantly derived from the expected consequence resulting from the gaze of others. With normative influence, individuals conform to what they perceive as being the norm for fear of standing out. This process stems from people's need to be accepted and valued by others.

In contrast, informational influence refers to cases wherein individuals would conform to what they perceive to be the behavior or standards of many, not out of fear of being left out, but rather out of a motivation to being correct, to not making errors. Others are believed to be more knowledgeable. Behaviors and beliefs are attuned, internally even, to the wisdom of the many in a rational endeavor. Informational influence arises in conditions of uncertainty, where individuals are unclear as to how to act, what to think, or how to feel. They willingly follow others, not for their social protection, but for the haven offered by their cognitive shield to their selves (and offspring).

These two types of influence are certainly intertwined. Their distinction, however, not only highlights a number of occurrences taking place in the specific journey of motherhood, but it participates in understanding the diffusion of normative motherhood. Their distinction allows us to better comprehend its diffusion to the new mothers opening the gate to an unknown, to-be-discovered realm, feeling exhaustingly confused as to how to proceed. It allows us to understand the diffusion of normative motherhood to all mothers exposed to novel emerging situations; its diffusion to those feeling as if walking a thin line of right and wrong in their every act in front of a judging audience, which will condemn them at that very moment and time, or await till the dreaded emergence of inappropriate behavior in their children, the flaws of the offspring as public testimony of their failure in their quest for maternal perfection (see Almond; O'Reilly).

Normative and informational influences reveal the motives underlying individuals' attention to the behaviors and attitudes of the many. Let us now examine the notion of social norms and the processes participating in their diffusion and maintenance. As mentioned earlier, normative motherhood refers to the attitudes and behaviours typically associated with individuals performing motherwork—"the relational and logistical work of child rearing" (Arendell 1192).[2] While straightforward, this characterization justifies at least two acceptations of normative motherhood depending on the standpoint considered. The first one is phenomenological, and refers to the actual, direct experience of mothers who do the motherwork (i.e., mothering as different from the institution of motherhood). The second is more indirect—a projected and thereby social understanding of what this experience is or, most often, should be. A set of beliefs then as to what mothers think, do, and feel. Said differently, normative motherhood in this latter sense refers to perceived social norms[3] (*social* social norms, also called metarepresentations, see Portelinha and Elcheroth). In its quality of social representation, normative motherhood is always socially situated. Normative motherhood cannot but refer to a given social group—that is, to a specific community of discourse. In other words, many (possible) normative motherhoods exist. Our inclination to refer to one type of normative motherhood undeniably speaks to the hegemony of said representation. In what follows, I focus on white-supremacist, heteronormative, and ableist representations of motherhood to better circumscribe its diffusion and maintenance. This emphasis is driven by the acknowledged limitations of my experiences.

As perceived social norms, as beliefs, normative motherhood is remarkably powerful for its ability to remain impervious and endure beyond inconsistencies concerning its phenomenological acceptance. Indeed, perceived social norms affect attitudes and behaviours even when people's beliefs regarding what others think are inaccurate (e.g., Prentice and Miller). This is notably illustrated by social psychology research on pluralistic ignorance (Miller and McFarland), which corresponds to a situation in which individuals privately disagree with what they perceive to be the norm yet go along with it, as they presume it to be accepted by most other group members. Pluralistic ignorance relating to normative motherhood can take the form of mothers believing other mothers to not only embrace patriarchal normative motherhood but to enjoy and uphold it, despite most mothers acting privately against the perceived (injunctive) norm[4]. Ironically, a false belief that relevant others tolerate and even endorse an oppressive set of practices (perceived as socially dictated)—in this case, motherhood as institution (Rich)—can lead to the actual strengthening of such a system, as this false belief comes to affect people's behaviour. As mothers are watched as they perform (and thus embody the institution of) motherhood, and as mothers remain publicly silent when exposed to those who deviate from the script of motherhood—the "mother outlaws" (Rich)—mothers and their inaccurate beliefs contribute to the upholding of motherhood as an institution. This perspective is derived from Noelle Neumann's classic spiral of silence theory, which posits that people's reading of the surrounding political climate affects their willingness to express their personal views. When individuals perceive their own attitudes conflicting with those of the majority, they are more likely to remain silent. This spiral of silence affects the potential for opinion change, as public behaviours developed on this basis alter in turn others' perceptions of the political climate. Eventually, aggregate political outcomes paradoxically come to reflect people's (possibly ill-informed) beliefs about the majority's opinions rather than their previously deeply held attitudes (Portelinha and Elcheroth).

Normative Motherhood and its Resistance

Thus far, this chapter has explored how social influence processes help to maintain normative motherhood—that is, the hegemonic representation of mothering in patriarchy. Although these considerations focused on the ways mothers can contribute with their beliefs, behaviours, and silences to the maintenance of the institution of motherhood, this is not to suggest that mothers are the cause of their oppression. In its intent to move beyond the silencing of women, this chapter proposes to participate in the articulation and theorizing of the voices of mothers, and to amplify them. But it also involves understanding those deliberate silences, beyond those imposed, and comprehending their emergence (or lack thereof) as well as their potential.

Silences can be instances of resistance, as it can take different forms. In its idealized representation, resistance is overt, intended, and collective (Vinthagen and Johansson). This is notably the case of practices and representations of childrearing operating not only in actual opposition to normative motherhood but also outside its realm. This is a non-normative, and thereby prefigurative, caring, as is the case with certain queer forms of mothering and kinship (see Park).

Alternative forms of non-normative motherhood are representations and practices of mothering that disrupt Western-centric, normative representations of mothering. These disruptions of normative renderings of motherhood make visible some of the ideological assumptions underlying it—assumptions that are often silenced and naturalized through their normalization and apparent ordinariness. The childrearing work of mothers who rely on nonpatriarchal (and often deprecated) practices of mothering fall into this category, such as the shared parenting of working mothers, the communal/othermothering of African American and Indigenous mothers, and the fictive kin of stepmothers (O'Reilly, *Matricentric Feminism*). In Andrea O'Reilly's words:

> Mothers come from all races and ethnicities, that mothers are both young or old, that mothers are both urban and rural, straight and queer, partnered and single, that many women mother with disabilities, that many mothers are poor or working class, that most mothers work outside the home in paid employment, that social and political activism is a part of many mothers' lives, that women mother older children as well as young children, that some mothers live apart from their children, that many women raise children with whom they have no biological relation as with adoption and in blended families and finally that all these mothers are good mothers who raise their children with love and care equal to that of the normative/idealized "good" mother. (O'Reilly, *Mothers* 3)

While the psychology literature tends to understand resistance as a binary category, with its presence or absence, resistance to the institution of motherhood can be any oppositional activity that allows those carrying out motherwork to hold space. It concerns those activities that talk back to unjust power relations and say "no" to the logics of oppression (Rosales and Langhout). In this sense, resistance in its everyday attire is neither pure nor separate from power. It can undermine some forms of power while simultaneously upholding other forms (Vinthagen and Johansson). Practically, everyday resistance to motherhood dynamically takes on different shapes, as it responds to and emerges in specific, situated contexts: from silence to songs and humour, from angry gestures to laissez-faire attitudes, from verbose complaints to sighs and shrugs, from blunt, unmasked exhaustion, anxiety to gossip and questioning (e.g., Collins; Cruz; Davis; Federici).

Everyday resistance to the institution of motherhood is everywhere. Sometimes heard. Seldom listened to. For our beliefs, our normative beliefs as to what other mothers feel, do, and value remain unchanged, their voices silenced, as the spectral presence of the "go(o)d mother"[5], with its ubiquity, maintains its hold. This, the perceptive paradox, is of importance. It certainly reveals the pervasive influence of patriarchy, of the power of its structural agents, be these of the social, legal, political, or economic domains. It similarly bespeaks the virulence of its ideological assumptions (see O'Reilly), which are woven into each pore of our societal bodies, and illustrates the repetition of thoughts and practices performing patriarchy and the maintenance of a power system in which marginalization and complicity are at times inexorably intertwined.

Everyday resistance is widespread, and our failure not so much to hear it but to represent it in our mind and beyond ordinary. Everyday resistance is raw, unadorned. It going unnoticed allows for the crude backbone of mothering to be removed from the public view and narrative (see Ruth Robbins cited in O'Reilly, *We Need to Talk*)—as are the ills, as are the dead. The muffling is almost unremarkable. It is in the dramatic indignation of the new mothers blaming previous generations of women for not warning them enough of the difficulty of the mothering task. It is in the common matrophobic utterance[6], whereby women vocalize their fear of becoming their own mother. It is in the humorous references to the dementia of the impossible mother-in-law. It is in the uneventful encounter at the morning school drop off, which already escapes the confines of memory by mid-morning. At the core of these examples though lie mothers' voices, blunt killjoy-like utterances and behaviours (Ahmed), unpleasant and often distant echoes of the fallen masks (Maushart).

To understand how and why the voices of resistance go unheard, to facilitate the emergence of these voices and the stifling of the spiral of silence, to ensure the context of their expression allows for them to be heard, is but essential for feminist work. As Audre Lorde puts it, "Where the words of women are crying to be heard, we must each of us recognize our responsibility to seek those words out, to read them and share them and examine them in their pertinence to our lives" (43). And she continues: "That we not hide behind the mockeries of separations that have been imposed upon us and which so often we accept as our own.... And all the other endless ways in which we rob ourselves of ourselves and each other" (43).

The perceptive paradox illustrates how in a context of pluralistic ignorance, the explicit, vocal expression of discontent vis-à-vis the (injunctive and perceived descriptive) norm is simply not enough to uproot inaccurate, non-representative normative beliefs (wherein the perceived descriptive norm does not match what people do). At least two further requirements are to be met. First, authors of the discontent are to be perceived as legitimate group members. As the prototypical, hegemonic representation of the "go(o)d mother" remains that of the white, cisgender, heterosexual, and middle-to-upper class married mother, the resistance of most, whichever its form, often goes unheard.

Furthermore, beyond the (improbable) inclusion of the odd killjoy in the mother group, the alteration of normative beliefs is likely contingent upon another requirement: The resistance is to be perceived as representative of other group members. The resistance cannot be merely individual and thereby pathological (or pathologized) in its occurrence. The resistance is to be understood as collective, however minimally. This would allow for the normative beliefs held by the others (i.e., meta-meta-beliefs) to be perceived as similarly amended; the mothering of the perceiver finally deemed safe from the collective surveillant gaze.

Resisting Resistance to Normative Motherhood

The process leading to the alteration of normative beliefs is contingent upon our ability to listen. If simmers of resistance are indeed everywhere, then the general quietness of the many transcribes a lack of harmonization, a lack of synchronicity among and beyond those currently oppressed. Which individual factors then participate in inducing such a lack of symbiosis, in permitting the ghost of the "go(o)d mother" to permeate our minds and bodies when in solitude and overworked?

In the global North, we could first of course invoke high levels of self-centeredness or narcissism. The sighs, humor, pain of others would remain unheard because of an inability to be enthralled by anything beyond ourselves, an inability to focus on beings situated outside our microworld, all because of unhealthy levels of self-esteem among recent generations (see Twenge et al.). Our capacity to hear and listen would thereby be minimal, and so would our ability to be moved to the point of representation and ultimately action. This tendency would be all the more exacerbated, given mothers' own hectic circumstances and motherhood-related challenges.

Temporality can also be understood as an important component of the absence of synchronicity. Mothering, as a practice, is not a linear or monolithic experience. It is a diverse, never-ending journey characterized by random, emergent occurrences, which incessantly disrupt hoped-for routines. Despite the societal focus on and adoration for children's first years, the physical and sociopsychological experience of mothering stretches over time, well beyond toddler years. The everyday entails its set of, if not issues, at least challenges to solve at once. As previous stages are passed and new ones reached, the specifics of our earlier, so recent experiences vanish before the acute urgency of the day. The pain associated with previous times becomes less perceptible, its intensity mitigated as well. Minds and hearts are now leaning towards the unknown to come, away, disconnected from those others located at different milestones on the mothering journey. Although individuals who move on to later stages can still cognitively mobilize their memories, the little resources they have available—in terms of time, attention, and energy—limit their ability to empathize and ultimately to hear.

In the Western world, voices can also fail to be heard because of the widespread tendency to associate people's difficulties with their personal qualities (or lack thereof). In the psychology literature, this tendency is referred to as the fundamental attribution error (Ross). Individuals tend to explain people's behaviours by resorting to dispositional attributes to the detriment of contextual ones. Said differently, others are seen as responsible for their behaviours and for what happens to them (see also Lerner). In practice, such cognitive tendency is likely to lead mothers to dissociate the narratives of their peers from their own. Discourses of struggle are reframed into discourses of unadjusted, incorrect mothering practice, attributed to personal shortcomings. Here, then, this missed occasion to join and be in communion, to synchronize mothering experiences, not only contributes to the silencing of voices but also allows normative motherhood to remain unscathed and endure.

In examining why the simmers of everyday resistance are seldom listened to, we have so far focused on individual characteristics: self-esteem, perception of time, self-serving comparisons, and representations of mothering. Let us however not fall prey to the fundamental attribution error since the tendency to silence others and ourselves can be first and foremost rooted in a social context that relentlessly desolidarizes our humanity, erects ramparts between bodies and minds, and commodifies all aspects of our lives.

For many, mothering is an isolated practice. This isolation is that of the walls of our apartments and houses, that of the boundaries of our families and (present or virtual) communities as well. It is isolation within the geography of our homes, where the crudeness of mothering is more and more aestheticized, the backdrop of the masquerade being more attuned to the farce at play. Ironically, the gradual takeover from the private sphere—with its apolitical perception—of an ever more depoliticized public sphere allows the masquerade to thrive in an almost placid and amenable environment. Isolation also exists between caregivers and cared for, where the burden of life-determining charge is confined to the abled adults.

Isolation, however, goes well beyond the mothering world, for its universe is the neoliberal culture of possessive individualism. This realm is replete with disconnected, parallel selves, each on a multichoice path of ongoing development, who idolize negative freedom, a freedom from—that is, the liberty to be let alone with one's belongings. These selves tolerate the protective arms and gaze of state authority so long as the tutelary power defends their freedom from, their comfort, and, in so doing, alleviates the nervousness that accompanies this form of liberty (Pensky). Negative freedom is then freedom for the self and its extension in the form of offspring, from the interference of others. It implies the liberty to enjoy one's possessions, a freedom from constraints that also reflects a desire for and possible experience of radical abstraction from context (Adams et al.). By ricochet, however, the focalization on the self, its close family, and belongings (provided that progeny is differentiated from property) affects its surroundings, local and distant, as the individualistic centration and grip foster social and economic injustice (for the role of legacy, see Fremeaux).

In the words of Tocqueville, individualism

> disposes each member of the community to sever himself from the mass of his fellows and to draw apart with his family… so that after he has thus formed a little circle of his own, he willingly leaves society at large to itself; selfishness blights the germ of all virtue; individualism, at first, only saps the virtue of public life, but in the long run it attacks and destroys all others and is at length absorbed in downright selfishness. (482)

Individualism is then to be distinguished from any personal disposition and from selfishness among others. We, mothers and non-mothers alike are the effects of liberal social and political institutions and of the epistemic and ontological hegemon these accompany. Individualism, Tocqueville suggests, corresponds to a mode of subjectivity, one that takes the form of an ambivalent set of contradictory yearnings. In individualism, we develop a fervent fondness for an assortment of pleasures that we see as both ignominious and taxing, as these satisfactions turn into a form of labour in the long run. As individuals, we yearn similarly for material wealth, the lasting value of which we paradoxically concurrently suspect. Social status appears as both critical and trivial, while our economic prospect engenders indomitable anxiety and inconstant optimism all at once. The individuals, as they simultaneously laud and despise the indetermination and vagueness of their pecuniary future, fall prey to an entrenched bitterness over structural economic comparative loss, which is strictly understood through an interpersonal lens. We are vehemently attached to a form of equality that is concurrently outraged and reinforced by the potential of deviance in others. Individuals look up to their political leadership with the unwavering expectation that it will competently assume its public duties, unperturbed by the oddity of exchanging their political freedom for the prospect of increased material comfort and wellbeing for themselves. They demand that their autonomy be unbroken, as they long for an omnipotent authority that takes care of their grievances in response to their perceived inequities (Tocqueville; Pensky).

In their quality of subjects of the liberal power then, beings of the individualism culture experience contradictory longings. These longings are in a way reminiscent of the phenomenology of the everyday mothering journey, and in particular of the perceptive paradox that allows the unflickered, albeit perturbing coexistence of the voices of mothers with that of the "go(o)d mother". The conflicting expectations regarding autonomy and political deference on the part of liberal subjects are similarly not without reminding the canon of intensive (also responsive) mothering, wherein children's individual needs are constantly anticipated and responded to while assuring their growing independence. This echo lays bare a process of systemic reproduction and regeneration of political subjectivity through reproductive work. Individualism and the institution of motherhood that sustains it allow, on one hand, its material contribution to successful individuation and, on the other, its simultaneous imposition of homogeneity and conformity on all subjects (Pensky).

Individualism then not only provides the context of mothering. Its values and epistemology infuse motherwork, its experience and practice. The contemporary global context of mothering features the neoliberal form of individualism, which stresses freedom from constraints on growth and self-expression above other liberal values (e.g., equality and civic obligation) (Deleuze and Guattari; see Adams et al.). In ecologies of neoliberal individualism, quotidian life is experienced through the lens of opportunities for choice and behavior conceived as resulting from one's choices (Adams et al.; Teo). The emphasis placed on freedom and self-determination is appealing, particularly for those engaged in upward mobility aspirations, in an everlasting search of constraints transcendence. Importantly, neo-liberalism extends the logic of market-based liberal capitalism to all aspects of life (e.g., Klein). Individuals, as entrepreneurial selves, groom themselves and their progeny as products to respond to the demands of the social and economic marketplace (Foucault; Gershon). Their ever-growing busyness with its innumerable projects, undertakings and enterprises bespeaks the frantic temporality of the market, where business as productivity denotes survivance.

This state of affairs is illustrated in the generalized proclivity to certainly understand ourselves and our mothering practice in comparison with others (see social comparison; Festinger) and through a can-do-better mentality, whereby one's practice can and is to be perfected though cognitive and individual adjustments. This is the realm of the mother-entrepreneur. Motherwork, its success and future, is apprehended as mildly affected by context and mostly dependent on our abilities to renew and adapt our practice and ultimately our personalities and ourselves. This work calls for the identification and implementation of (performing) performance strategies, which are, coincidentally, at our (expensive) disposal and ready to be picked from the vast and prolific market of hands-on solutions – available on shelves and couches. Paradoxically, then, the legitimacy of our experience is lost; the voice within silenced in a spiral of perfectionization. As we proudly climb the expertization ladder, the paroxysm of our past difficulties is soon overlooked—until the next ones, experienced in the isolation of our hardly-gained, select expertise, until the next ones then, which will not fail to mobilize unsolved experiential memories.

The marketization is not limited to the (performant) performing of the self, as the perfectibility of body, mind, behaviour, and even offspring become not only accessible but also self-determined. Children's flawlessness appears as the foreseeable expected outcome of maternal and mothering perfection (Almond). The marketization spreads to the social stage of the entrepreneurial selves, where others are tolerated insofar as they sustain the selves' growth. The masks mothers and non-mothers put on then, which "deny and repress what [they] experience, misrepresent it, even to [themselves]" (Maushart 1-2) attest to the aesthetical quest, standardization, and to the incessant appraisal and ultimately commodification of all. Everyday resistance as it arises through the voices of the others is heard in its usefulness for the entrepreneurial self, not beyond. As masks irremediably fuse with their vehicle and as normativity becomes internalized, the (authentic) waters of the (internal or remote) simmers recede, rendering their presence more inaudible still.

In the value-laden realm of neoliberal subjectivity, the prospect of individual economic and psychological wealth gain dictates a forward, though lonely, trajectory in a market-formed universe, where the perceived norm is evidently that of self-interest. Incidentally, missed encounters with the voices of everyday mothers who resist bear the potential to further deepen the trenches of individualized mothering. This is the case when what is retained from the encounter takes the form of a self-esteem booster. When away from the other, what is remembered is that the "I" is fine. The "I" is not as desperate. It is in a better situation. It is better. Again, the other's voice is unheard. The focus turns on the self and towards the "go(o)d mother". Still, distrust in the potential person who would overuse others comes to legitimize preemptive monitoring, in both its formal and informal forms. Masks then are further held onto as they maintain the disciplinary power at bay. In parallel starts the pathologization of the unstandardized, the exposed or market-free/-outlaw barbarians.

Normative motherhood then, its maintenance and resistance, far from resting on the dispositional shortcomings of atomized agents, are but the foreseeable outcome of a context of neoliberal individualism, wherein negative freedom, comparative personal growth, and advantage, as well as physical and psychological comfort, accompany a marketized subjectivity of barely noticed, though depleting ambivalent contrasts, caught in an apoliticization spiral. If this context transpires in motherhood as institution, it is its infusion in mothering, in the phenomenology of motherwork, and in the motives then for and processes against everyday resistance, which needs to retain our attention if the overcoming of normative motherhood is to be achieved. In this vein, for instance, the foregrounding of the discomfort arising from the irreconcilable disconnect between the "go(o)d mother" and mothering—be this identifiable through the voices of the others or ours—in some way calls for the intervention of an authority, which would ensure psychological and physical safety. The longing for a formal, inflexible type of equality in comfort and undisturbedness similarly epitomizes the voice of the neoliberal individualist within us (Tocqueville; see Pensky; Schulman), for this further contributes to the dissociation of our future from that of the collective. An individual and thereby complicit form of resisting.

Let us, therefore, hold on to the discomfort, for the phenomenology of mothering lays bare the disempowering, politically depleting nature of the neoliberal context of our experience. This discomfort holds a radical mobilizing potential, an opportunity for the privileged to join in, through and beyond the experience of (some) hurting and violence, to work towards the emergence of another form of being, a different subjectivity. The discomfort, suffered collectively, allows for the direness of a systemic change to be experienced not as an aggregate, but in togetherness.

As it reproduces, legitimizes, and reinforces the authority of neoliberalism and its colonization of everyday life (Adams et al.), psychology, in its disciplinary conceptualization of normative processes, apprehends the others in their (social or cognitive) usefulness to the self, thereby essentializing a (perceived) self-interest norm. Such comprehension of the other, however, is far from inescapable. Suffice it to turn our gaze to forms of queer mothering (Park) in which the norm, in its interpersonal utility, is abandoned—not in a betterment enterprise but in the mere transcendence of normativity. There, the "go(o)d mother" is no more. The "go(o)d mother" is dead.

If queering prefigures alternative kinds of subjectivity, normative forms of mothering are not without presenting seeds of hope, as occurrences of selflessness and experience of interdependence apparent in the human expression of devotion to the progeny, remind us that love, as stronghold of the private sphere, remains unparadoxically a critical and yet often silenced stronghold of the political.

Conclusion

Normative motherhood is inseparable from the sociopolitical context in which it is rooted and evolves. So are its diffusion, maintenance, and resistance. Any serious endeavour to resist normative motherhood, thus, entails resisting neoliberal individualism, its epistemic and ontological hegemon, as well as the subjectivity it brings about. This project is not concerned with extinguishing the fire of our burning house (Baldwin). It is concerned with radically deconstructing our house, with finding new materials to allow, welcome, and embrace collective experiencing. It calls for the death of the "go(o)d mother" in order to give birth to the expanded subjectivity of the collective work of politics, to the potential of exercising political freedom in concert, intersubjectively, as embedded in ordinary life and its collective experience (Arendt; Pensky; Shulman; Tocqueville). Only then will the voices within be finally heard and honoured.

Endnotes

1. Intensive parenting (also called responsive or sensitive parenting) corresponds to a child-centred approach in which the caregiver's constant involvement, their reactivity (both verbal and emotional), and systematic presentations of age-appropriate and personality-

adapted stimulations are critical for a child's healthy development (see Nomaguchi and Milkie).

2. A distinction is made in the sociopsychological literature between descriptive norms, that is, what in-group members typically do, and injunctive norms, that is, what in-group members approve or disapprove of (see Cialdini).

3. Patriarchal normative motherhood refers to a series of ideological assumptions (O'Reilly), among these: the beliefs that all women want to be mothers and that maternity is the basis of female identity; that maternal ability and motherlove are innate to all mothers; that all mothers find joy and purpose in motherhood; that the birth mother is the real and authentic mother; that motherwork is confined to the reproductive realm of the home; and that the nuclear family is the specific domain of maternal identity and practice. Childrearing should also be expert driven and a nonpolitical undertaking.

4. The term "god mother" is used to foreground the pervasiveness and influence of the representation of the "good mother," an anxiety-triggering representation revered through omission. The invocation of the "god mother," as epitome of the injunctive norm, sheds light on the beliefs and behaviors attributed to others in the realm of motherhood—that is, normative beliefs. Other mothers' attitudes, values, and behaviours are understood through the lens of their presumed adhesion to the figure of the "god mother," an adhesion analogous to religious faith. It is perceived then that many revere the figure of the "god mother." The relationship between believers and the "god mother" is not only individual in nature; it is seen as firm, unshakable, and unquestionable. Assuming that other mothers are devoted believers leads to perceiving them as striving to abide by the "god mother's" precepts, just as the faithful act as guardians of the holy. The "god mother" is reminiscent of, in Freudian conceptualization, the voice of the superego, the internalization of the commands of the fatherly figure, which are representative of cultural law.

5. Pluralistic ignorance entails the perception of a descriptive norm, which does not correspond to people's actual behaviors or attitudes. The fact that individuals in a situation of pluralistic ignorance

do not abide by the injunctive norm may arise in part from the practical impossibility of doing so, or from attitudinal disalignment with the norm.

6. Matrophobic refers to the fear of becoming one's mother (Rich).

Works Cited

Adams, Glenn, et al. "The Psychology of Neoliberalism and the Neoliberalism of Psychology." *Journal of Social Issues*, vol. 75, no. 1, 2019, pp. 189-216.

Ahmed, Sara. *Living a Feminist Life*. Duke University Press, 2017.

Almond, Barbara. *The Monster Within: The Hidden Side of Motherhood*. University of California Press, 2010.

Arendt, Hannah. *On Revolution*. Penguin, 1963.

Arendell, Terry. "Conceiving and Investigating Motherhood: The Decade's Scholarship." *Journal of Marriage and Family*, vol. 62, no. 4, 2000, pp. 1192-1207.

Baldwin, James. *The Fire Next Time*. Dial Press, 1963.

Belsky, Jay, Richard Lerner, and Graham Spanier. *The Child in the Family*. Addison-Wesley/Addison Wesley Longman, 1984.

Cialdini, Robert B. "Crafting Normative Messages to Protect the Environment." *Current Directions in Psychological Science*, vol. 12, no. 4, 2003, pp. 105-09.

Collins, Patricia H. *Fighting Words: Black Women and the Search for Justice*. University of Minnesota Press, 2018.

Criado-Perez, Caroline. *Invisible Women: Exposing Data Bias in a World Designed for Men*. Harry N. Abrams, 2019.

Crittenden, Ann. *The Price of Motherhood: Why the Most Important Job the World is Still the Least Valued*. Henry Holt and Company, 2001.

Cruz, Cindy. "When Does Resistance Begin." *Cracks in the Schoolyard: Confronting Latino Educational Inequality* edited by Gilberto Conchas and Briana Hinga, Teachers College Press, 2016, pp. 131-43.

Davis, Angela. "Reflections on the Black Woman's Role in the Community of Slaves." *The Black Scholar*, vol. 12, no. 6, 1981, pp. 2-15.

Deleuze, Gilles, and Felix Guattari. *A Thousand Plateaus: Capitalism and*

Schizophrenia. University of Minnesota, 1987.

Faircloth, Charlotte. "Intensive Parenting and the Expansion of Parenting." *Parenting Culture Studies*, edited by Ellie Lee, et al., Palgrave Macmillan, 2014, pp. 25-50.

Federici, Silvia. *Witch, Witch-Hunting, and Women*. PM Press, 2018.

Festinger, Leon. "A Theory of Social Comparison Processes." *Human Relations*, vol. 7, no. 2, 1954, pp. 117-140.

Foucault, Michel. *The Birth of Biopolitics*. Palgrave Macmillan, 2008.

Fremeaux, Nicolas. *Les Nouveaux Héritiers*. Seuil, 2018.

Gershon, Ilana. "Neoliberal Agency." *Current Anthropology*, vol. 52, no. 4, 2011, pp. 537555.

Hank Karsten, and Anja Steinbach. "The Virus Changed Everything, Didn't It? Couples' Division of Housework and Childcare before and during the Corona Crisis." *Journal of Family Research*, vol. 33, no. 1, 2021, pp. 99-114.

Hays, Sharon. *The Cultural Contradictions of Motherhood*. Yale University Press, 1996.

Klein, Elise. *Developing Minds: Psychology, Neoliberalism and Power*. Routledge, 2016.

Maushart, Susan. *The Mask of Motherhood*. Penguin Books, 2000.

Lerner, Melvin J., and Carolyn H. Simmons. "Observer's Reaction to the 'Innocent Victim': Compassion or Rejection?" *Journal of Personality and Social Psychology*, vol. 4, no. 2, 1966, p. 203.

Lorde, Audre. "The Transformation of Silence into Language and Action." *Identity Politics in the Women's Movement*, 1977, pp. 81-84.

Miller, Dale T., and Cathy McFarland. "Pluralistic Ignorance: When Similarity Is Interpreted as Dissimilarity." *Journal of Personality and Social Psychology*, vol. 53, no. 2, 1987, p. 298.

Nomaguchi, Kei, and Milkie, Melissa. "Parenthood and Well-Being: A Decade in Review." *Journal of Marriage and the Family*, vol. 82, no. 1, 2020, pp. 198-223.

Noelle-Neumann, Elisabeth. *The Spiral of Silence: Public Opinion—Our Social Skin*. University of Chicago Press, 1993.

O'Reilly, Andrea. *Matricentric Feminism: Theory, Activism, and Practice*. Demeter Press, 2016.

O'Reilly, Andrea. *Mothers, Mothering and Motherhood Across Cultural Differences: A Reader.* Demeter Press, 2014.

O'Reilly, Andrea. "We Need to Talk about Patriarchal Motherhood: Essentialization, Naturalization and Idealization in Lionel Shriver's We Need to Talk about Kevin". *Journal of the Motherhood Initiative for Research and Community Involvement,* vol. 7, no. 1, 2016.

Park, Shelley. "Queering and Querying Motherhood." *The Routledge Companion to Motherhood,* edited by Andrea O'Reilly, Routledge, 2019, pp. 63-76.

Pensky, Max. "Radical Critique and Late Epistemology." *Authoritarianism: Three Inquiries in Critical Theory,* edited by Wendy Brown, Peter E. Gordon, and Max Pensky. University of Chicago Press, 2018, pp 85-124.

Portelinha, Isabelle, and Guy Elcheroth. "From Marginal to Mainstream: The Role of Perceived Social Norms in the Rise of a Far Right Movement." *European Journal of Social Psychology,* vol. 46, no. 6, 2016, pp. 661-71.

Prentice, Deborah A., and Dale T. Miller. "Pluralistic Ignorance and Alcohol Use on Campus: Some Consequences of Misperceiving the Social Norm." *Journal of Personality and Social Psychology,* vol. 64, no. 2, 1993, p. 243.

Rich, Adrienne. *Of Woman Born: Motherhood as Experience and Institution.* Norton, 1986.

Rosales, Christine, and Regina Day Langhout. "Just Because We Don't See It, Doesn't Mean It's Not There: Everyday Resistance in Psychology." *Social and Personality Psychology Compass,* vol. 14, no. 1, 2020, p. e12508.

Ross, Lee. "The Intuitive Psychologist and His Shortcomings: Distortions in the Attribution Process." *Advances in Experimental Social Psychology,* edited by L/ Berkowitz, Academic Press, 1977, pp. 173-220.

Shulman, George. "Rethinking Equality." *International Social Science Journal,* vol. 67, pp. 223-24, 2017, pp. 11-20.

Teo, Thomas. "Homo Neoliberalus: From Personality to Forms of Subjectivity." *Theory & Psychology,* vol. 28, no. 5, 2018, pp. 581-99.

Tocqueville, Alexis. *Democracy in America.* Winthrop D. 2000.

Twenge, Jean M., et al. "Egos Inflating Over Time: A Cross Temporal Meta Analysis of the Narcissistic Personality Inventory." *Journal of Personality*, vol. 76, no. 4, 2008, pp. 875-902.

Vinthagen, Stellan, and Anna Johansson. "Everyday Resistance: Exploration of a Concept and Its Theories." *Resistance Studies Magazine*, vol. 1, no. 1, 2013, pp. 1-46.

Wall, Glenda. "'Love Builds Brains': Representations of Attachment and Children's Brain Development in Parenting Education Material." *Sociology of Health & Illness*, vol. 40, no. 3, 2018, pp. 395-409.

Chapter 12.

Supermom's Support Group: Exploring and Resisting Normative Motherhood

Rachel E. Stough and Elizabeth A. Bennett

The internal push and pull between acceding to and actively resisting the expectation to mother selflessly, intensively, and exclusively is a source of suffering for many mothers. The unforgiving standards of the motherhood ideal prescribe the dissolution of one's sense of self in favor of a oneness with one's children (Parker). Although raising children is a challenging task for all parents, it is particularly formidable for those assigned the mother role (by self-assignment and/or by social assignment). Empirical data demonstrate that mothers have a significantly lower sense of wellbeing (e.g., less happiness, more stress, and more fatigue) as compared with fathers (Musick, Meier, and Flood). This finding is decidedly related to the aspect of ideal motherhood, which requires an abandonment of one's needs and desires and, therefore, one's sense of wellness. A motherhood that approximates the ideal "demands of mothers maternal 'instinct' rather than intelligence, selflessness rather than self-realization, relation to others rather than the creation of self" (Rich 42). Certainly not all mothers attempt to reach this ideal to the same extent. Importantly, many mothers cannot afford to mother exclusively, as doing so requires various degrees of privilege (e.g., financial security). However, the pressure to approximate the ideal, regardless of privilege or the capacity to fulfill the imperative, affects the lives of mothers almost universally. Despite the ubiquity of this experience, normative support spaces for mothers often enforce the maternal ideal by facilitating comparison and judgment between mothers. Given that mothers experience needs rooted in the universality of the human condition (i.e., mothers are human beings too), the social pressure to mother in a way that emulates the ideal, coupled with the inevitable failure to fulfill this impossible task, often opposes personal growth, a sense of presence, and overall life satisfaction. Grounded in our lived experience as working mothers to young children—struggling to navigate normative motherhood authentically and often feeling unsupported in that struggle—we argue that nurturing relationships between mothers and critical dialogue are imperative in resisting the deleterious effects of the motherhood ideal.

In this chapter, we contextualize the sociopolitical origins of the maternal ideal, explicate the role of normative mothers' support groups in reinforcing that ideal, and critique the resulting imperative for mothers to become supermoms to meet the demands of the ideal. Following this critique of supermotherhood, we share our experiences of living in relation to this phenomenon in the form of creative nonfiction; our writing is grounded in our identities as mother-scholars and practicing psychotherapists. Using a well-worn hallmark of modern mothering—the mom group—we play with the metaphor of a supermom support group to explore the complexities and controversies of challenging normative motherhood in community with other mothers. In doing so, we highlight the ways in which normative motherhood isolates mothers in their suffering even in the face of potential supports. Finally, as an antidote to normative motherhood, we call for a mother community—which advocates for a subversion of the oppressive ideal and a fostering of resilience through resonance with other mothers and radical acceptance of one's ambivalence.

The Sociopolitical Birth of the Ideal Mother and Her Legacy

Prior to the Industrial Revolution, the home was a place of work for the whole family and, thus, women's lives did not centre on mothering. Additionally, because adult children and extended family members tended to remain in the home, childrearing was a community effort, offering mothers built-in support (Chodorow). This critical support was lost beginning in the mid-eighteenth century when industrialization relocated work outside of the home, fracturing the community, as family members followed jobs to new locations (Rich). Amid this social shift, women were "idolized for their service" and regarded as "domestic guardians of the nation's moral and spiritual well-being" for remaining at home to raise their children alone (Parker 174). Based on this new ideology, motherhood became conflated with womanhood, and more limited gender roles solidified the moral and social imperative for exclusive and intensive mothering.

One might assume that in contemporary society, mothers have been liberated by the loosening of gender roles and an increased appreciation for non-normative family structures. However, although social ideology and economic needs have evolved over the last few centuries, raising a child is still largely considered a maternal duty. Although many more fathers have become involved in sharing these responsibilities today, they do not face the same judgment or social pressure to parent in a way that risks alienation from their selfhood. Furthermore, our current economy necessitates more than one income for many families, and, as such, many mothers are working mothers. This norm violates ideal motherhood, as many families rely on childcare workers to help raise children (O'Reilly; Ridgeway and Correll). Mothers remain unsupported in the workplace, expected to effortlessly manage work and mothering without one impeding the other. As a result, mothers are often valued less than other workers and many experience significant wage and opportunity gaps (Abetz and Moore). Whether a working mom or a stay-at-home mom, most mothers are forced to find creative ways to do it all, whereas partners, family members, and employers take this impossible standard of motherhood for granted.

Isolation in normative motherhood is partially because our culture widely accepts a biologically deterministic view, which posits that mothers are naturally better parents than fathers and thus should carry the bulk of the child-rearing responsibilities for the well-being of the children. Such assumptions result in lower social support for mothers, which often leads to lower life satisfaction, greater stress, and more intense and persistent psychological distress (Rizzo, Schiffrin, and Liss). This essentialist view is reified by the professionals who detect and treat psychological distress. The medical community, in its goal of eliminating health risks for young children, often positions mothers as solely responsible for their children's health, making excessive worry a maternal duty (Menkedick). Similarly, various foundational theories of psychology problematically essentialize mothering, such that the problems of living are grounded in the dysfunctional mother-child relationship. Implied here is that mothers do not experience development; rather, mothering is static and a natural disposition—a mother is either good or bad. In other words, behind every psychotherapy client is a mother who failed to meet the ideal (Baraitser and Noack). Because these social structures uncritically maintain the dated standards of ideal motherhood, contemporary normative motherhood demands the fulfillment of eighteenth-century childrearing without the social or economic support necessary today.

Mothers' Support Groups Reinforce the Motherhood Ideal

Although adequate support for mothers is increasingly rare, there are various forms of normative mothers' support groups, including groups based on particular occupations (e.g., Mothers in Academia) and mothering skill-building groups (e.g., La Leche League) (Kawash). However, by simply offering support rather than raising critical consciousness, these groups tend to orient mothers towards the maternal ideal by helping them to meet social expectations rather than challenge them. Perhaps most notably, Mothers of Preschoolers (MOPS) International is a network of mothering groups based in religious communities. Although the intended goal of MOPS groups is to offer a space to critically explore motherhood, one explicit objective is to remind "mothers that they are doing 'the most important job in the world'" (Newman and Henderson 485). This reflects the conceptualization of motherhood as a political and moral duty and implies that a mother who experiences ambivalence about her job is failing to fulfill that duty. While support groups like these do offer the opportunity for much needed connection, they may also leave mothers vulnerable to surveillance of any thoughts or behaviours that are misaligned with the group's particular orientation to the mothering ideal. Without actively critiquing the ideal, these groups risk reorienting mothers towards a particular way of mothering that ultimately threatens their wellbeing.

The Cost of Achieving Supermotherhood

With rigid social structures and mothers policing one another relative to the ideal, the private is always public in motherhood. In a dizzying irony, "today's mother...is faced with a set of normative prescriptions about what she *should* do coupled with the assertions that there are *no* hard and fast rules about mother[ing], and that childrearing should be an individual, private affair" (Parker 67). For many mothers, the impossibility of intensive mothering while maintaining a full-time career sets them up for inadequacy in both realms and alienation from their personal and embodied needs. In other words, avoiding burnout and successfully rising to the impossible challenge of ideal motherhood requires disembodiment, or rather the adoption of a super body that transcends humanly needs—a supermom.

To be called a supermom is both a compliment and a curse. The supermom fulfills each of her duties without fumbling (at least not in a way that is outwardly perceptible). She is unilaterally perfect and necessarily transcends her humanity. This metaphor, which prizes pure altruism and complete devotion to mothering without attention to one's own desires as an embodied, psychologically nuanced being, unequivocally serves the patriarchal maternal ideal.

The supermom trope is derived from the superheroines that appeared in comics from the 1960s to the 1980s. Superheroines, representing the second-wave feminist mantra that women can do it all, were characteristically strong and independent and were normatively beautiful. Albeit inspirational for women and girls to see themselves represented in this popular art form, superheroines in comics were subversive in their strength and independence, but they still preserved traditional gender roles and mothering ideals in their protectiveness, nurturing, and selflessness. They were also isolated in their specialness—or perhaps, tokenness—represented as the only superwoman among supermen. This parallels the isolation of maternal performance in pursuit of the ideal. These characters were born out of the identity of the working mom, who straddles public and private realms in order to find a nontraditional way to achieve the ideal. One must accept all aspects of the maternal ideal in order to successfully do it all (D'Amore).

An Illustration of the Pitfalls of Supermotherhood

Through the medium of creative writing, we offer below our personal experiences of attempting supermotherhood with the hopes that the reader may not only gain insight into the binds of normative motherhood but may also feel an embodied resonance with our experiences, bringing the reader into dialogue with these norms along with us. The first narrative is written by Rachel, a first-time mother of a young toddler navigating motherhood while training to become a psychotherapist and completing a doctorate in clinical psychology. The second narrative belongs to Elizabeth, a mother to a young child and a toddler, who balances her mothering with an academic career while also working as a licensed clinical psychologist. Each creative nonfiction piece is a recounting of the internal monologues of shame resulting from incidents of falling short relative to the maternal ideal, revealing our unworthiness of the supermom title. Despite how common it is for mothers to have such self-deprecating reactions to ordinary experiences, even when given the opportunity to seek support, mothers tend to internalize these experiences and suffer alone for fear of outing themselves as inadequate. Here, we share just a sampling of the many moments in which we, as two moms trying to do it all, have felt oppressed by normative mothering standards and alone in our mothering.

Supermoms' Support Group

[1]

On an asteroid not too far away and within audio range of the nap-time monitor, supermom entered the waiting room, reluctant and ready. She doffed her unlaundered, milk-stained cape and shuffled through the rack of similarly worn capes searching for a vacant but expecting hanger. "Is this usually a yoga studio?" she wondered. "I'll have to find out for some time down the road when I get back into it." Although she knew that road was long, she always added hopeful stops along the way. Finally resting her cape, she folded herself to attend to her boots—the red patent leather was tighter around her toes than she remembered. She peeled them off with relief and situated them on the rack next to a tattered and dulled purple pair. "At least mine still stand upright," she thought with an eyebrow raise of fleeting conceit. As supermom turned towards the door, she noted that below the sign designating this "Supermoms' Support Group" read an invitation to leave one's mask at the door. With no intention of removing her mask, she scoffed, "I'd have put on concealer today to hide these eyebags if I was willing to remove my mask." Her self-deprecation dissolved in a sighed reminder: "I should really get more sleep."

With her next inhale, supermom pushed through the door to the chilled, echoey room and took her place within the circle of plastic folding chairs holding the sunken, overburdened bodies of other still-masked supermoms. Our heroine had come here for the first time looking for a place to unashamedly feel out loud. Yet after a litany of shame-laced stories beginning with "He's a good dad, but..." and "I love my baby, but...," it seemed that these other moms were not here for the same purpose. Emboldened by dissent, supermom sat up in her chair, removed her mask (revealing her unconcealed exhaustion), inhaled heavily, and began to say..."

A tiny but forceful objection cuts through my fantasy, and I am brought back to this moment. Was I zoning out now of all times? I should really go to bed earlier. Cold, fat drops of rain slip down my arm while the darkened sky shakes with a continuous roar. I am sitting halfway into the back seat of my car in the daycare parking lot in the middle of a thunderstorm, battling my most worthy adversary—my toddler. He has been refusing to sit down in his car seat for the last half-hour. With every passing parent and teacher, I sink further into embarrassment and despair. I remind him gently, while doing my best to conceal my growing exasperation, that I hear his "no" and that Mommy's job is to keep him safe on the ride home by putting him in his chair. He does not accept this plea and counters with his newest, most effective weapon, "NO!" He goes stiff-legged and rolls off to the side. He hits. He bites. Until I give up and I hold him to my chest. He holds me back. He giggles. He plays with my unkempt, increasingly frizzing curls as we sit half in the rain. I sing him a song about puppies through silent tears. "I used to fit back here," I think, "I should really workout more. I've got to get to bed earlier so that I can get more sleep so that I can work out more."

After a brief cessation and a cuddle, the battle begins again. My child continues to reject my attempts to secure him and screams as if in pain. I panic and look around hoping that no one thinks that I would harm my child. What if I am harming my child? What if I'm holding him too tightly and he gets a bruise, and someone is called and they take him away from me. We pause again. I hold and shush us both for comfort. His little hand rubs my wet shoulder, and he says, "Rain!" I didn't know he knew that word. He's getting so big. I'm so proud until I remind myself that his teacher taught him that, not me. I have the audacity to be in school and to work, and I failed to teach him the word "rain" myself. We begin again.

Here, in this parking lot, I dodge both flailing arms from my child and judgmental glances from mothers who must have forgotten that they once fought this fight. Or maybe they just see through me. Perhaps they can tell that I haven't the supernatural powers of a supermom. That I loathe the isolation of my secret lair, and I struggle to maintain the limitless beneficence of my oath. I realize then how utterly alone I am in my motherhood. Moreover, how the weight of these (thankfully) infrequent skirmishes seem to outweigh what I should know as a fact—that I have been a loving mother to my son. I once fought back the demons of crushing fear and anxiety through the infant stage and came out victorious. Yet all my successes fall away as I call my husband to come rescue us from me an hour into this epic struggle.

Once we load our child into his dad's car, I unload myself back into mine, and I follow them home. In an effort to retain a composed look on my face in the event that my husband scans for distress in his rearview mirror, I drift off back to that circle of chairs in that chilled, echoey room in my mind.

I remove my mask, inhale heavily, and say, "I don't belong here. And neither do you." Aghast, the other supermoms look around, but no one responds, and their silence is deafening. I continue, "We inherited the lie that we should do and be it all for our children. We suffer in the exclusivity of it all, feigning strength where we feel powerless. Dutifully, we take up the narrative that motherhood is natural, all the while feeling so unnatural, so alien in a mothering that never seems to look like it's supposed to. We come together to trade tips for how to do it better—how to be more effective, more efficient, and cleaner in our mothering. By donning these capes, we deny ourselves our fallibility. By wearing these masks, we invite one another to keep their humanity hidden. Who are we saving and from whom are they being saved? Who even started this whole supermom thing!?" With another long overdue breath, I look around just enough to notice the darting glances of both recognition and concern. I don't linger to decipher the hushed murmurs and instead I see myself out, clumsily pulling on my boots and snagging my cape on the way.

I return to myself, profoundly alone and following behind the car of our hero and the now-happy child securely fastened in his car seat. Only half-believing, I remind myself, "I am a good mom. I know how to care for my child. I will just try to sleep more."

* * *

[2]

It is 5:29 p.m. I have slammed the car into park and am gasping for air as I whip open the back door to procure the toddler whose daycare closes first. We are here for baby brother, whose daycare ends *Promptly At 5:30 P.M. Daily, Thank You For Your Cooperation*!! I repeat the last line of our monthly daycare newsletter under my breath as I text his teachers to let them know that I am On Time and Not a Shit Mother. Oh, and that I am also Not Guilty of the $3 Per Minute Penalty for inferior moms who get stuck in traffic after racing out of work. I have decided my colleagues think I am a sort of Tasmanian devil with the freneticism of my attempts at mothering and work (the desperate, spinning cartoon version, although the real-life screeching marsupial also describes me well). My toddler might feel this way too as we run, run, run down the steps to the daycare entrance. "Mama we are so, so fast!"

"I wonder if they see how relatable it is for me to arrive just before group starts," another supermom thinks as she scoots past the Supermoms' Support Group sign. "So sad that some moms always seem so be running la...Jesus CHRIST I have to stop this comparison!" she whispers as she hangs her cape. "I have been coming to this group for almost a year, and it wasn't until last week, when that mom totally snapped and said aloud what we have all been thinking. I wish I really knew these other women better. Or at all. We were our own people before we became mothers, like I had a name before I was Mom—and now all we have are these fucking capes and a weekly meeting that smells like yoga mats." Pausing before entering the circle of competitive, disembodied, self-protectiveness, she touched her mask. "I am so tired, just like that mom from last time. Who was she? How was she so brave?" Her hand hovers over her mask. "Wait, that is stupid. Of course we are all brave. This is a literal support group for

heroines." And yet! "I feel so alone here, as if I could crack into a million pieces if someone asks me the wrong developmental stages question."

"How many two-word simple sentences is the baby stringing together?" [Shit, he just babbles and eats yogurt noisily. He is supposed to be speaking in sentences?]

"Oh you know, like 'me go' and 'more juice'—just simple things, like most babies say by this time." The mom across the room smiles warmly, with the encouraging face of a psychologist who is about to tell you your child is delayed.

[You know, it's funny. I think the "most babies" and "by this time" were what I was supposed to latch onto. I'm too tired to remember all these stages. At least he won't say "more juice" because we don't drink juice in our house! Briefly touching my hand to my mask—I kept it on today after all—I am victorious in the end. All moms know: simple sugar is the greater sin.]

"Ah, hi Mom! Squeezing in right at 5:30 p.m. again—this must be your superpower!" I smile, joking that yes indeed, we all have to be good at something I suppose. Being the very last mom to collect my baby from the fluorescent lighting of his basement daycare classroom before I accrue latte-equivalent fees is not nothing. It is also, however, not lost on me that my internal comparison of me to all the other moms who are able to pick up their babies far ahead of the very last moment, must look a little more motherly to the well-socialized eyes of the daycare personnel. But I reassure myself. He and his sister may spend nine hours a day in someone else's care while I work in a job that rarely feels worth the time we sacrifice together. But at least he doesn't drink juice.

Conclusion: A Norming of Maternal Ambivalence and a Call for Mother-Community

In juxtaposing normative motherhood, via the metaphor of a supermom support group, with our lived experiences as an actual-mom counterpoint, we bring into question the psychological impacts of normative motherhood and call for a resistance to the pressuring siren song of the mothering ideal. The above narratives are characterized by our ambivalent voices navigating the simultaneous beauty and heartbreak in each moment of mothering. Rozsika Parker writes that maternal ambivalence is a central feature of matrescence, the developmental process of becoming a mother. Through ambivalence, mothers navigate feelings of both love and hate for their children, inviting a reflexivity that is ultimately growthful as a mother learns to carry out her mothering duties and develop relationships authentically. Supermoms, however, are not afforded ambivalence. According to Parker, "[Our] culture plays a part in producing the difficulties virtually prohibiting the kind of full discussion and exploration that would reveal the hidden contribution to creative mothering that maternal ambivalence can make" (1). Ambivalence in the pursuit of supermotherhood (ideal motherhood) results in "feelings of shame, confusion, self-reproach and anger" even as a mother "finds herself in a *losing* battle to maintain any solid sense of choice or desire" (Barautser and Noack 179). In normative motherhood, ambivalence becomes intolerable, unmanageable, and threatening, even though "[ambivalence] itself is emphatically not the problem; the issue is how a mother manages the guilt and anxiety ambivalence provokes" (Parker 8). When mothers can release themselves from the pursuit of the ideal and welcome nuance and complexity into their mothering experience, ambivalence increases psychological resilience, fosters flexibility, and creates congruence between a mother's sense of self and her choices in mothering.

Through recognizing that motherhood is socially constructed rather than biologically determined, we can begin to challenge the social and political structures that uniquely oppress mothers. In recognizing mothers' humanity, we might begin to consider the processes of maternal development as well as the potential impact of a mother community in offering a village in which mothers support "themselves emotionally by supporting and reconstituting *one another*" (Chodorow 36). The potential of such structured mother community is quite rich. What could it mean for the possibility of more fully and flexibly exploring matrescence if mothers could do this via genuine relational, embodied support? We conceptualize this as a sort of motherhood consciousness raising. What if the mothers really did take off their masks, attend vulnerably to self and other, and prioritize the humanity of each mother in the support group circle—a sort of womb of reconstitution? What could this movement do in response to the ways in which mothering norms are constructed and enacted in our current attempts at community? We welcome the shifts in this direction that mothers make in small ways—for example, by speaking honestly to each other about challenges (removing masks!) and by intentionally setting and resetting aside the temptation to compare as a means of validating one's own maternal choices. Addressing and deconstructing mothering norms simply cannot begin without a communal eschewing of the supermom archetype to which we are compared. We propose that emphasizing nurturing, rather than policing, in mothering relationships and engaging critically with the oppressive structures of normative motherhood comprise the radical and liberatory movement that contemporary mothers need in order to reclaim their selfhood in mothering.

Works Cited

Abetz, Jenna, and Julia Moore. "'Welcome to the Mommy Wars, Ladies': Making Sense of the Ideology of Combative Mothering in Mommy Blogs." *Communication Culture & Critique*, vol. 11, no. 2, 2018, pp. 265-81.

Baraitser, Lisa, and Amélie Noack. "Mother Courage: Reflections on Maternal Resilience." *British Journal of Psychotherapy*, vol. 23, no. 2, 2007, pp. 171-88.

Chodorow, Nancy. *The Reproduction of Mothering*. University of California Press, 1978.

D'Amore, Laura Mattoon. "The Accidental Supermom: Superheroines and Maternal Performativity, 1963–1980." *The Journal of Popular Culture*, vol. 45, no. 6, 2012, pp. 1226-48.

Kawash, S. "New Directions in Motherhood Studies." *Signs: Journal of Women in Culture and Society*, vol. 36, no. 4, 2011, pp. 969-1003.

Menkedick, Sarah. *Ordinary Insanity: Fear and the Silent Crisis of Motherhood in America*. Pantheon, 2020.

Musick, Kelly, Ann Meier, and Sarah Flood. "How Parents Fare: Mothers' and Fathers' Subjective Well-Being in Time with Children." *American Sociological Review*, vol. 81, no. 5, 2016, pp. 1069-95.

Newman, H. D., and A. C. Henderson. "The Modern Mystique: Institutional Mediation of Hegemonic Motherhood." *Sociological Inquiry*, vol. 84, no. 3, 2014, pp. 472-491.

O'Reilly, Andrea. "Matricentric Feminism: A Feminism for Mothers." *Journal of the Motherhood Initiative for Research and Community Involvement*, vol. 10, no. 1-2, https://jarm.journals.yorku.ca/index.php/jarm/article/view/40551. Accessed 11 Feb. 2023.

Parker, Rozsika. *Torn in Two: The Experience of Maternal Ambivalence.* Virago, 2005.

Rich, Adrienne. *Of Woman Born: Motherhood as Experience and Institution.* W.W. Norton & Company, 1995.

Ridgeway, Cecilia L., and Shelley J. Correll. "Motherhood as a Status Characteristic." *Journal of Social Issues*, vol. 60, no. 4, 2004, pp. 683-700.

Rizzo, Kathryn M., Hollow H. Schiffrin, and Miriam Liss. "Insight into the Parenthood Paradox: Mental Health Outcomes of Intensive Mothering." *Journal of Child and Family Studies*, vol. 22, no. 5, 2013, pp. 614-20.

Chapter 13.

The Art of Mothering with a Disability: Challenging Normative Motherhood

Amy Wagner, Susan Smith, and Amy Crocker

Introduction

Many ideals exist that define normative motherhood. Normative motherhood, represented by the "ideal" or "natural" mother, as defined by dominant cultures, is a narrow one that portrays what the good mother should be. This includes multiple idealized facets, such as thirty-something-years-old, married, heterosexual, middle class, and able bodied. This does not necessarily reflect the diversity of identities and lived experiences of all mothers and is noninclusive. The visibility of disabled mothers, for example, may play a role in role modelling mothering for other women with a disability, whether in person or through popular media (Malone 201). These ideals of motherhood—such as being ever present, selfless, and nurturing (O'Reilly, *Matricentric Feminism*)—are learned and role modelled by others, as well as represented in culture such as art.

This chapter will explore the double cultural critique of both mothers with disabilities and artists, who also may promote visibility and representation. These identities of disability and being an artist challenge the concept of normative motherhood. A mother with a disability may be able to resist the dominant cultural discourse through her visibility and inclusion. Increased visibility and nonerasure of the disabled mother are important in recognizing and affirming the disabled mother.

By challenging the norms of motherhood, a difference-centred perspective (Malone 206) may shed new light on diverse ways of mothering. Malone reinforces this view by stating: "Thinking about mothering from a difference-centered perspective reflects the dynamic and changing needs of families and of mothers and creates a space for valuing and honoring the variety of mothering arrangements and abilities that exist" (207). This chapter will explore disabled motherhood as a challenge to normative motherhood through a normative motherhood framework and matricentric feminist lenses, which will be defined next. The following topics will be discussed: (1) the lived experience of disabled motherhood; (2) models of disability, including medical, social, hybrid and ecological models, and their relationship to normative motherhood; and (3) disabled motherhood and art, highlighting the example of Alison Lapper. These topics will highlight how mothers with disabilities challenge current notions of normative motherhood.

Normative Motherhood

What is ideal motherhood? Who represents normative motherhood and who is excluded in representing this ideal? A dominant view post-World War II is that of sacrificial motherhood and intensive mothering where the mother is the central caregiver (O'Reilly, "Maternal Theory" 24). Andrea O'Reilly's ten dictates of normative motherhood—"essentialization, privatization, individualization, naturalization, normalization, idealization, biologicalization, expertization, intensification, and depoliticization" (O'Reilly, *Matricentric Feminism* 9)—will be integrated into this chapter. Normative motherhood excludes mothers who are non-normative, for example, older, single, or disabled. Normative motherhood may also be associated with natural motherhood, which assumes a selfless, maternal love, and a "single-minded identity" (Rich 22).

A part of the ideal of normative motherhood also includes ability or able-bodiedness. The binary of disabled-nondisabled categorizes mothers as either one or the other and leaves little room for a continuum of able-bodiedness. Robert McRuer discusses "compulsory able-bodiedness" as an ideal portrayed by society (Campbell, "Ability" 13).

Ableism involves the marginalization of those with a form of difference, including discrimination and the noninclusion of the mother with a disability. Fiona Campbell states that "the concept of the normative" is key to a system of ableism (13). This applies to normative motherhood as well. Disability and disabled motherhood will be further discussed in this chapter and will be a central focus in exploring normative motherhood.

Feminist Mothering, Empowered Mothering, and Matricentric Feminism

It is important to define terms central to motherhood and normative motherhood. The term "motherhood" is understood as related to patriarchal institutions (O'Reilly, "Feminist Mothering" 185). Feminist mothering, however, is defined as a negation of patriarchal motherhood and is empowering to women (187). The institution of motherhood under patriarchy ensures that women "remain under male control" (Hallstein, O'Reilly, and Giles 1-2). Mothering, in contrast, is a construct that is related to the work of mothering and relates to women's empowered lived experiences of mothering.

It is through empowered mothering that women can mitigate patriarchal motherhood (O'Reilly, "Maternal Theory" 29) and transform ways that the patriarchy limits them (30). Empowered mothering also "counters the normative discourse of motherhood" (e.g., middle-class, married, heterosexual, and able bodied) to broaden and be more inclusive of other types of mothering (non-normative mothering) and maternal practices and identities (31). Empowered mothering could also involve self-expression as seen through art. It is empowered maternal practices (Hallstein, O'Reilly, and Giles 3) that are seen in the art and work of mothering as described in this chapter.

Matricentric feminism views mothering as a practice rather than a fixed identity (O'Reilly, *Matricentric Feminism* 26). Matricentric feminism does not "disavow motherhood" but rather views motherhood as socially constructed and "integral to a mother's sense of self and her experience of the world" (27). This is shown in the valuing of motherhood and the mother-baby dyad. As an example, mother and artist Allegra Holmes describes her art in terms of matricentric feminism: "Art and art practice materialize matricentric feminist concepts" (219). In this chapter, the work of artist Alison Lapper, a mother with a disability, specifically, will be explored in depth in terms of normative motherhood and matricentric feminism. Finally, matricentric feminism explores maternal diversity, including ability, age, etc. (O'Reilly, *Matricentric Feminism* 47). A matricentric feminist perspective will be utilized in this chapter to celebrate the diversity of motherhood across all spectrums of ability.

Lived Experience of Disabled Motherhood

Disability represents an extremely diverse and broad umbrella of different abilities and may be difficult to generalize. Tom Shakespeare discusses disability as "a multidimensional concept, which should be understood in terms of a continuum" (5) as opposed to a binary construct. Disability may include physical disability, mental or intellectual disability, or sensory disability (such as vision or hearing). "Who is disabled" is an important question that may affect policy, identity, and activism (Filax and Taylor, "Disabled Mothers"; *Mothers* 145). Gill defines disability as a "social distinction ... a marginalized status" (Gill 44) with this status assigned by a majority culture (Filax and Taylor, "Disabled Mothers"; *Mothers* 145).

Perceptions about sexuality of the disabled mother may also be a source of discrimination—in that the mother with a disability may be seen as asexual (Hayward et al., "Reproductive" 413) or have difficulty accessing contraceptive resources, experience sexual abuse, or be seen as passive (Peta and Ned). In fact, femaleness has historically been associated with disability (Thompson 19). "Validation of the reproductive capacity" is critical to full inclusion for disabled mothers, according to Judith Rogers (xi). Sexuality will also be addressed later during the discussion of the use of nudity in the *Alison Lapper Pregnant* statue and in Lapper's self-portrait work.

Some disabled women achieve pregnancy and become mothers. As of 2005, around 12 per cent of women of childbearing age in the United States "have some type of disability," and they reproduce at nearly the same rate as mothers without a disability, according to one recent study (Horner-Johnson et al. 529.e1). However, disabled mothers may experience barriers to prenatal care, including lack of provider or staff training, inaccessible facilities, and lack of information or clinical guidelines for mothers with a disability (Mitra et al. 447). It is imperative for these mothers to be provided with adequate care, which may include training of healthcare providers and staff as well as increasing access to clinics and providing the necessary equipment and assistance to optimize their ability to mother. Amy Wint, Diane Smith, and Lisa Iezzoni found that mothers with a physical disability were able to care for their infant through adaptation of their environment and use of adaptive equipment, such as babywearing wraps for carrying their infant, furniture adaptations, and caregiver assistance (1). Such adaptive devices and assistance are critical to promote full inclusion in mothering for women with a disability.

The mother with a disability may challenge the binary view of motherhood as good-bad and serve as a lens that expands the horizons of what it means to mother through emphasizing the full continuum of mothering that exists. The disabled mother "offers insights to feminist practices of mothering" (Filax and Taylor, "Disabled Mothers"; *Mothers* 143) and may "illuminate the workings of the dominant culture," and serve as a cultural diagnosis, acting as a critique (151). The disabled mother indeed acts as a cultural critique, a "site of resistance, and source of cultural agency" from which we may learn (Filax and Taylor, "Disabled Mothers," *Routledge Companion to Motherhood* 81). This counters the able-bodied norm for motherhood of the dominant culture narrative.

Julia Daniels describes the "assumption of able-bodied motherhood … to shed light on the beliefs, principles, and standards underpinning the infeasible articulation of the 'ideal mother'" (115). She describes the "approved" or ideal mother as physically having dexterity, endless energy, physical stability, and being independent and autonomous (116). This ideal of normative motherhood contrasts with the ability of the disabled mother to demonstrate unique attributes, such as "interdependence, cooperation, and connection" (120). These attributes counteract and contradict the patriarchal concept of individualism (Holmes 228). The mother with a disability may spend additional time interacting with her child (such as diaper changes), and "challenge Western society's construction of ideal motherhood" (Filax and Taylor, "Disabled Mothers"; *Mothers* 153-54). It is through her unique aspects of mothering that the disabled mother can challenge the dominant culture and patriarchal individualistic values and also promote feminine/maternal values, such as connection and community.

Models of Disability (Social, Medical, Ecological)

Models of disability have power. These models not only define disability and create frameworks for viewing individuals with disabilities but also have an influence on individuals with disabilities. Much of the work of healthcare practitioners, researchers, policymakers, and educators is guided by the model of disability to which they subscribe. This section will describe the medical model, the social model, a hybrid model, and the ecological model of disability as frameworks for viewing disability and their relationship to normative motherhood.

From around the mid-1800s, as there were significant advances in the field of medicine, the medical model of disability replaced the oldest model of disability, the moral or religious model, which asserted that disability was punishment from an all-powerful entity (Retief and Letšosa). The medical model defined disability as a medical problem within an individual and viewed those with disabilities as having deviated from biomedical or cognitive norms, being dependent on others, and needing cures from their physical impairments (Smart). According to this model, individuals with disabilities deviate from what is seen as normal and are not comparable to able-bodied individuals, and in the context of normative motherhood, a disabled woman might not only be excused from traditional roles, such as wife or mother, but may be perceived as not capable of fulfilling those roles (Hayward, "It's a Miracle" 73). Concepts related to the medical model of disability and normative motherhood are essentialization (the ability to mother is related to biology), individualization (the issue of being disabled/a disabled mother is an individual one rather than societal), and idealization (physical abled-bodied ideals become the ideal norm).

In contrast to the medical model, the social model of disability was introduced in the 1980s during the beginning of the disability rights movement in the United Kingdom and North America and moved from viewing disability as a problem in the individual to a focus on societal barriers (Retief and Letšosa; Shakespeare 12-13). Rather than seeing the individual as needing to be fixed as in the medical model, the social model centres on addressing these barriers to participation that are asserted to be the result of ableist environmental and social factors (Retief and Letšosa). Centred on how the physical environment and social environment impose barriers, this model decreases the focus on the individual and their body, and, in the context of normative motherhood, the disabled mother's individual experiences may be devalued or not considered. In the medical model, the mother with a disability would be viewed as impaired and in need of being individually improved in order to be able to mother. The social model of disability would, however, provide acceptance and inclusion of the disabled mother as she is and would focus on providing societal support to facilitate mothering. The social model also challenges one of the tenets of normative motherhood, depoliticization, in that it promotes politicization—bringing issues of disability, including disabled motherhood, into the arena of social policy changes to improve access and participation in mothering for those with a disability.

However, a criticism of the social model, by individuals within and outside of the disability community is its disregard of the psychological and physical pain associated with impairments (Hayward, "It's a Miracle" 73). This led to discussion and formation of the International Classification of Functioning, Disability and Health (ICF), a biopsychosocial framework that integrates both the medical and social models of disability (Kostanjsek; Roush and Sharby; Shakespeare; Ustün et al.; World Health Organization). The ICF, approved by the World Health Assembly in May 2001, marked a shift in the way disability and health were understood and incorporated not only biological impairments but also restrictions to participation (ability to perform social roles such as mothering) in society as well as contextual factors, such as attitudes of others and environmental access (Kostanjsek; Roush and Sharby 1719). Shakespeare discussed the need for such a hybrid model, which moves away from the dichotomy of either a social or medical model and sees disability as multifactorial (21). This hybrid view of disability allows the person with a disability to benefit from improved access and removal of barriers while also acknowledging their individual needs. Thus, in the hybrid view, a mother with a disability could both access healthcare to address physical pain or other impairments and receive accommodations and equipment to facilitate her ability to mother.

This shift towards a biopsychosocial model opened up opportunities for those with a disability, including mothers, to receive health benefits, such as the use of assistive devices, psychological support, legal protections, and other benefits that increase, not decrease, personal agency. An example of this would be the use of childcare aids and adaptive techniques that are "central to the [disabled] mother's successful involvement in childcare" (Kaiser, Boschen, and Reid 104). Healthcare services and resources are critical to facilitate the success of disabled mothers during conception, pregnancy, birth, and mothering.

A fourth model of disability, the ecological model, based on Urie Bronfenbrenner's child developmental framework, is more universalistic, promoting policies that would benefit all (Hayward, "It's a Miracle" 74). The ecological model defines disability in terms of the "interaction between the individual and the environment under a particular context at different points in time" (74) with ability and disability viewed on a spectrum that is dependent upon those interactions. At the centre is the individual, with progressive "rings" moving outwards, which represent their immediate community and support system (microsystem), work and home (mesosystem), healthcare system (exosystem), and the overarching beliefs and values (macro-system) of those around them (Bronfenbrenner). The chronosystem is what makes this model unique, which in the context of normative motherhood represents changes that occur throughout the lifespan of the disabled mother (Hayward, "It's a Miracle" 74). Thus, as a mother with a disability experiencing different aspects of mothering throughout her lifetime, such as pregnancy through mothering an adult child, the different support systems in the "rings" would provide needed support for the mother and offer inclusion in the mothering experience.

Art and Disabled Motherhood

Maternal art and art created by mothers have historically been underrepresented (Chernick and Klein 148), as has the representation of female artists in general. Maternal art brings to light and makes visible the invisible work of mothering, such as childcaring or changes to the body that occur during and after pregnancy. Niki de Saint Phalle's work, *Hon*, a room-sized, larger-than-life piece of a pregnant woman, is one of the earliest feminist works representing the embodiment of pregnancy and motherhood in the feminist era. Feminist/maternal artists, such as Judy Chicago, have also pioneered the art of motherhood (childbirth in particular) and the artistic representation of the female body and womanhood in multiple mediums. However, despite the increased proliferation of art reflecting mothering, there is a need for increased visibility of mothering in art, particularly mothers who are "non-normative," such as mothers with a disability.

The artist, in general, requires considerable space and time to work, which are not always as available for mothers compared to male artists (Chernick and Klein 153). In addition to the time required to produce one's art, separate spheres of motherhood (private realm), work, and the art world may be seen as disparate (Gosling, Robinson, and Tobin 202). Feminist mothering has been addressed in art to analyze social expectations (212). The next section will focus on artist Alison Lapper, who is a disabled mother and artist, as well as the subject of art: herself. She is an example of a mother and artist who challenges normative motherhood.

Artist Alison Lapper

Alison Lapper is an artist who was born with congenital limb deformities; she has two very short legs and is missing both arms. The hospital encouraged her mother to leave her in the care of the state. She resided in a children's home where the children were often referred to as "the strange little creatures" (Lapper and Feldman 20). At age four, she was reunited with her mother but had a strained and distant relationship. Alison's mother expressed disdain for the prosthetics she used, and Alison often felt like an inconvenience. Her time at the children's home was not particularly pleasant, with caregivers who often were unkind to both Alison and the other children. When she finally left the children's home as a teenager, she moved to London and began pursuing her art career. She graduated from Brighton University in 1993 and was made a full member of the Mouth and Foot Painters Association, which was a pivotal moment for her as she was then able to make her own income as an artist (189).

Much of Alison's portfolio consists of self-portraits that include nudity. Portraying her body and the beauty of her differences has been a major focus of her work. To this end, she has received criticism that she is not a good artist. Although Alison does not agree with the criticism, she does understand the difficulty others have with her work. Differences are revered in nature but not in humans (Lapper and Feldman 235). She feels that, maybe, the world is not ready to view the art that she is producing.

One of Alison's most notable pieces is titled *Angel* and features her nude bust with angel wings set on a mystical background. Her body is thrusting upwards in a nod to winged figures from classical mythology akin to the likes of the winged Nike (Millett-Gallant 407). This juxtaposition between the stereotypes of disability and goddess is seen throughout much of Alison's work and speaks to her desire to reform the public's perception of disability.

In 1999, when Alison was pregnant with her son, she faced much criticism. People doubted her ability to parent and questioned whether her child would have the same disability she had. Once her son, Parys, was born, Alison continued to face obstacles; social services told her that if she did not have help taking care of the baby, they would remove him from her care (Lapper and Feldman 208). Alison hired several helpers to assist her with caring for Parys, but social services continued to question her ability to properly parent. One worker wrote a report outlining how inept she was as a parent, and although the details of the report were disputed and eventually social services agreed to step back, they refused to throw out the report, and it remains on file to this day. Despite many obstacles, Alison Lapper has brought awareness to her ability to demonstrate non-normative motherhood and to other disabled mothers. Shakespeare states, "From the start, creative work has been part of the advocacy and resistance of the disabled people's movement" (147). Alison Lapper has helped to push the boundaries of normative motherhood through personal agency, and is an exemplar of matricentric feminism, and feminist and empowered mothering.

Alison Lapper Pregnant Statue

When Alison first met artist Marc Quinn, she was a bit unsure and wary. She did not understand why he would want to create statues of disabled bodies. Marc began speaking of older statues that had lost a limb or various parts due to the wear and tear of time and explained how those statues have been universally accepted as beautiful and valuable (Lapper and Feldman 235). He wanted to show the beauty of those who were born with limb differences. She was not yet pregnant when they met, so when he contacted her in 2000, asking if she was still interested in being his muse, she was surprised when he reacted so positively to her pregnancy. He felt that showing her as both pregnant and with a limb difference would be extremely impactful. He later created three more statues of Alison, including one with her son when he was five months old. In 2005, the statue was enlarged to sixteen feet tall and titled *Alison Lapper Pregnant*. The statue was displayed in London on the Fourth Plinth in Trafalgar Square for eighteen months and later was reinterpreted as an inflatable replica as the centerpiece for the 2012 London Paralympic Games opening ceremony (Quinn).

The statue of *Alison Lapper Pregnant* has important implications for exploring normative motherhood. The statue itself represents the artist nude. There have been positive and negative potential consequences of the portrayal of female nudity in art, depending on the context. Holmes describes imagery of the female body as linked to patriarchy and potentially problematic; however, the use of one's own body is disruptive to patriarchal forces in art (Holmes 220-21).

The use of neoclassical style and marble and the location of the Lapper statue are all important elements of the piece that contribute to the interpretation and meaning of disability and normative motherhood. Lapper's pose, seated with head erect and slightly turned and gazing into the distance, is on par with heroes and military leaders (Tveite 53) as is the location, Trafalgar Square in London, which represents the city site for war hero monuments and political activism (87). The armless figure also correlates to other Greco-Roman art of mythical and heroic figures, increasing the heroism motif in the piece (19). Marble itself is associated with cultural and social acceptance as well as heroes (83) and memorial art (Betterton 86). The statue on public display challenges the notion of physical perfection (86), and "enables us to imagine different kinds of practices and values through which to figure maternal bodies" (96). The public nature of the art also conveys Lapper as a representative of both disability and motherhood; her body is a living monument to "bodies and identities that have been socially devalued, shamed, and excluded from public life historically" (Millett-Gallant 399). Lapper states, "I regard it as a modern tribute to femininity, disability and motherhood" (399).

Surveillance may be experienced by the disabled in general (Filax and Taylor, "Disabled Mothers" Routledge 82). This is also experienced through the "gaze of others" (O'Reilly, *Matricentric Feminism* 59). This surveillance, or gaze, puts the mother with a disability under the eye of public scrutiny and judgment while being seen as outside the norm. The act of being an artist as well as the subject of art may subvert the surveillance and the gaze of others while illuminating the physicality and embodiment of what it means to be a disabled mother.

Women who are subjects of art may be subject to the male gaze, in which men view women as the passive bearers of meaning (Tveite 49). In contrast to the male gaze, Bracha Ettinger describes the matrixial (matrix = womb) gaze. What Ettinger refers to as the "matrixial borderspace" is considered trans-subjective and according to Ettinger, "designates woman not as the Other, but as co-emerging self with the m/Other, and *link* rather than object" ("Matrixial Trans-subjectivity" 218). The statue of *Alison Lapper Pregnant* could represent witnessing together or wit(h)nessing (Ettinger, *The Matrixial Borderspace* 145). Thus, the statue portrays the matrixial bordersphere, where her work is transformative and linking as opposed to being a passive subject.

Alison Lapper is both the artist and the subject of artwork. *Alison Lapper Pregnant* is an important artwork in portraying and representing non-normative motherhood in a public arena, using an artform associated with heroism. Rosemary Betterton states, "She rejects the label 'disabled mother' and ... gives birth to images of herself and her child in an imaginative process of transformation" (89). Alison Lapper represents an artist and mother who through her personal agency and empowered mothering has subverted the dominant (normative) narrative about disabled motherhood. Her own artwork and that of Marc Quinn represent a type of resistance against normative motherhood. As the subject, Alison Lapper has promoted visibility of mothers with a disability in multiple ways. As an artist and advocate, she has broken down barriers and challenged cultural norms of motherhood.

Conclusion

The ideals of normative motherhood are noninclusive. Mothers with a disability challenge the normative discourse of motherhood, act as a cultural critique, and illuminate the full continuum of motherhood that exists, including the promotion of mothering with a variety of able bodiedness. Changing models of disability can promote more access, policies, and inclusion for the mother with a disability, enabling and facilitating her participation in the role of mothering. Artists such as Alison Lapper challenge normative motherhood and shed light on representations of motherhood that are unique, diverse, and promote empowered, diverse motherhood. Through increased public representation and visibility, the diversity of all mothers can shine forth.

Works Cited

Betterton, Rosemary. "Promising Monsters: Pregnant Bodies, Artistic Subjectivity, and Maternal Imagination." *Hypatia*, vol. 21, no. 1, 2006, pp. 80-100.

Bronfenbrenner, Urie. "Ecological Models of Human Development." *Readings on the Development of Children*, 4th edition, edited by Mary Gauvain and Michael Cole, Worth Publishers, 2005, pp. 3-8.

Campbell, Fiona Kumari. "Ability." *Keywords for Disability Studies*, edited by Rachel Adams, Benjamin Reiss, and David Serlin, New York University Press, 2015, pp. 12-14.

Chernick, Myrel and Jennie Klein. "Feminist Art and Motherhood: An Overview." *The Routledge Companion to Motherhood*, edited by Lynn O'Brien Hallstein, Andrea O'Reilly, and Melinda Vandenbeld Giles, Routledge, 2020, pp. 147-155.

Daniels, Julia N. "Disabled Mothering? Outlawed, Overlooked and Severely Prohibited: Interrogating Ableism in Motherhood." *Social Inclusion*, vol. 7, no. 1, 2019, pp. 114-23.

Ettinger, Bracha L. "Matrixial Trans-Subjectivity." *Theory, Culture & Society*, vol. 23, no. 2-3, 2006, pp. 218-22.

Ettinger, Bracha L. *The Matrixial Borderspace*. University of Minnesota Press, 2006.

Filax, Gloria, and Dena Taylor. "Disabled Mothers." *Mothers, Mothering, and Motherhood across Cultural Differences—A Reader*, edited by Andrea O'Reilly, Demeter Press, 2014, pp. 143-60.

Filax, Gloria, and Dena Taylor. "Disabled Mothers." *The Routledge Companion to Motherhood*. Eds. Lynn O'Brien Hallstein, Andrea O'Reilly, and Melinda Vandenbeld Giles. Routledge, 2020, pp. 77-88.

Gill, Carol J. "Questioning Continuum." *The Ragged Edge: The Disability Experience from the Pages of the First Fifteen Years of The Disability Rag*, edited by Barrett Shaw, The Advocado Press, 1994, pp. 42-49.

Gosling, Lucinda, Hilary Robinson, and Amy Tobin. *The Art of Feminism: Images that Shaped the Fight for Equality, 1857–2017*. Chronicle Books, 2018.

Hallstein, Lynn O'Brien, Andrea O'Reilly, and Melinda Vandenbeld Giles, eds. *The Routledge Companion to Motherhood*. Routledge, 2020.

Hayward, Katharine. "It's a Miracle." *Disabled Mothers: Stories and Scholarship by and About Mothers with Disabilities*, edited by Gloria Filax and Dena Taylor, Demeter Press, 2014, pp. 71-86.

Hayward, Katharine, et al. "Reproductive Healthcare Experiences of Women with Cerebral Palsy." *Disability and Health Journal*, vol. 10. no. 3, 2017, pp. 413-18.

Holmes, Allegra. "The Gift: Matricentric Feminism, Physiological Mothering, and Art Practice." *Journal of the Motherhood Initiative for Research and Community Involvement*, vol. 10, no. 1-2, 2019, pp. 219-32.

Horner-Johnson, Willi, et al. "Pregnancy Among US Women: Differences by Presence, Type, and Complexity of Disability." *American Journal of Obstetrics and Gynecology*, vol. 214, no. 4, 2016, pp. 529-e1–529e9.

Kaiser, Anita, Kathryn Boschen, and Denise Reid. "Use of Aids and Adaptations in Childcare for Mothers with Spinal Cord Injury." *Disabled Mothers: Stories and Scholarship by and about Mothers with Disabilities*, edited by Gloria Filax and Dena Taylor, Demeter Press, 2014, pp. 87-107.

Kostanjsek, Nenad. "Use of the International Classification of Functioning, Disability and Health (ICF) as a Conceptual Framework and Common Language for Disability Statistics and Health Information Systems." *BMC Public Health*, vol. 11, no. 4, 2011, pp. 1-6.

Lapper, Alison, and Guy Feldman. *My Life in My Hands*. Simon & Schuster, 2005.

Malone, Amanda. "Ideal Motherhood and Surveillance: Young Mothers with Intellectual Disabilities Share Their Stories." *Disabled Mothers: Stories and Scholarship by and about Mothers with Disabilities*, edited by Gloria Filax and Dena Taylor, Demeter Press, 2014, pp. 195-213.

Millett-Gallant, Ann. "Sculpting Body Ideals: Alison Lapper Pregnant and the Public Display of Disability." *The Disability Studies Reader*, 4th edition, edited by Lennard J. Davis. Routledge, 2013, pp. 398-410.

Mitra, Monika, et al. "Barriers to Providing Maternity Care to Women with Physical Disabilities: Perspectives from Health Care Practitioners." *Disability and Health Journal*, vol. 10, no. 3, 2017, pp. 445-50.

O'Reilly, Andrea. "Feminist Mothering." *Mothers, Mothering, and Motherhood across Cultural Differences—A Reader*, edited by Andrea O'Reilly, Demeter Press, 2014, pp. 183-205.

O'Reilly, Andrea. "Maternal Theory: Patriarchal Motherhood and Empowered Mothering." *The Routledge Companion to Motherhood*, edited by Lynn O'Brien Hallstein, Andrea O'Reilly, and Melinda Vandenbeld Giles, Routledge, 2020, pp. 19-35.

O'Reilly, Andrea. *Matricentric Feminism: Theory, Activism, Practice*. 2nd ed. Demeter Press, 2021.

Peta, Christine, and Lieketseng, Ned. "So from Here Where Do We Go? A Focus on the Sexuality of Women with Disabilities in Africa: A Narrative Review." *Sexuality & Culture: An Interdisciplinary Quarterly*, vol. 23, no. 3, 2019, pp. 978-1009.

Quinn, Marc. "Alison Lapper." *Marc Quinn*, 20 Sept. 2015, marcquinn.com/artworks/alison-lapper. Accessed 2 Feb. 2023.

Retief, Marno, and Rantoa Letšosa. "Models of Disability: A Brief Overview." *HTS Teologiese Studies/Theological Studies*, vol. 74, no. 1, 2018, pp. 1-8.

Rich, Adrienne. *Of Woman Born: Motherhood as Institution and Experience*. W.W. Norton & Company, 1995.

Rogers, Judith. *The Disabled Woman's Guide to Pregnancy and Birth*. Demos Medical Publishing, 2006.

Roush, Susan E., and Nancy Sharby. "Disability Reconsidered: The Paradox of Physical Therapy." *Physical Therapy*, vol. 91, no. 12, 2011, pp. 1715-27.

Shakespeare, Tom. *Disability: The Basics*. Routledge, 2018.

Smart, Julie F. "The Power of Models of Disability." *Journal of Rehabilitation*, vol. 75, no. 2, 2009, pp. 3-11.

Thompson, Rosemarie Garland. *Extraordinary Bodies: Figuring Physical Disability in American Culture and Literature*. Columbia University Press, 1997.

Tveite, Elisabeth. "A Contemporary Body in Classical Guise: Representation of Disability in Classical Form and Contemporary Beauty Norm in *Alison Lapper Pregnant*." MA Thesis. University of Bergen, 2014.

Ustün, T. Bedirhan et al. "The International Classification of Functioning, Disability and Health: A New Tool for Understanding Disability and Health." *Disability and Rehabilitation*, vol. 25, no. 11-12, 2003, pp. 565-71.

Wint, Amy J., Diane L. Smith, and Lisa I. Iezzoni. "Mothers with Physical Disability: Childcare Adaptations at Home." *The American Journal of Occupational Therapy*, vol. 70, no. 6, 2016, pp. 7006220060p1–7006220060p7.

World Health Organization. *International Classification of Functioning, Disability, and Health: ICF*. World Health Organization, 2001.

Chapter 14.

Older First-Time Moms in Twenty-First-Century Canada: Challenging (and Changing) the Norms of Normative Early Motherhood

Rosann Edwards

Normal, Norm, and Normative

Normal, ordinary, common. Norm, average, median. Normative, conforming to norms, determining norms or standards. The modern ideal of normative motherhood is the 'good mother'. She (she is always unquestionably a she) mothers above all else, intensively, single mindedly, sacrificing all (but not ALL all, as she still needs to be a good role model—stay in shape, eat healthy, be happy). She is engaged in her children's community and activities. She breastfeeds (sometimes tandem). She may work (but that never interferes with her mothering), and she is not too young but also not too old. She is just right (Ennis; Horwitz; O'Reilly). The 1990s saw both the emergence of the contemporary ideal of intensive mothering, which persists to this day, as the normative Western view of the good mother (Horwitz; O'Reilly) and a shift in demographics in many Western countries towards women waiting later in life to have their first babies (Canadian Institute for Health Information [CIHI]).

Using a multifaceted lens, this chapter examines childbearing over the age of thirty-five in Canada from a historical perspective, in relation to the medicalization of pregnancy and childbirth, and from a sociocultural perspective exploring why women wait to have children later. And, finally, it explores the experiences of early motherhood that begin with trying to live up to the good mother and ultimately moving towards empowered mothering practices. Despite initially being true believers in the core elements of intensive motherhood, older first-time mothers in the latter half of this chapter are rebelling against the loss of self and putting up active resistance to all-in mothering by seeking balance and embracing good enough as truly good enough.

In my thirteen years as a frontline public health nurse and lactation consultant, I encountered countless older mothers who expressed feelings of grief, guilt, anger, resentment, disappointment, anxiety, and depression when discussing their breastfeeding and their mothering experiences. They desperately wanted to be the good mother, the intensively mothering mother they had envisioned themselves to be during pregnancy. For so many of these new mothers, the disconnect between expectations and realities of early motherhood contributed to adverse maternal mental health outcomes, negatively affecting the mother-infant relationship, and acted as a contributing factor to early weaning and to their overall misery as human beings. The ideals that these women had internalized of how they must mother to be successful mothers (not just good) would have been impossible for anyone short of a deity to live up to. I wanted to know why older mothers were seen as so unusual and somehow abnormal. Why did these accomplished, independent, self-described feminists, and high achievers torture themselves with the need to practice intensive mothering even to the detriment of their own mental health?

The irony is that although many social roles and expectations for women (especially white, cis-gendered heterosexual women) have loosened over the past thirty years, norms surrounding motherhood have moved in the opposite direction, embracing the restrictive ideology and practices of intensive mothering (Ennis; Horwitz; O'Reilly). The women I worked with as a public health nurse led to my doctoral research exploring the expectations, experiences, and decision-making processes related to breastfeeding of first-time mothers who were thirty-five and older. It became clear early on in the study that breastfeeding and mothering were inseparable in the early postpartum period for the twenty-three mothers who shared their experiences with me. It was also clear that these new mothers (all highly educated and high career achievers) had internalized the normative good mother, and for the most of them, things were not going as planned. By the second interviews, three to four months later, the mothers in my study had mostly rejected the good mother ideal and had taken ownership of their baby feeding and mothering practices. They were moving into the realm of empowered mothering, much like the mothers in Horwitz's work on empowered motherhood; they too were resisting the ideal and actively questioning the status quo.

Delayed Childbearing

Since the 1990s there has been a growing trend in developed countries towards women delaying childbearing, with increasing numbers of new mothers being over the age of thirty-five at the time of first live birth (Best Start [BS]; CIHI; Mills et al.). For example, in Canada by 2018 one in five live births (23 per cent of total births) was to a mother over the age of thirty-five; this was 47 per cent higher than a decade ago in 1998, with first births to women over thirty-five accounting for only 11 per cent of those births (CIHI; Society of Obstetricians and Gynecologists of Canada [SOGC]; Statistics Canada, *Live Birth*). Between 2014 and 2016 in Ontario (Canada's most populous province), births to women over thirty-five years of age accounted for nearly a quarter of all births, with 15.1 per cent of those births being to first-time moms (Better Outcomes Registry and Network [BORN] Ontario)

It should be noted that while this chapter examines the fertility and birth trends in Canada, the statistics from other high income/developed countries, including the United States, England, and Australia, share similar trends and patterns over the last three decades, with increasing rates of first live births to women thirty-five years of age and older (Matthews and Hamilton; Rindfuss et al.; SOGC; Statistics Canada, *Fertility Overview*). For example, in the United States (US), the average age of women having their first baby has been steadily increasing over the past forty years, and first births to women thirty-five and older have increased since the mid-1970s (Matthews and Hamilton). The United States National Centre for Health Statistics (NCHS) reports that from 2000 to 2012, first live births to women thirty-five to thirty-nine years of age rose by 24 per cent, and first live births to women forty to forty-four years of age rose by 35 per cent in most states (Matthews and Hamilton). In the US, as in Canada, first live births to younger women (especially those under twenty years of age) have steadily declined over the same period, as first births to older mothers have been increasing (Matthews and Hamilton; Provencher et al.).

Until the mid-1800s, Canada was a mainly rural society with high fertility rates; for example, the estimated total fertility rate in 1851 was 6.56 children per woman (Statistics Canada, *Fertility*). Large families were normal, and women had children from the time they were married (typically in their twenties) until the end of their reproductive years (Statistics Canada, *Fertility*). Women having children into their early forties was common in Canada until the 1970s and is not a new development (Veniza and Turcotte). What is new in the past thirty years is the increasing numbers of women having their first child in their mid-thirties and forties (BS; SOGC; Statistics Canada, *Fertility*; Veniza and Turcotte).

There were fluctuations in the fertility rate in Canada throughout the late 1800s and early to mid-1900s. These fluctuations were influenced by a multitude of factors, including increasing urbanization, the rising cost of raising children, the Great Depression, two world wars, the declining influence of organized religion, the postwar baby boom, reliable and available contraception, as well as education and employment opportunities for women (Provencher et al.; SOGC; Statistics Canada, *Fertility Review*). For example, the estimated total fertility rate in Canada in 1937 was 2.64 children per woman, as compared to 3.94 children per woman in 1959 at the peak of the baby boom; it then began to significantly decline in the late 1960s and was down to 1.54 children per woman in 2016 (Provencher et al.; Statistics Canada, Fertility Review). The record low was tied between 2000 and 2002 with 1.51 children per woman (SC *Fertility*).

The last year that the replacement-level fertility was reached in Canada was 1971, with a rate of 2.1 children per woman. Every year since 1971, the Canadian fertility rate has failed to meet the requisite 2 children per woman required, not for population growth through births, but rather to avoid population decline as deaths begin to outnumber births in any given year (Statistics Canada, *Fertility*). This correlates with another Canadian trend that began in the mid-1970s, namely women marrying later (Statistics Canada, *Fertility*; Veniza and Turcotte). By the 1970s and 1980s, with the ability to better control family planning, the number of years within which women had their children shrank. Instead of the average woman's childbearing years being roughly two decades (providing one did not die in childbirth or due to pregnancy-related causes), women were now actively planning their families, and as a result, they had fewer children, had those children closer together, and were generally finished having their families younger than previous generations (BS; Statistics Canada, *Fertility*). In the 1990s, another new trend emerged, with women still having fewer children but waiting until they were older to have their first child (BS; Statistics Canada, *Fertility*).

When examining the age-specific fertility and birth rates in Canada, two significant trends emerge in the 1990s. The first is that the birth rate to women at the youngest end of the reproductive spectrum, those nineteen years of age and under, began steadily declining (BORN; Statistics Canada, *Fertility*). In 2016, for the first time in Canadian history, the youngest mothers were having fewer babies than the oldest mothers (Statistics Canada, *Fertility Overview*). The second trend is that at the older end of the reproductive spectrum, the fertility rate for women thirty-five to forty-four years of age began steadily increasing, with many of these births being to first-time mothers (Provencher et al.; Statistics Canada, *Fertility Overview*). In 2010, for the first time in Canadian history, the number of births to women aged thirty-five to thirty-nine surpassed the number of births to women aged twenty to twenty-four (Statistics Canada, *Fertility Overview*). The birth rate for Canadian women over thirty-five doubled between 1990 and 2003 (BS).

It is important to reiterate that women having babies in their mid-thirties to forties is not a new phenomenon in Canada. However, the growing number of women having their first child in their mid-thirties to forties is new, and along with all mothers who feel shut outside the club of normative motherhood, older first-time mothers are challenging the decades-held good mother ideal in their mothering practices.

More and More Canadian Women Are Waiting Longer to Have Babies: Why and So What?

Upon establishing that there is a growing trend towards delayed childbearing in Canada and other developed countries over the past three decades, it is necessary to ask, so what? Is there really anything different other than age between a woman who has her children in her twenties and a woman who does not begin having hers until her thirties or even forties? In the age of the internet and mass media, are there factors outside of those historically influencing the decisions on when to time childbearing for women in the new millennium? For example, in their examination of portrayals of older mothers in the British media, Rachel Shaw and David Giles found older mothers were overwhelmingly framed as being outside of the norm and painted as being selfish, needy, and even accused of violating "the natural order" (221).

Are these new moms stepping outside the boundaries of normative mothering? Are they being perceived as outside the boundaries of normative mothering? If so, then does this affect how they mother? Does this affect how they experience pregnancy, childbirth, and early motherhood? But first, why wait?

Social, Economic, and Cultural Factors

This section could be summarized as "every other norm seems to change in the favour of women except motherhood." When the question of why people postpone parenthood was explored, current research found that increasingly high levels of education for women was one of the primary factors driving the trend towards delayed childbearing in most of the Organization for Economic Co-Operation and Development countries (Lemoine and Ravitsky; Mills et al.; Southby et al.). Surrounding educational attainment was a cluster of other underlying social forces and factors, including effective and accessible contraceptive options, career path options, financial pressures, waiting for the right time to have children (that is, having secure finances, finding the right partner, and establishing a career), individualistic family models, and the continued uneven distribution of household labour (Lemoine and Ravitsky; Mills et al.; Southby et al.). Many of these factors are not always, if ever, within an individual woman's control (Guedes and Canavarro).

Thus, the decision to delay childbearing is not always a conscious one; rather in many cases, it is the outcome of external social forces and changing norms and values outside of the existing dominant norms of motherhood. For example, the societal shift over the last few generations towards extended adolescence (well into a person's twenties) and the delaying of many life stages (some due to the increasing educational and professional requirements for career advancement and economic security) is beyond the control of the individual who is living within the circumstances and expectations of their peers, family, and society as a whole (Cooke et al; Friese et al.; Shaw and Giles; Statistics Canada, *Fertility Overview*).

For many women in Canada, gender equality is increasingly a lived reality. Provided they have the economic, social, and structural resources, women have the same general opportunities as men to enter most professions and to pursue most educational paths. The pursuit of many educational and career paths requires large amounts of time devoted to study and professional advancement. It is challenging for women to achieve the same level as their male counterparts if they have children (Mills et al.). This is especially true as the bulk of the burden of household tasks and childcare still primarily falls to women, and childcare or the help of extended family is not always readily available (Mills et al.; Veniza and Turcotte).

The search for the ideal partner and changes to marital realities (including second marriages) are also contributing to the phenomenon of delayed childbearing (BS; Cooke et al.; Power; Nislem et al.; Mills et al.; Southby et al.). Jennifer Power argues that this is part of a broad social and historical process in developed countries, where pressures around career and education exist and expectations concerning romantic relationships have changed. Marriage in the twenty-first century is less central to the social and economic lives of young adults. Their expectations of the relationship within marriage, when they do marry, are different from those of previous generations, with young adults seeking emotional and sexual fulfillment as opposed to social and economic security (Power). The by-product of these changing expectations in a life partnership is that relationships become more transient, as self-actualization becomes an important goal (Power). The pattern of shorter, more transient relationships is correlated with women waiting longer to have their first children (BS; Cooke et al.; Power; Mills et al.; Nislem et al; Southby et al.). Andrea O'Reilly calls the rise of intensive mothering a "backlash to feminism" (13). One of the central tenets of intensive mothering—that mothering takes much of one's time, energy, and material resources—runs directly counter to the fulfilment and self-actualization sought after in long-term relationships by the women later chasing the ideal of the good mother.

That is not to discount that educational attainment was the primary driver influencing women's decisions related to the timing of their first child. Mireille Verniza and Martin Turcotte's secondary analysis of the Canadian 2006 census data related to age, education, professions, and births supports the assertion that education is a primary factor influencing the decision to delay childbearing for many Canadian women. They argue that societal changes have resulted in the bar being higher for educational attainment to enter many professions, and as a result, many women are staying in school longer.

Perhaps not surprisingly, Verniza and Turcotte found that the highest numbers of first-time mothers over thirty in Canada were those who belonged to professions that required the longest number of years of postsecondary education and residencies. Women over forty who were physicians, engineers, lawyers, and university professors were the most likely to have been a first-time parent over the age of thirty-five. Physicians had the highest rates of delayed childbearing; 22 per cent of female physicians in Canada over forty parented children who were preschool aged or younger.

At the same time that intensive motherhood was becoming the normative practice of mothering in Canada, options around life decisions—such as marriage, the seeking of personal fulfillment, and choosing when to become, or if to become, a parent—were becoming more flexible for many Canadians due to the breakdown in the strict constraints of socially accepted roles (Friese et al.; Guedes and Canavarro). Over the last thirty years, expectations about the normative life course have shifted, and for many, women's social roles were less rigid (Friese et al.; Guedes and Canavarro; Power). Carrie Friese et al. make the case for older motherhood as part of the phenomenon of the new possibilities emerging in response to changing social, cultural, economic, and physical (since women in their forties are often in good physical health) realities and, in turn, part of the "profile of the new middle age" (66).

Pregnancy and Childbirth: Starting Out on the Outside of the (Perceived) Medical Norms of Motherhood

This section could be summed up as "if you are over thirty-five and pregnant with your first baby your doctor probably thinks you are old, and there are going to be repercussions." The terms "advanced maternal age," "late maternal age," "elderly primps," or the currently accepted term "delayed childbearing" all refer to the phenomenon of women who have children closer to the end of their natural reproductive cycle, or over the age of thirty-five (SOGC). The SOGC statement "delayed childbearing is associated with increased risk of infertility, maternal comorbidity, pregnancy and birth complications, and increased maternal and fetal morbidity and mortality" (1) is a typical example of how the medical profession frames being older and pregnant as inherently risky and outside the norm of the healthy pregnancy of a younger woman.

What the SOGC terms as the "consequences" of delayed childbearing fall into three categories termed by healthcare professionals as risks. The first category is risk to fertility. This is simple biology: As women age, their fertility naturally declines until menopause. For most women, fertility begins to decline in their early thirties, and both subfecundability (not being able to conceive naturally within one menstrual cycle) and the incidence of miscarriage for women who do conceive spontaneously increase (SOGC). Compared to their younger counterparts, older women do have increased incidences of preexisting medical conditions, including endometriosis, fibroids, polyps, obesity, hypertension, and diabetes, which may negatively affect fertility (CIHI; SOGC). Increased incidents of risk factors does not mean all (or even the majority of) women thirty-five and older are at risk for adverse pregnancy outcomes preconception; it simply means that older women are statistically more likely to have issues than younger women.

The second category of risk is to the fetus. Maternal age-related risks to the fetus include an increased incidence of genetic conditions, congenital anomalies, and suboptimal birth outcomes (CIHI; SOGC). The incidence of chromosomal aneuploidy (primarily trisomies), gene abnormalities, and some congenital malformations (including cardiac defects, hypospadias, and craniostynosis) all increase as maternal age increases (CIHI; SOGC). For example, the rate of chromosomal disorders for women over thirty-five years of age was four times higher than those of women twenty to thirty-four years of age (SOGC). Again, even before the baby is born, older mothers, simply by virtue of choosing to carry a pregnancy at an advanced age, are perceived as putting the health of their infant at risk, which goes against the risk-averse normative good mother discourse.

The third category of perceived risk includes those related to maternal health, pregnancy, and birth-related outcomes. Women over the age of thirty-five are at higher risk for most adverse pregnancy and birth-related outcomes including (but not restricted to) miscarriage, small for gestational age and low-birth-weight babies, preterm labour, placenta abnormalities, ectopic pregnancy, pregnancy-induced hypertension, preeclampsia, induction, multiple births, interventions during labour, and delivery via caesarean section (CIHI; Statistics Canada, *Live Birth*; SOGC). Most notable are the increased rates of caesarean sections, gestational diabetes, and placenta previa in women over forty (Bayrampour and Heaman; CIHI; SOGC). The incidence of placenta previa was found to be ten times higher in nulliparous (first-time mothers) women over forty compared to those between twenty and twenty-nine years of age, and the incidence of caesarean section in women over the age of forty is over 50 per cent compared to the rates in the general obstetrical population of approximately 25 per cent (SOGC).

Marie-Eve Lemoine and Vardit Ravitsky go so far as to assert that the growing phenomena of delayed childbearing and advanced maternal age in developed countries is in fact a public health issue and should be addressed by governments and public health authorities. They argue that the multitude of issues associated with increasing numbers of women delaying childbearing into their mid-thirties and forties places a higher burden (aka financial cost) on the healthcare system (CIHI; SOGC). Lemoine and Ravitsky question how well informed the public (that is, women) is about the risks of delayed childbearing. They do acknowledge that there is a fine line between advocating for earlier motherhood and impinging on women's autonomy and reproductive rights, but they argue that due to the reality of the medical risks and the lack of information that women receive on those risks (including the risks and cost of artificial reproductive technologies), there needs to be social, economic, and political support to empower women to have children earlier.

On the flip side, many researchers are actively questioning the significance of the rates of risk (for example the frequency of interventions during pregnancy, labour, and birth). They theorize that physicians may have an unnecessary lower threshold for interventions when providing care to older mothers due to preconceived notions of elevated risk and may intervene sooner (and thus more frequently), especially concerning relatively routine procedures, such as caesarean sections and inductions (Bayrampour and Heaman; Marques et al). Recent studies found no statistically significant levels of correlation between advanced maternal age and the rates of birth defects, prematurity, and low birth weight in their analysis of older mothers as compared to their younger counterparts (Carolan et al. and Marques et al). The emphasis by healthcare professionals on medical risk when managing pregnancies and births for otherwise healthy older women may be a significant contributing factor to the high levels of anxiety experienced during the perinatal period among this population and may also be contributing to the delayed transition to the maternal role, as these mothers may see themselves as abnormal and in need of extra attention and worry (Carolan and Nelson).

Mary Carolan and Sioban Nelson argue that current perinatal healthcare regimes do not meet the needs of otherwise healthy but older women and may be leading to self-fulfilling prophecies through increased levels of routine interventions (including caesarean sections, prenatal screening, and induction of labour), leading to clinically poorer outcomes, which reinforces for these mothers that they and their infants are, in fact, less healthy or more fragile than younger mothers and their infants. Compounded by exposure to negative framing of older mothers in the media and social discourses (Shaw and Giles), the increased medicalization of older motherhood may be a major contributing factor to the increased levels of anxiety and need to prove that they are indeed good mothers for this population of women.

Realities of Early Postpartum and Challenging Intensive Mothering

Reality of Life after Baby

Research supports the assertion that for many older first-time mothers, the reality of motherhood is wildly different from what they expected

(Aasheim et al.; Carolan; Edwards et al.; Shelton and Johnson). The dominant discourse internalized by these new mothers in the contemporary literature is that of the attachment-focused, child-centred, and intensively mothering good mother (Edwards et al.; Shelton and Johnson). The mythos of the good mother comes in many forms depending on the cultural context, but generally it is consistent with the discourses around Western normative mothering. She (remember she is always a she) is a mother who instinctively knows how to care for her newborn. Mothering comes completely naturally for her, and she is the all-giving and all-sacrificing nucleus of a happy family. Her baby also fits the ideal of the quiet infant who sleeps well and breastfeeds well—the good baby (Shelton and Johnson).

Since many older first-time mothers are found to lack any alternate discourse of what real motherhood looks and feels like, the reality is a shock. They report high levels feelings of failure and anxiety—feelings that they are not meeting expectations, and inadequacy in the early maternal role when neither they nor their infants fit the myth (Carolan; Shelton and Johnson). Carolan has characterized this shock as the "nightmare of early mothering" (769). This experience inevitably leaves a void for many new mothers in which they do not have a social discourse that matches how they feel to help them come to terms with their new reality or how to navigate that reality with their sense of themselves intact (Aasheim et al.; Fisher et al.; Shelton and Johnson).

Not surprisingly, given the overwhelming disconnect between the expectations and realities of early motherhood, anxiety and worry are common threads throughout the studies exploring the experiences of older first-time mothers (Carolan and Nelson; Southby et al.). Clara Southby et al. found that the idea of "now or never" was central to the experience of older first-time mothers. This sense of urgency—that this may be their last chance to have a baby and do it right—puts a pressure on early motherhood compounded by striving to live up to the bar set by intensive mothering practices.

As explored in the previous section, healthcare professionals may be setting the tone for this anxiety during pregnancy with increased surveillance and testing of older mothers, even for women with minimal risk factors (Carolan; SOGC). The use of risk-laden language by healthcare professionals when describing the pregnancies and possible birth outcomes for older mothers may also be compounding the social discourse of risk that this group of mothers is already exposed to in the media and broader cultural narratives. As argued in the previous section, healthcare professionals may inadvertently be reinforcing the cultural message to these mothers that they are different; they deviate from the norm while their babies are still in utero and for some even before conception (Carolan and Nelson; Shaw and Giles; Southby et al.).

Many older first-time mothers went from living life with a strong sense of independence and a fully formed adult identity to a life of seeming confinement, chaos, and never-ending demands in their new role as mother (Aasheim et al.; Fisher et al.; Shelton and Johnson). Despite having internalized the normative discourse of the good mother, stories from older first-time mothers reflect resistance and ambivalence towards the dominant discourse of the good mother and what they should be doing during early motherhood (Edwards et al; Shelton and Johnson).

Many older mothers (especially those in professional positions) tried to balance maintaining some of their previous existence and their new maternal responsibilities (Edwards et al.; Shelton and Johnson). In the early postpartum period, seeking balance between the intensity of caring for the new baby and often unsupportive, demanding, or inflexible workplace cultures was a struggle for many women (Kim et al.; Metcalfe et al.). In my own doctoral work, by four to six months postpartum, older first-time mothers realized not only that their baby was a unique person but also that they had to find their own definitions of motherhood that fit them as unique persons, allowing for balance between their mothering and their preexisting self and life goals (Edwards et al.; Carolan; Aasheim et al.)

Challenging Intensive Mothering

In Ramona Mercer's theory of becoming a mother, the transition to motherhood occurs under the central assumption that in each person, there exists a relatively stable core self. This self evolves in the cultural context of the individual over the lifespan and determines how an individual defines and reacts to situations and life changes—motherhood being a pivotal life change (Mercer). For the mothers in my work, the first six weeks of motherhood were a period of instability; their notion of self was threatened by the sudden loss of autonomy due to the intensity of early breastfeeding and the loss of their well-established, pre-baby lives. By four to six months postpartum, the mothers were firmly entrenched in the active process of redefining their core selves as mothers, which included changing their mothering practices to allow them to mother as the person they were before the baby. By taking control and ownership over their mothering practices, they moved away from the constraints of intensive mothering towards actively practicing empowered mothering. They gave the proverbial (and for one of the mothers in my doctoral study the literal) middle finger to intensive mothering and the constraints of the good mother mythos.

The mothers in my study resisted and rebelled against intensive mothering in their own deeply personal way. These women, all accomplished human beings before motherhood, emotionally invested in living up to the ideal of intensive mothering through the act of breastfeeding. They concluded that they had to find their own way back to who they were as a person in order to be a mother. These acts of resistance came in a multitude of seemingly small forms, including giving their babies formula, cosleeping, choosing to exclusively pump breastmilk (and in two cases give the milk to other mothers too), going out without their baby from time to time, and acting against direct medical advice by not waking their babies up to feed every three hours at night.

One common thread was the act of doing their own research on common breastfeeding and early parenting issues. In the first three months of motherhood, almost all of the mothers talked about being heavily reliant on the advice of the healthcare providers in all aspects of feeding and caring for their baby—this was a way to ensure things were done right. Nurses, lactation consultants, and physicians were all gatekeepers to good mothering, which for the mothers in my study came mostly through breastfeeding supports.

By the four-to-six-month mark, most of the mothers in our study had come to lose trust in the healthcare professionals and the rhetoric of intensive mothering that they found was a subtext to all the health information and promotion. Now they were choosing to seek out others that they identified with online, in the community, and in their circles of friends. Others validated their choices to be good enough, to give a bottle of formula sometimes, to take time for themselves, to not always be thrilled with their baby, to sometimes be bored to death with their baby, to complain about the things that sucked about being a mom, and to even still care about their careers. They were choosing through small acts of everyday rebellion to mother unapologetically as fully formed adult human beings.

Final Thoughts

The 1990s saw the rise of both intensive mothering and a shift towards more and more women waiting until their mid-thirties to early forties to have their first baby. Like the prevailing discourse of intensive mothering, the growing trend of delaying childbearing in Canada and many other developed nations has been driven by a multitude of complex and interrelated social, economic, and cultural forces. While bearing children into one's forties is not a new phenomenon, even before their babies are born, older mothers are labelled as outside the norm, and as inherently risk laden in both their pregnancies and births. This view of women thirty-five and over as risk takers, which is against the ideals of the good mother, may be reinforcing the anxieties of many women who practice intensive mothering to prove they are not bad mothers, simply by being older. Older first-time mothers may have internalized the normative discourse of the good mother. They are also found to be pushing against the norm and creating their own versions of empowered mothering that fit with their lives, aspirations, and selves as mothers.

Works Cited

Aasheim, Vigdis, et al. "Satisfaction with life during pregnancy and early motherhood in first-time mothers of advanced maternal age: A population-based longitudinal study." *BMC Pregnancy & Childbirth*, vol. 14, no. 86, 2014, pp. 1-9.

Bayrampour, Hamideh, and Maureen Heaman. "Comparison of Demographic and Obstetric Characteristics of Canadian Primiparous Women of Advanced Maternal Age and Younger Age." *Journal of Obstetrics and Gynecology Canada*, vol. 3, no. 8, 2011, pp. 820-829.

Best Start. *Pregnancy after Age 35: Trends in Timing of First Pregnancy*, 2015, www.beststart.org/resources/rep_health/pdf/bs_pregnancy_age35.pdf. Accessed 2 Feb. 2023.

Canadian Institute for Health Information. *In Due Time: Why Maternal Age Matters*, 2011, www.secure.cihi.ca/estore/productfamily.htm . Accessed 2 Feb. 2023.

Carolan, Mary. "Health Literacy and the Information Needs and Dilemmas of First-Time Mothers over 35 Years." *Journal of Clinical Nursing*, vol. 16, no. 6, 2007, pp. 1162-72.

Carolan, Mary, et al. "Older Maternal Age and Intervention in Labor: A Population-Based Study Comparing Older and Younger First-Time Mothers in Victoria, Australia." *Birth*, vol. 38, no. 1, 2011, pp. 24-29.

Carolan, Mary, and Sioban Nelson. "First mothering over 35 Years: Questioning the Association of Maternal Age and Pregnancy Risk." *Health Care for Women International*, vol. 28, 2007, pp. 534-55.

Cooke, Alison, et al. "'Informed and Uninformed Decision Making': Women's Reasoning, Experiences and Perceptions with regard to Advanced Maternal Age and Delayed Childbearing: A Meta-Synthesis." *International Journal of Nursing Studies*, vol. 47, 2010, pp. 317-29.

Cooke, Alison, et al. "Advanced Maternal Age: Delayed Childbearing Is Rarely a Conscious Choice: A Qualitative Study of Women's Views and Experiences." *International Journal of Nursing Studies*, vol. 49, no. 1, 2012, pp. 20-39.

Edwards, Rosann, et al. "The Breastfeeding Experiences of Older First-time Mothers: A Constructivist Grounded Theory Study." *Midwifery*, vol. 96, 2021, www.sciencedirect.com/science/article/abs/pii/S0266613821000243. Accessed 2 Feb. 2023.

Ennis, Linda Rose. *Intensive Mothering: The Cultural Contradictions of Modern Motherhood*. Demeter Press, 2014.

Fisher, Jane, et al. "Assisted Conception, Maternal Age and Breastfeeding: An Australian Cohort Study." *Acta Paediatrica*, 102, no. 10, 2013, pp. 970-76.

Friese, Carrie, et al. "Older Motherhood and the Changing Life Course in the Era of Assisted Reproductive Technologies." *Journal of Aging Studies*, 22, no. 1, 2008, pp. 65-73.

Guedes, Maryse, and Maria Cristina Canavarro. "Psychosocial Adjustment of Couples to First-Time Parenthood at Advanced Maternal

Age: An Exploratory Longitudinal Study." *Journal of Reproductive and Infant Psychology*, vol. 32, no. 5, 2014, pp. 425-40.

Horwitz, Erika. *Through the Maze of Empowered Motherhood: Empowered Mothers Speak*. Demeter Press, 2011.

Kim, Theresa H., et al. "Characteristics of Social Support among Teenage, Optimal Age, and Advanced Age Women in Canada: An Analysis of the National Longitudinal Survey of Children and Youth." *Journal of Maternal and Child Health*, vol. 21, no. 6, 2017, pp. 1417-27.

Lemoine, Marie-Eve, and Vardit Ravitsky. "Sleepwalking into Infertility: The Need for a Public Health Approach toward Advanced Maternal Age." *The American Journal of Bioethics*, vol. 15, no. 11, 2015, pp. 37-48.

Marquis, Barbara, et al. "Being a Mother after 35 Years: Will It Be Different?" *Acta Medica Portuguesa*, vol. 30, no. 9, 2017, 615-22.

Mathews, T. J., and Brady Hamilton. "First Births to Older Women Continue to Rise." *National Center for Health Statistics: NCHS Data Brief*, vol. 152, 2014, pp. 1-7.

Metcalfe, Amy, et al. "Educational Attainment, Perception of Workplace Support and Its Influence on Timing of Childbearing for Canadian Women: A Cross-Sectional Study." *Journal of Maternal & Child Health*, vol. 18, 2014, pp. 1675-82.

Mercer, Ramona. *First-Time Motherhood: Experiences from Teens to Forties*. Springer Publishing Company, 1986.

Mills, Tracey, et al. *Younger Mothers and Older Mothers: Maternal Age and Maternity Care*. Quay Books, 2012.

Morgan, Patricia Ann, et al. "Triple Whammy: Women's Perceptions of Midlife Mothering." *The American Journal of Maternal/Child Nursing*, vol. 37, no. 3, 2012, pp. 156-62.

Nilson, Ann Britt Vika, et al. "Characteristics of Women Who Are Pregnant with Their First Baby at an Advanced Maternal Age." *Acta Obstertricia et Gynecologica Scandinavica / Nordic Federation of Societies of Obstetrics and Gynecology*, vol. 91, 2012, pp. 353-362.

O'Reilly, Andrea. *Matricentric Feminism: Theory, Activism, and Practice*. 2nd edition. Demeter Press, 2021.

Power, Jennifer. "Not Finding the Right Partner Is a Social Phenomenon Affecting Advanced Maternal Age." *The American Journal of Bioethics,* vol. 15, no. 11, 2015, pp. 60-62.

Shaw, Rachel, and David C. Giles. "Motherhood on Ice? A Media Framing Analysis of Older Mothers in UK News." *Psychology and Health,* vol. 24, no. 2, 2009, pp. 221-36.

Mills, Melinda, et al. "Why Do People Postpone Parenthood? Reasons and Social Policy Incentives." *Human Reproduction Update Journal of Community and Applied Social Psychology,* vol. 16, no. 6, 2006, pp. 316-30.

Society of Obstetricians and Gynaecologists of Canada. "Delayed Child-Bearing: SOGC Committee Opinion." *Journal of Obstetrics and Gynaecology Canada,* vol. 34, no. 1, 2012, pp. 80-93.

Southby, Clara, et al. "It's Now or Never—Nulliparous Women's Experiences of Pregnancy at Advanced Maternal Age: A Grounded Theory Study." *Midwifery,* vol. 68, 2019, pp. 1-8.

Statistics Canada. *Live Birth, by Age of Mother,* 2018, www.150.statcan.gc.ca/t1/tbl1/en/tv.action?pid=1310041601. Accessed 2 Feb. 2023.

Statistics Canada. *Fertility Overview 2012–2016,* 2018, www.150.statcan.gc.ca/n1/pub/91-209-x/2018001/article/54956-eng.pdf. Accessed 2 Feb. 2023.

Statistics Canada. *Fertility: Fewer Children, Older Moms,* 2018, www150.statcan.gc.ca/n1/pub/11-630-x/11-630-x2014002-eng.htm. Accessed 2 Feb. 2023.

Vezina, Mireille, and Martin Turcotte. "Forty-Year-Old Mothers of Preschool Children: A Profile." *Statistics Canada,* 2009, www150.statcan.gc.ca/n1/pub/11-008-x/2009002/article/10918-eng.htm. Accessed 2 Feb. 2023.

Chapter 15.

Throw Down Your Bundles: An Anishinaabeg Mother's Perspective on Anishinaabeg Normative Motherhood

Renée E. Mazinegiizhigoo-kwe Bédard

Opening the Bundle

In the beginning was thought, and her name was Woman. The Mother, the Grandmother, recognized from earliest times into the present among those peoples of the Americas who kept to the eldest traditions, is celebrated in social structures, architecture, law, customs, and the oral tradition. To her we owe our lives, and from her comes our ability to endure, regardless of the concerted assaults on our, on Her, being, for the past five hundred years of colonization. She is the Old Woman who tends the fires of life. She is the Old Woman Spider who weaves us together in a fabric of interconnection. She is the Eldest God, the one who Remembers and Re-members; and though the history of the past five hundred years has taught us bitterness and helpless rage, we endure into the present, alive, certain of our significance, certain of her centrality, her identity as the Sacred Hoop of Be-ing. (Gunn-Allen 11)

I have always been inspired by the words and gynocentric theories of Keres Pueblo/Sioux scholar Paula Gunn-Allen that place Indigenous feminine and maternal normativity at the forefront of her writings. Her chapter "When Women Throw Down Bundles, Strong Women Make Strong Nations" became the inspiration for this paper. When I think of that phrase "Throw Down Bundles," I think of my own Anishinaabeg (Ojibwe/Nipissing/Omàmiwininiwak) and Kanien'kehá:ka (Mohawk) mother, Shirley Ida Bédard, fighting for her Anishinaabeg identity, treaty rights, connections to her traditional territory, and membership to her mother's community at Okikendawt (Dokis First Nation), along with the those of her four children. To throw down our bundles is a metaphor for asserting our cultural ways of living and fighting to live as Anishinaabeg mothers and women. My mother threw down her bundle to assert her agency as an Anishinaabeg, a mother, and to show her children how to be Anishinaabeg and her daughters how to be women, mothers, and leaders. Anishinaabeg women are fiercely protective of their children, their territories, and their cultures. For this reason, Anishinaabeg maternal normativity is rooted in protecting and nurturing the relationship between mother and child, which are embedded in the teachings of "madjimadzuin," (Jenness 90)—meaning the chain of relations that binds us from generation to generation through our mothers.

What is normative motherhood for an Anishinaabeg mother? For the women in my family, it is a constant process of decolonization, cultural reclamation, and rebuilding of what has been lost or forgotten for a time. In this chapter, I will explore what it metaphorically and symbolically means for Anishinaabeg women to "throw down our bundles." Furthermore, I will highlight the Seven Grandmother (or Grandfather) teachings—also called the Niizhwaaswi-gichitwaa-miigiwewinan (Seven Sacred Gifts)—that come to us through the Niizhwaaso-ishkoden Ningaanaajimowin (Seven Fires Prophecy). Anishinaabeg mothers learn to carry these teachings in our maternal bundles to guide us in our roles as mothers so that we can practice mothering and motherhood in a good way. This chapter will discuss maternal normativity through the lens of Anishinaabeg motherhood, womanhood, and the feminine gender spectrum as we navigate not only the rigours of colonization and "degynocratization" (Gunn-Allen 42) but also the good work of decolonization, regynocratization, resurgence, and renewal.

Anishinaabeg Maternal Normativity

Anishinaabe maternal normativity is rooted in the axiology of our ancestral grandmothers who learned how to be Anishinaabeg mothers by living in specific ecosystems over generations, spanning back through time and space, and over thousands of years. Our First Teacher and First Mother in Creation is Aki, whom we watch every day and model how to be mothers—that is, creators, teachers, leaders, nourishers, sustainers, and nurturers. As Anishinaabeg scholar Basil Johnston-*ban*[1] states:

> Learning comes not only from books but from the earth and our surroundings as well. Indeed, learning from the mountains, valleys, forest and meadows anteceded book knowledge. What our people know about life and living, good and evil, laws and the purposes of insects, birds, animals and fish comes from the earth, the weather, the seasons, the plants and the other beings. The earth is a book; the days its pages; the seasons, paragraphs; the years, chapters. The earth is a book, alive with events that occur over and over for our benefit. Mother Earth has formed our beliefs, attitudes, insights, outlooks, values and institutions. We owe the earth our all, more than we can take in, more than we can say. (Johnston, *Honour* v)

Anishinaabeg normativity is grounded in our language learned from living on the land, which came to us as a miigiwewin (gift) from the natural and the beings of the Spirit realm: the birds, the insects, the wind, the plants, the animals, and the manidoowag (spirit beings). Anishinaabeg maternal identity encompasses all biological, LGBTTI QQ2SA+,[2] two-spirited, and Indigiqueer persons, who identify along the female gender spectrum or naazhe, the feminine gendered aspects of human beings. In Anishinaabemowin, the female gender spectrum includes a multitude of gender terminology for female. All are important to gender normativity within the Anishinaabeg worldview. Kwe, or Ikwe, is the larger umbrella of a person who is ever changing, and it is a fluid identity. It is not bound or confined to mere biology, and all are key to maternal normativity. For instance, Awanigiizhik Bruce offers the following list of linguistic terms: naazhe (noun; female child-bearing body); ikwe(wag) (noun; biological female, female identity;

indigokwe(wag) (noun; like a woman); dagokwewi (noun; woman spirit within a man); dago-ininiwi (verb; man spirit within a woman); e-ikwewi (verb; both spirits are female, aspic femme lesbian); eyekwe/aayekwe/aayaakwe/eyaakwe(wag) (noun; experience as a woman); ikwewaadizi (verb; has the nature of a woman); ininikonye (verb; dress like a man, feminine cross-dressing); ikwekonye (verb; dress like a woman, masculine cross-dressing); and babkaani-inaadizi/baakaanizi (verb; their actions are different, with positive, respectful connotations) (Bruce). There are likely other terms that have been lost to time, but in order to articulate maternal normativity, it is critical to acknowledge Anishinaabeg feminine normativity in all its complexity.

Most often, in everyday language, Anishinaabeg tend to use Kwe, or Ikwe, to name the feminine and maternal because of its open, expansive, and ever-changing quality. Kwe has meaning within its nature to the fluidity of time and space, connecting us to the creative forces or energies of the universe. That may mean the ability to give birth, or it may mean the ability to create with our hands, such as food for our families, a basket, a fishing net, clothing, snowshoes, and so on. In this chapter, all maternal figures who define themselves under the female gender spectrum are going to be referred to as Kwe, but I carry all these terms in my mother's bundle for my daughters in case they feel that one of these terms best describes their identity and connects more with their heart or spirit. However, I also understand that maternal normativity was also inclusive of those naabe-nini (males; men) who took up the responsibilities and duties traditionally performed by women or the passing down of knowledge that they knew was exclusive to women for the sake of the children, such as daughters. There is also the positionality of adoptive mothers, the ogikaawinag. These are the aunties, grandmothers, and community members (female or male gender spectrum), who are seen within Anishinaabeg culture as maternal figures.

As a mother, I normalize all these terms and the gender inclusive spectrum they offer within my own Anishinaabeg maternal contexts. I want my daughters to each walk confidently down their own individual miikana-bimaadizi (path of life), especially in this colonial world that normalizes only two genders, to the exclusion of all others. They need to understand that the Anishinaabeg worldview is complex, fluid, and inclusive of their identities and jiichaag (soul-spirits) as human beings.

From Kwe (woman) to Kwe, these Anishinaabeg maternal normative teachings were miigiwewinan (gifts) stored in our gichitwaa-gash kibijiganan (sacred bundles) containing the embedded wisdom of our maternal ancestors on how to be women and mothers (or know basic mothering practices, understand adoption, and being an auntie or a grannie). Anishinaabeg maternal axiology—those ethical ways of knowing, being, seeing, learning, and relating to one Creation—represented sacred bundles carried by the mothers. Gashkibijiganan (bundles) are sacred repositories used to carry not only our ceremonial items but also our maternal stories, memories, women's plant medicines, tools, and traditional customs of the Anishinaabe-kwewag (women) that gave them to us or led us to them: our grandmothers, mothers, Elders, aunties, and mentors. Each bundle is different, and the carrier of the bundle puts in all that they hold sacred to their life path. Many of these items will go with them to the grave to be carried on their journey down the Jiibay-Miikana (Path of Spirits) to the realm of the Spirits.

When we open our bundle and lay it out, we are doing so purposefully and with a reason. Bundles are not placed down unless it is of grave importance to take them out. These items are not used without intention or purpose. Furthermore, the items in an Anishinaabeg bundle awaken and connect us to the sacred, our ancestors, our spirit guardians, the land, and to all of Creation. To work with those items is to call forth a host of allies, guardians, and familial relations that do not exist in this realm but in the realm of Spirit. To call them forth is a great burden on them and their journey through the afterlife. Our items and knowledge with the bundles are regarded as an aspect of an individual's connection to the madjimadzuin, the great cosmic chain or lifeline that connects us to Gizhew-Manidoo and Creation itself.

In his research among the Anishinaabeg peoples of Wasauksing First Nation (Parry Island, Ontario), anthropologist Diamond Jenness was given key teachings on the nature of madjimadzuin, which when translated refers to a "chain of ancestors connecting those who have gone before with those who follow, the line of ancestors and descendants together with all the inheritance factors they carry with them" (90). Madjimadzuin embodies the teaching of the "moving life" or the "life line" (Jenness 90). The concept of the cosmic-chain, or life line, is connected to those maternal umbilical cord teachings we are given at puberty and then again as pregnant mothers. Pregnant mothers receive specific teachings on the madjimadzuin as the way of coming to understand their sacred complex nature of feminine normativity: our fertility, pregnancy, motherhood, parenting children, grandmotherhood, and Eldership. We learn about our role as leaders, teachers, nourishers, providers, and life sustainers. Furthermore, we are instructed how to mentally and spiritually connect ourselves through that life line to not just our babies but also to our cosmic-sense of ourselves-in-relation to all life in the universe as well as all Anishinaabeg that have come before or will come in the future. Wasauksing community members and knowledge holders talked to Jenness about the Milky Way (Jiibay-Miikana) as representative of the madjimadzuin (Jenness 90). The Jiibay-Miikana, or Path of Souls, the route the souls take to return to or come out of the realms of the spirits connects to our earthly reality. The Anishinaabeg of Wasauksing described the madjimadzuin as an "enormous bucket-handle that holds the earth in place" (Jenness 90) They told Jenness that "if it ever breaks the world will come to an end. The 'life line' (madjimadzuin: 'moving life') is a human Milky Way" (Jenness 90). It is the chain connecting all Anishinaabeg across time, space, and dimensions (Jenness 90). Mothers hold up the universe through our connection to the madjimadzuin. We usher children across that Milky Way, through the eastern doorway of life, and into this world. We give each of our children one link in that great cosmic chain of existence and teach them, as their first teachers, how to honour their madjimadzuin. Their belly buttons are a physical reminder of their indinawemaaganag—a sense of self in relation to others. Maternal normativity is rooted in the teachings of madjimadzuin and our roles as teachers in its ceremonial practices and philosophies.

As mothers, we will refer to this from a maternal worldview and perspectives through the lens of madjimadzuin kwewag, which embodies the chain of relations connecting one mother to the next through time and space and over generations. It binds us to all mothers and women that have come before, those with us now, and those yet to be born. Madjimadzuin is a spiritual energy or connection between all the women, the mothers, grandmothers, aunties, and to the Earth Aki, as First-Mother-in-Creation, but also to the Earth's plants, animals, birds, insects, air, and the waterways. All women, all human beings, are connected through the generations by way of the madjimadzuin—

reaching back as far as the moment of Creation and forward to the end of everything. It is for this reason that Anishinaabeg Elder Art Solomon wrote the following:

> the women were the present and the future
> because without them their could be no
> future for the nations; the cycles of life
> could have no continuity;
> the Creator's plans for human beings
> would end. (qtd. in Posluns 34)

Madjimadzuin kwewag is the way I think of and name my mother's bundle. It carries the power of many generations of women who came before me, and I utilize that strength of those women to grow my own traditional knowledge, to protect my family, and to fight for my people.

Due to the rigours of colonization, some of our women put away, hid, buried, and even forgot where they put some of these bundles used to guide their mino-miikana-bimaadiziwin (good path of living) as mothers. They had thrown their bundles down to protect their families, themselves, and their people, but in doing so, we are now left sometimes staggering around looking for our lost ways. We sometimes find it, and other times we are left piecing together new bundles of knowledge out of the ruins of those things that have survived.

In my family, there are old stories shared with my mother by her own aunties, which told her of how some of the people of Okikendawt would hide their valuables in or under the trees, under stumps, and bury them in secret locations in the bush. They hid them from the priests, Indian agents, and white people that would come through the reserve looking to confiscate or sometimes steal. One summer when I was a small child, we were visiting the old graveyards of our ancestors in Franks Bay. We saw a white family with armloads of silver items and bags of stuff that they had dug up. That day, I witnessed these strangers to our territory steal our bundles. The fears of our ancestors had come true.

Colonization has resulted in the repression, theft, and extermination of maternal culture among Anishinaabeg women. Gunn-Allen refers to this as a "program of degynocraticization" and an attack on "gynocentricity" grounded within Indigenous cultures (42). It has disrupted the holistic intergenerational movements of knowledge and wisdom between kwewag. Anishinaabeg mothers' sense of intergenerational maternal normativity is grounded in our ethical relationality with the land over generations. It is recorded in our traditions, the land, language, ceremonies, and systems of governance that had once prioritized women's status in Anishinaabeg communities as the "center of everything" (Posluns 34-35). Elder Solomon wrote the following:

> The woman is the foundation of which
> Nations are built.
> She is the heart of her nation.
> If that heart is weak, the people are weak.
> If her heart is strong and her mind is clear,
> Then the nation is strong and knows its purpose.
> The woman is the centre of everything. (qtd. in Posluns 35)

As the foundation of our families and communities, Anishinaabeg women have been forced to fight to return our inherent rights, culture, and lands to our people. Due to the Indian Act of 1876, many of our women lost their status for marrying non-status non-Indigenous men and non-status Indigenous men. My grandmother Roseann Dokis Sheppard lost her Indian status under the Indian Act and the 1850 Robinson-Huron Treaty because on October 8, 1929, she married a non-status Kanien'kehá:ka (Mohawk) man who had not been registered with his mother's community of Wahta First Nation. That choice by my great-grandmother Elizabeth Larivere set in motion a set of events that would extinguish her daughter-in-law's Treaty rights and those vested within the Indian Act. Roseann was removed from the Federal Indian Status Registry and from her band enrollment list, lost her rights to land, and other treaty rights. Finally, she was forced to leave the reserve with a small amount of money to support herself. She was cast adrift by the Indian agent, chief and council, who expelled her from the community. Family members rallied to her aid and helped her, and Edward purchased a bit of land just off the reserve, a short distance by boat. Then, in the 1990s, my mother, her sisters, brothers, and my own sister began compiling documents to regain their Indian status under the amendment to the Indian Act, under the 1985 *Bill C-31: An Act to Amend the Indian Act*. Metaphorically, she threw down her bundle to protect her family and stand up for her rights, not just to the government but also to her mother's community who at times sought to deny her the treaty rights, land rights, and Indian status she should have never been denied. She also stood up for her children and her future grandchildren's rights. Because she stood up and put her bundle down, regained her Indian status for herself and her children, we were able to find our way back to our traditional territory and culture.

As a family, we never really left our traditional territory because of that nearby land purchase by my grandmother and grandfather. We remained near the reserve, and visited every summer when we returned from the city during all the kids' summer school break. We still harvested, fished, hunted, and collected plant medicines like our grandmothers before us. Our connections to land and territory always remained a constant despite the government's expulsion of my grandmother from her home community. She carried her bundle with her when she left and proceeded to throw that bundle down, right next to the reserve. Decades later, her children were able to go back, and her bundle was picked back up.

Today, my children are now able to apply for their Indian status and feel the impact of their treaty rights responsibilities in the amendment to the Indian Act under the 2017 *Bill S-3: Act to Amend the Indian Act in response to the Superior Court of Quebec decision in Descheneaux c. Canada (Procureur général)*, which further eliminates gender-based inequities in registration for First Nations[3] women. Gaining Indian status and treaty rights does not make us more or less Anishinaabeg and Indigenous because that is work that we personally do for ourselves on our individual lifepaths as Kwewag (women) and Niniwag (men). In fact, the return of my familial rooted Indian status and legal rights to territory returned my familial political rights and land rights, which had been strategically taken from First Nations women to reduce the population size of First Nations reserve communities, thus expediting the decline of Indigenous peoples, which would eventually allow the federal government to seize the land and resources that had once been stew-arded by the original peoples of Turtle Island (North America). As the great-great-great granddaughter of Michel Eagle Dokis—known by his Anishinaabeg name as Petawachuan (also Biidwewejiwan), meaning "He Who Hears the Rapids Far Away," and a signatory to the 1850 Robinson-Huron Treaty and a man who fought to save as much of the traditional hunting and ceremonial territory of the Anishinaabeg of the French River waterway—I am glad that I have my rights back so as to slow the government down from the continual colonization and theft of my grandmother's ancestral lands. I pick up her bundle and Petawa-chuan's bundle and add them to my own.

What we carry in our bundles represents our tools to renew and build our future. I carry the ethics of the Anishinaabeg inside me, which I use to guide my daughters on the nature of being kwezensag (girls). I tell them the old stories and the prophecy teachings known as the Niizhwaaso-ishkoden Ningaanaajimowin (Seven Fires Prophecy). Within the prophecy teachings are instructions known as the Niizhwaaswi-gichitwaa-miigiwewinan (Seven Sacred Gifts), or the Seven Grandmother (or Grandfather) teachings. We use them to guide us through the difficult work of following the mino-miikana-bimaadizi (good path of life) as human beings. They teach us the knowledge of Anishinaabeg-bimaadiziwin (living as human beings) within the order of Creation, finding balance with the scheme of everything in our ecosystems or traditional territories, and knowing that we carry responsibilities to guard the land. I will share with you a story about how mothers came to learn these teachings and how they became important parts of our bundles. When we metaphorically "throw down our bundles," we are telling the world we are enacting our responsibilities given to us by Gizhew-manidoo, the Creator.

Nookomis-Asabikeshiinh miinawaa Anishinaabeg Bawaajige-Nagwaaganan: Grandmother Spider and the Anishinaabeg Dream Catchers

Before the sun even crests the horizon Nookoomis-Asabikeshiinh, Grandmother Spider, the Great Net Maker who makes and weaves the threads that hold the universe together, begins building her morning web to catch and hold Giizis, Grandfather Sun.

Grandmother Spider wakes before dawn arrives and begins spinning her net of silken silver threads. The net is composed of intricate entwined and interlaced threads. The silk lines harden into a sticky snare for her prey, Giizis. Her web is a trap lighter than mist or a feather floating on the breeze. Grandmother Spider watches and waits from the edges of her web, hidden from her prey. Each thread is used to catch and hold Giizis' rays of light, holding them to the sky above. The threads restrain and guide Giizis from east to west across the sky until it disappears over the horizon, and it is time for Nookomis-Dibiki-Giizis, Grandmother Moon, to ascend upwards into the night sky.

One morning while Grandmother Spider was finishing up her morning web, some Anishinaabeg mothers and children from the nearby village approached her with sad expressions on their faces. One of the mothers was openly weeping, which worried Grandmother Spider.

"Why are you weeping granddaughter? What has happened to make you so upset?" asked Grandmother Spider.

One of the mothers named Ziigwan-waabigwan-kwe (Spring Flower Woman) stepped forwards to answer Grandmother Spider: "Grandmother, Seven Prophets gifted our village with instructions from Gizhew-Manidoo about where and how the Anishinaabeg should live on Aki. They carried with them warnings from their grandmother and teachings, which they called the seven gifts. They told us to take these gifts and leave the east or face destruction. We are to go westwards. Many of us do not want to go, and we are scared. We trust that the Prophets want what is best for us. Most of us are leaving to go west. Grandmother, will you come with us?"

"Oh! That is very upsetting. I am very sad now. My granddaughters! My granddaughters!" Grandmother Spider cried out. "I am afraid I can't come with you. I will miss you all very much, but I know you must follow the words of the Prophets and Gizhew-Manidoo's wisdom."

The mothers and Grandmother Spider wept together as the sun rose into the sky. A mother named Mizhakwan-kwe (Clear Day Woman) looked up at Grandmother Spider in her morning web that glistened with dew and begged her: "Please come with us Grandmother! We want you to be with us. We would miss you too much if you stayed. If you stay here in the east, you will not be there to visit our babies and protect them with your asabikeshiwasab-nagwaaganan (spider web snares) on their dikinaagan-aagiingwe'onaakoon (cradleboard hoops) from those Spirits that would come to steal their jichaag (soul-spirits) away. You have taught us so much about motherhood and protected us. Who will be there for us if you go?"

Some of the other mothers fell to their knees in utter despair and sobbed at the coming loss.

When Grandmother Spider spoke, her voice shook with great

emotion: "Granddaughters, my blessed granddaughters, I will not be travelling with you on your westward journey because I have responsibilities here in the east. I must be here to catch Giizis in the morning and guide it across the sky to light the world. My role is to remain in the east to guard the doorway of life for the mothers and children yet to come. I must be there to catch, greet, and guide those young spirits as they enter the eastern doorway so that they might find their way to their parents. I can't leave them alone to find their way all by themselves. They are so little and new.

Her answer brought more tears among the mothers, but Ozaawi-Memengwaa-kwe (Orange Butterfly Woman) spoke up: "We understand Grandmother. Some of our people are remaining to guard the eastern doorway and keep the eastern fires burning. They will keep you company and aid you in your work. We will miss you, your guidance, and protection."

Grandmother Spider told the young mothers that she would send her kin and children with them to help their future infants' spirits come into the world in a good way. They would keep their spirits safe. She added: "When you see spiders in your lodges near you, know that I am close, and you are protected. Do not harm them but learn from them and remember me. To give you solace and protection for your babies, I will teach you to weave sacred hoops of webbing to protect your children's jiichaag (soul-spirits)." She then instructed them to gather miskwaabiimizh-wadikwanan (red willow branches), ojiitaad (sinew), and miigwanag (feathers). The women left and came back with all their supplies.

When they returned, she gave them teachings on constructing the dreamcatchers, which she told them to hang on all the babies' dikinaaganan (cradleboards) as protection or in openings to the lodges in order to keep bad spirits out and away from their families. She said, "You will first cut the branches to make a small tear shape the size of the palm of your hand. The tear shape is to mark the sadness of our parting and to remind you of the pain that comes with watching our children grow up and grow away from us. The sinew will be used to weave the threads of the net that will catch the Spirits and repel illness. In honour of the prophecy teachings and our relationship, the number of points where the web connects to the red-willow-hoop should number seven for the Seven Prophecies, with one extra loop to hang the dreamcatcher as a reminder to women of the number eight for spider's eight legs. The webbing represents the madjimadzuin, the cosmic lifeline that connects mothers to their children, human beings to the Spirit World and the Great Mystery of Gizhew-Manidoo (the Creator). It will connect you and the baby to me but also to waawiyekamig (the universe) and to the Gchi-asabikeshiwasab-bimaadizi (Great Web-of-Life), which connects everything in creation. As it hangs, the dreamcatcher will filter out all the bad bawaajiganan (dreams) and only allow good energies and thoughts to enter the minds of abinoojiinyag (children). You will leave a small hole in the centre of each dream catcher where those good bawadjige may come through. With the first rays of sunlight, the maji-bawaajiganan (bad dreams) will perish. Lastly, you will add a feather to the dreamcatcher to warn you when they are near so that you might hold your babies close to your heart until they pass by. You will call these little webs bawaajige-nagwaa-ganan (dreamcatchers), and they will only allow pleasant dreams to enter your babies' minds as they sleep. The web will connect you and the baby to me but also to waawiyekamig (the universe) and to the Gchi-asabikeshiwasab-bimaadizi (Great Web-of-Life), which connects everything in creation. The dream catcher will remind you that you are connected." The mothers who had brought their babies in dikinaaganan (cradleboards) tied the new dream catchers to the dikinaagan-aagiingwe'onaakoon (cradleboard hoops) or the negweyaab (rainbow), as it is also known. It is a bent wood piece that protects the child from injury if the dikinaaganan were to topple over, as well as allow a mother to attach a covering to shield the child from rain, wind, or snow. Attaching the dreamcatcher to the rainbow hoop protects the child from leaving across the jiibay-miikana (path of Souls) to the Spirit realm with a manidoo (Spirit being) or jiibay (spirit of a deceased person). Further, it is a reminder of the madjimadzuin, the cosmic spider web thread that connects a child to their mother and to Gizhew-Manidoo (Creator).

All day long, the mothers sat in front of Nookomis-Asabikeshiinh making many dreamcatchers. Grandmother Spider shared many stories and helped them understand the meaning of the seven gifts of the Grandmother prophets but also how to situate it in their lives as mothers, women, and for their families. More importantly, Grandmother Spider taught them to see the teachings of dabasendiziwin (humility), gwayakwaadiziwin (honesty), minaadendamowin (respect), zoongide'ewin (bravery or courage), nibwaakaawin (wisdom), debwewin (truth), and, lastly, zaagi'idiwin (love) through the view of a mother's heart, mind, body, and spirit. She continued to speak to the women till the sun fell below the horizon.

"Go now my Granddaughters. Make the bawaajige-nagwaaganan and remember the teachings I have given you. Carry them in your bundles. Know that I hold you dear to my heart and will be watching over you," Nookomis-Asabikeshiinh said softly.

The Anishinaabeg have no word for goodbye, but one of the eldest grandmothers stepped forwards and offered these words: "Nookomis-Asabikeshiinh. Baanimaa miinawaa odisaabandamang giga-waabandimin (Grandmother-Spider. The spirits will decide when we will meet each other again). If we do not see each other in this world, then we will see each other in the next."

The women parted as Nookomis-Dibiki-Giizis, Grandmother Moon, ascended into the sky to light their way back to their lodges. The next day, the Anishinaabeg embarked on their journey westwards. On their journey, they saw the children of Grandmother-Spider watching over them and reminding them of her teachings. Mothers passed down the teachings of Grandmother-Spider, and although many Anishinaabeg rarely offer their prayers or songs to Grandmother-Spider in today's world, the mothers pay respect to her when they make dreamcatchers and teach their daughters what it means to be a mother. I share her story so that the other mothers will once again remember to lay their tobacco down for her and thank Nookomis-Asabikeshiinh for her teachings.

A Mother's Perspective on the Niizhwaaswi-Gichitwaa-Miigiwewinan (Seven Sacred Gifts)

Over the years, I have picked up a lot of the pieces from the bundles my ancestral grandmothers threw down, including all that my grandmother and mother threw down in order to survive the onslaught of colonization or fight for rights in the face of unjust laws designed to eradicate First Nations cultures and peoples across Canada. I have repaired, recreated, revitalized, and renewed what used to exist. Along the way, I have added new knowledge so that my descendants can have a healthy bundle of their own. Yet while I pick up their bundles, I am still having to fight to rebuild and assert space in academic spheres so that the voices of the mothers are not silenced again. I still have to throw my bundle down to remind people that we are here, we demand to be heard, and we will not just survive but thrive. My bundle becomes a symbol of my woman's creatix and our powers for birthing and creating new pathways forward for our people. As Elder Solomon teaches us:

> The power of birth was given to the women.
> It was given by the Creator
> And it is an immutable law.
> It was given as sacred work
> and because it is a sacred work.
> Then a sacred way was given to the women...
> The woman is the foundation on which
> nations are built.
> (qtd. in Posluns 35)

Gunn-Allen adds to this positionality by stating that for generations, Indigenous women of Turtle Island have been the "creatix and shaper of existence in the tribe and on the earth, everyone knew that women played a separate and significant role in tribal reality" (30). When we metaphorically throw down our bundles, we are setting in motion the power of the creatix and become the shapers of existence, using our powers as women to rewrite the stories of colonization that have normalized the invisibility, disempowerment, dislocations, and terminations of feminine indigeneity. Gunn-Allen describes this state of decolonized femininity as "gynecentricity" and "[re-]gynocatiziation" (42). I would add it is also the "biskaabiiyang" (Geniusz 10), or the "returning to ourselves" (Geniusz 10), and resurgence of Indigenous sacred maternal-feminine cultures, identities, spirituality, ceremonies, stories, governance systems, histories, and experiences. In other words, it is the renewal and building new decolonized female bundles to give us life outside of the colonial lens or institutions that seek to extinguish Indigenous maternal normativity.

It is because of "degynocatization" (Gunn-Allen 42) that systems of white-settler patriarchal Christianity were normalized at the expense of Indigenous maternal intellectual traditions; this makes asserting the gifts of the seven grandmothers so fundamentally important. I carry the seven gifts in my bundle for my daughters so that they will not have to throw their bundles down but carry them peacefully with honour. As in the story, the gifts include dabasendiziwin (humility), gwayakwaadiziwin (honesty), minaadendamowin (respect), zoongide'ewin (bravery or courage), nibwaakaawin (wisdom), debwewin (truth), and zaagi'idiwin (love). These are Grandmother Spider's teachings for Anishinaabeg mothers to carry in their bundles as tools of maternal normativity.

The first gift I will share is dabasendiziwin (humility), which is a teaching that returns the primacy of Grandmother Spider to the lives of Anishinaabeg women. She is an old ally to the Anishinaabeg but more importantly to Anishinaabeg mothers and women (inclusive of those who are LGBTTIQQ2SA+, two-spirited, and Indigiqueer persons), who have been almost completely erased from the landscape of Anishinaabeg culture. We can find her buried in the teachings of the Anishinaabeg dreamcatchers hung on dikinaaganan (cradleboards). Guardian of the eastern doorway, Grandmother Spider guides mothers to understand dabasendiziwin. Every morning as the sun rises in the east, the power of creation is ignited. Every living creature is humbled by the need for the sun to rise. The sun's presence is necessary for living, and it makes us feel small, insignificant, and in awe that something is so important to our lives. The Anishinaabeg stories tell us that Grandmother Spider catches the sunlight every morning in the dew drops collected along her eyebigwasabiig (spider threads). Grandmother spider works to spin her web around each of the rays and guides it across the sky. David Bouchard and Joseph Martin write that human beings begin their "journey in the spring, in the east. East is where all life begins and yellow best represents my first teaching: humility.... For the betterment of yourself and all Creation, strive to be humble" (15).

As women, as mothers, we humble ourselves to the process of motherhood. We humble ourselves to the difficulties involved in the process of giving life and its contrast, death. Mothers look to the teachings of nooze-makwa (bear-mother; female bear) for lessons on maternal humility. We observe how nooze-makwa does not live for herself alone but for her cubs. Watch how she allows them to climb on her back, eat first, and stands between them and all danger. She does this out of humbling herself to the responsibilities of motherhood, caring for another's life, and deference to her role in Creation as a creatix, a life-maker, sustainer, nourisher, and nurturer. Nooze-makwa understands what a small but crucial part she plays in the ecosystem but also without her work, the next generation would not survive. She normalizes the humility of mothering.

The second gift of the grandmothers is gwayakwaadiziwin (honesty). These teachings centre around the lessons that Sabe, or Gchi-Sabe (Sasquatch), gave to human beings. These spirit beings, manidoowag, are surprisingly vital teachers to defining mothering in Anishinaabeg maternal culture. From what traditional stories tell us, Sabe exist in family units. They protect each other and live peacefully and honestly with the natural rhythms of the land. They maintain the inaakon-igewinan (natural laws) of the land. For many Anishinaabeg, we have been led off the path of living in accord with the natural laws of the land. Prophecy tells us this has happened now and again, but that we must always try to find our way back to the mino-miikana, that good path of life. The warnings, as well as instructions, are there in the prophecy teachings so that we survive as a people. Sabe reminds us of the prophecy for the sake of our families. Bouchard and Martin write that "Sabe reminds us to be ourselves and not someone we are not. An honest person is said to walk tall like kitchi-Sabe" (7). As mothers, we know that to revitalize Anishinaabeg ways of knowing for the well-being of our children, we must show them what honesty looks like by proudly modelling how to live mino-bimaadiziwin—a good way of living in accordance with natural laws. Normalizing traditional knowledge for our children in contemporary times returns them back to what it means to be Anishinaabeg outside of colonial contexts.

Next is the gift of minaadendamowin (respect). Every plant and animal on earth serves a purpose in the order of the ecosystem they live in. Anishinaabeg are told that if we do not maintain the balance and respect for a certain creature they would disappear. Today, there are fewer and fewer fish in Northern Ontario. When I was a child, there was more than enough fish to eat all spring and summer and then put away a supply for winter in the freezer. We wasted those fish and failed to maintain the balance. Bouchard and Martin explain further about these teachings: "Do not waste. Use all things wisely. Never take more than you need and always give away that which you do not use. And treat others as you would have them treat you, respectfully. learn respect and learn balance. What goes up will come down. What you do for others will be done for you. What you give away will always come back to you in the one Circle" (9).

The fourth gift is zoongide'ewin (bravery and courage). As women who choose to bring a child into the world and become a mother—or those guardians, aunties, or grannies of children who take on mothering roles—we have all taken the leap of faith to take on the responsibility of nurturing life. You do what is right for yourself and your family. Doing what is right does not always come easy, but we model this behaviour for our children, and this takes bravery and courage. The mother zii'amoonh (wood-duck) nests in cavities of the trees of wetlands. A day after hatching, the baby ducklings must leap from the tree to follow their mother to the water. Every female duckling must both jump as a duckling and then watch her babies jump down to the ground to her. Courage comes from within, but it is also modelled by mothers for our children, which we call gikinoo'waabanda'iwewin in Anishinaabemowin. This shows our children that life is not easy and that we must let courage within us awaken to grow, mature, and gain valuable life experience.

Then, there is the fifth gift, which is nibwaakaawin (wisdom). Wisdom comes from life experience; it is personally learned. Knowledge can be given to you from the experiences of others, but the teachings of nibwaakaawin tell us that mothers must allow children to step into the world and experience it. I remember watching my babies learn to walk. Their sense of triumph and awe at being about to make their little legs walk were life changing for both of us. Nibwaakaawin also means prudence or caution. With knowledge comes the responsibility to not abuse it, which leads to wisdom. Mothers teach their children to think not just of themselves but the impact they will have on others: family, community, and nature. Furthermore, mothers teach each of their children that we are all created special, with unique talents and gifts. In a forest, there are many trees, but each tree is different and performs different responsibilities in the forest. The maple does not envy the white pine. Together, they make each other and the forest stronger; similarly, allowing each child to express their talents makes them feel successful, leading to healthy family dynamics.

Debwewin (truth) is the sixth gift of the grandmother's teachings. Truth comes when we know and live all the gifts of the grandmothers.

We are reminded to think about these teachings when we look up to the moon, Nookomis Dibik-Giizis (Grandmother Moon). In the Anishinaabeg Creation story, Giizhigoo-kwe (Sky Woman) fell through a hole in the Sky World to the Earth below. Mishoomis-mishiikenh (Grandfather Turtle) offered his back for her to rest. The other animals brought her soil, which she placed on the back of a turtle, which expanded and became Turtle Island. Giizhigoo-kwe lived her life, and when she died, she returned to the sky as Nookomis Dibik-Giizis. In a year, there are thirteen moons, which mimic the plates of Mishoomis-mishiikenh's back. Every time my daughters and I see Grandmother Moon up in the sky, we are reminded as women to honour this ancestor and actively live the teachings of the Grandmother prophets.

The last of the seven Grandmother gifts I carry in my bundle as a mother is zaagi'idiwin (love). As a mother, my love for my children is boundless, but it is also my role to teach my children how to love as Anishinaabeg—for themselves, their family, community, nation, culture, the land, and all of Creation. They need to be taught how to self-love, along with mutual love. From the moment they were placed into my arms, and I held them to my breast to give them nourishment, they learned a mother's love as their first love. Our mutual love is rooted in the teachings of the madjimadzuin, which are rooted in Gizhew-Manidoo, the Creator of all life, whom we are all connected to through a cosmic umbilical cord that is unseen but is present inside of us as a cellular, even an atomic level. In the old stories, Grandmother Spider is responsible for weaving this cosmic umbilical cord through and into us at the moment of our birth. As we enter that eastern doorway, she quickly wraps her silken threads around us and tethers us to this realm, connecting all of us to the rest of the fabric of the universe or Great Web-of-Life spread throughout the cosmos. Just like the sun, she captures and guides across the sky each day, she does the same for us throughout our life along the miikana-bimaadizi, with her great love and caring spirit: zaagi'idiwin.

I share these teachings of my bundle. I throw down my bundle here so that I create a space for Anishinaabeg mothers and for allies to understand Anishinaabeg maternal normativity through the lens of an Anishinaabeg mother. The knowledge I share rewrites the discourse of the colonizer and frees the women of my family: mothers, daughters, granddaughters, and descendants. Carrying the gifts and using the gifts of the bundle mean committing to Anishinaabeg normativity, our values, and our goals for our families, communities, and nation.

Concluding Thoughts

Anishinaabeg maternal normativity is embedded in ancient teachings that come to Anishinaabeg mothers from the Gete-Anishinaabe-nookomisag—the grandmothers of long ago. They left us the wisdom of their bundles so that each generation passes on to the next the madjimadzuin kwewag tools of survival, renewal, resurgence, and blueprints to build our futures. The knowledge within my bundle is medicine that I give to my daughters to heal their wounds incurred by living under the mantle of colonization, but it can also act as medicine for others to witness the legacy of how colonization affects all of us within the land of Canada. It is not just the burden of my family. I extend a piece of my bundle in this chapter so that we can all begin to learn, heal, and build decolonized spaces of thought, creativity, and dreaming of better futures with a new decolonized maternal normativity. I end here with a poem for mothers.

Madjimadzuin kwewag, The Anishinaabeg Mother's Lifeline

I am daughter.
I am mother.
I am grandmother.
We are the pieces in the great and sacred hoop.... Grandmother Spider's web ... the chain of Creation.

I carry their bundles,
my mother's and grandmother's bundles,
I carry the bundles of my daughters and granddaughters yet to be born.
Their bundles are within me: beauty and spirits radiate from each cell.
Build, create, regenerate, and revitalize is the work of the Anishinaabeg mother's bundle.
I call out to the sacred daughters, mothers, and grandmothers to walk with me down the mino-miskwaa-miikana-bimaadiziwin.

I am daughter.
I am mother.
I am grandmother.
I am granddaughter.
I am the bundles of all the mothers who came before me.

Endnotes

1. In Anishinaabemowin, "-*ban*" or "-*ba*," is a preterite suffix that is added to a noun stem to indicate a past state, absence, or loss. For example, -*ban* is added to a noun to indicate that the person is now deceased. To honour that they have passed to the Spirit Realm, I have chosen to write it as -*ban* at the end of their name. To not bother or draw the attention of the Spirit of the deceased who is busy with their existence in that Spirit realm, Anishinaabeg are encouraged to alter or add to the name -*ban* or -*ba*. I have chosen not to attach it directly to the name of each deceased person repeatedly. Furthermore, I have chosen to italicize -*ban* to make it visually resonate as different and alter the name in the traditional manner.
2. LGBTTIQQ2SA+ means lesbian, gay, bisexual, transgender, transsexual, intersex, queer, questioning, two-spirited, and asexual.
3. First Nations or Indian peoples are defined by both the Indian Act (1876) and under Section 25 (2) of the Canadian Constitution (1982). First Nations is also defined as the original peoples of North American.

Works Cited

Government of Canada. "Background on Indian Registration." *Crown-Indigenous Relations and Northern Affairs Canada, Collaborative Process on Indian Registration, Band Membership and First Nation Citizenship: Consultation Plan*, www.rcaanc-cirnac.gc.ca/eng/1522949271019/15 68896763719. Accessed 11 Feb. 2023.

Bouchard, David, and Joseph Martin. *Seven Sacred Teachings Niizhwaaswi Gagiikwewin*. MTW Publishers, 2009.

Bruce, Awanigiizhik. "Anishinaabe Gender Terms." *Facebook*, https://m.facebook.com/awanigiizhik.art/photos/a.56290865412 8278/1375487209537081/?type=3. Accessed 11 Feb. 2023.

Gunn-Allen, Paula. *The Sacred Hoop: Recovering the Feminism in American Indian Traditions*. Beacon Press, 1986.

Jenness, Diamond. *The Ojibwa Indians of Parry Island, Their Social and Religious Life*. National Museum of Canada, 1935.

Posluns, Michael, ed. *Songs for the People: Teachings on the Natural Way, Poems and Essays of Arthur Solomon*. NC Press Limited, 1990.

Notes on Contributors

Editor

Andrea O'Reilly, PhD, is a full professor in the School of Gender, Sexuality, and Women's Studies at York University, founder/editor-in-chief of the *Journal of the Motherhood Initiative*, and publisher of Demeter Press. She is coeditor/editor of twenty-five plus books including *Feminist Parenting: Perspectives from Africa and Beyond* (2020), *Mothers, Mothering, and COVID-19: Dispatches from a Pandemic* (2021), *Maternal Theory, The 2nd Edition* (2021), *Monstrous Mothers; Troubling Tropes* (2021), *Maternal Regret: Resistances, Renunciations, and Reflections* (2022), and *Coming into Being: Mothers on Finding and Realizing Feminism* (2023). She is editor of the *Encyclopedia on Motherhood* (2010) and coeditor of the *Routledge Companion to Motherhood* (2019). She is author of *Toni Morrison and Motherhood: A Politics of the Heart* (2004); *Rocking the Cradle: Thoughts on Motherhood, Feminism, and the Possibility of Empowered Mothering* (2006); and *Matricentric Feminism: Theory, Activism, and Practice, The 2nd Edition* (2021). She is twice the recipient of York University's "Professor of the Year Award" for teaching excellence and is the 2019 recipient of the Status of Women and Equity Award of Distinction from OCUFA (Ontario Confederation of University Faculty Associations). She has received more than 1.5 million dollars in grant funding for her research projects including two current ones: "Older Young Mothers in Canada" and "Mothers and Returning to 'Normal': The Impact of the Pandemic on Mothering and Families."

Contributors

Renée E. Mazinegiizhigoo-kwe Bédard is of Anishinaabeg (Ojibwe/ Nipissing/ Omàmiwininiwag), Kanien'kehá:ka and French Canadian ancestry. She is a member of Okikendawdt Mnissing (Dokis First Nation). She holds a PhD from Trent University in Indigenous studies. Currently, she is an assistant professor at Western University in the Faculty of Education. Her areas of publication include practices of Anishinaabeg motherhood, maternal philosophy and spirituality, along with environmental issues, women's rights, Indigenous Elders, Anishinaabeg artistic expressions, and Indigenous education.

Elizabeth A. Bennett, PhD, is a clinical psychologist and mother-scholar in private practice. She specializes in work with maternal trauma (broadly understood), eating disorders, and somatic interventions. Her research foci include embodied traumas and poetic inquiry. Elizabeth is a mama of three young children: Elodie, Ambrose, and Leo.

Natalie Bruvels' art practice and theoretical research engage the intersection of motherhood studies and representations of mothers in visual culture and contemporary art practices. Bruvels holds a BSc in biology, an MFA in visual arts, and an MA in contemporary art theory from the University of Ottawa. She is the recipient of the Charles Gagnon and Michel Goulet prizes. Bruvels is currently a PhD candidate at the Feminist and Gender Studies Institute at the University of Ottawa. She is a member of Cat Attack Collective and is represented by Studio Sixty-Six.

Amy F. Crocker, PT, DPT, OCS, FNAP, is the director of Social Accountability and Experiential Learning and associate professor in the School of Physical Therapy at the University of the Incarnate Word in San Antonio, Texas. Dr. Crocker's areas of interest and research include social accountability, interprofessional education and collaborative practice, and experiential learning. She creates partnerships with local community organizations to promote future healthcare providers' engagement with individuals of all abilities.

Rosann Edwards, RN IBCLC MScN PhD, is an assistant professor in the Department of Nursing and Health Sciences at the University of New Brunswick Saint John. In her research and community involve-ment, she seeks to better understand the ways of mothering. Rosann's work focuses on breastfeeding, m/othering under the external influences of systems, and exploring how nurses can empower vulnerable populations of women and their children while improving health outcomes. Rosann is also an experienced front line public health nurse, a lactation consultant, a lover of karate, and a mother of boys.

Denise Y. Hill is a teaching professor in the Department of English at Arizona State University, Tempe. She holds a PhD in composition, rhetoric, and the teaching of English from the University of Arizona. Her research interests revolve around rhetorics of motherhood and (dis)ability studies. She brings these two passions together as a volunteer mentor for mothers whose children were recently diagnosed with autism, helping them navigate the complexities of the healthcare system.

May Isaac's successful corporate career and her first attempt at a PhD were both upended by motherhood. Her lived experience over a fourteen-year hiatus motivated her to complete a new doctoral study investigating motherhood in a contemporary career context. With that completed, she is now busy being the change she wishes to see. Her research interests are gender equity, intersectionality, and neoliberal feminism.

Karla Knutson is a full professor of English and women's and gender studies at Concordia College in Moorhead, Minnesota. She teaches courses in feminist literature, depictions of women and children in literature, and the English language as well as ethnography and autoethnography. Her publications explore the rhetoric of lactation production, academic motherhood, and the mothers of only children.

Lori E. Koelsch, PhD, is an associate professor of psychology and director of undergraduate programs at Duquesne University. Her research interests include qualitative methodology, with a particular focus on poetic inquiry. She brings a background in feminist psychology and an attunement to equity and inclusion to her work. Of equal importance, Dr. Koelsch is the mother of two young children, who bring her much joy and keep her busy.

Dr. Zsuzsanna Lénárt-Muszka teaches at the North American Department of the Institute of English and American Studies, University of Debrecen, Hungary. She received her doctorate from the University of Debrecen (2021); the title of her dissertation is *Mothers in the Wake of Slavery: The Im/possibility of Motherhood in Post-1980 African American Women's Prose*. Her research interests include the representations of violence and embodiment in contemporary North American short fiction.

Sônia Maria de Magalhães is a historian, amateur chef, and mom. She is an associate professor in the Faculty of History at Goiás Federal University/Brazil (UFG). She is also coordinator of the Professional Master's Program in History (ProfHistória) at UFG, coordinator of the Women Scientists and Plural Maternities Workgroup by National Council for Scientific and Technological Development/Brazil, coordinator of the Working Group on the History of Health and Diseases of the Brazilian Association of History (Goiás regional section), and a member of the DIAITA Food Heritage of Lusophony.

Vanessa Marr is an artist and academic, fellow of the Royal Society of Arts (RSA), and principal lecturer at the University of Brighton, UK. She is best known for her experimental autoethnographic practice, drawing with thread onto commonplace objects to phenomenologically embody her gendered, lived experience. Marr is drawn to cloth as a medium that holds the legacy of so-called women's work and its potential for subversion and quiet activism. Her work is published and exhibited world-wide.

Megan Marshall, PhD, is an assistant professor of English and the coordinator of the Composition Program at Marshall University. She teaches various writing, pedagogy, and humanities courses and centres her research within (and across) the fields of dis/ability studies, young adult literature, adaptation theory, and critical pedagogies. She lives with her family in the otherworldly hills of West Virginia, where her children swing on vines and keep eyes out for Mothman.

Isabelle Portelinha holds a PhD in psychology from the University of Paris and is associated with New York University. She teaches multiple courses in graduate and undergraduate programs in social science. Her research and writing explore questions relating to political behaviour, broadly understood, and sociopsychological processes that maintain or resist the status quo. While grounded in social psychology, her work is at the intersection of psychology, sociology, cultural anthropology, and philosophy.

Ana Carolina Eiras Coelho Soares is a feminist, writer, mom, poet, columnist of the "Mom's Chronicles" for the Brazilian women's magazine *Revista Cláudia*, historian, belly dancer, and tree planter. She was the director of the Women and Diversities of the Inclusion Secretary of the Rectory of Goiás Federal University/Brazil (UFG) in the first semester of 2022 and associate professor in the Faculty of History at UFG. She is also a coordinator of the Women Scientists and Plural Maternities Workgroup by the National Council for Scientific and Technological Development/Brazil and a coordinator of the Research Group on Gender Relations (CNPq/BR).

Susan N. Smith, PT, DPT, PCS is an associate professor in the School of Physical Therapy at the University of the Incarnate Word in San Antonio, Texas. Dr. Smith's areas of interest and research include infant powered mobility, babywear for children with special needs, and experiential learning in physical therapy education. She is a clinical director for the Special Olympics FUNfitness program and an advocate for both children and adults with developmental disabilities.

Rachel E. Stough is a mother and a clinical psychology doctoral candidate at Point Park University. In her research and clinical work, she is interested in mothering experiences, collective and complex traumas, and healing in community.

Amy Wagner, PT, DPT, PhD, GCS, is a professor in the School of Physical Therapy at University of the Incarnate Word in San Antonio, TX. She has scholarly interests in the areas of motherhood, postpartum health, aging, disability studies, and health humanities. She has presented at several national conferences previously, including the topic of disability and motherhood. Dr. Wagner holds several leadership positions in the American Physical Therapy Association.

Deepest appreciation to
Demeter's monthly Donors

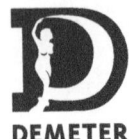

DEMETER

Daughters
Rebecca Bromwich
Summer Cunningham
Tatjana Takseva
Debbie Byrd
Fiona Green
Tanya Cassidy
Vicki Noble
Myrel Chernick

Sisters
Amber Kinser
Nicole Willey

Grandmother
Tina Powell